From
Stonehenge
to
Santa Claus

The Evolution of Christmas

From Stonehenge to Santa Claus

The Evolution of Christmas

PAUL FRODSHAM

For

Katie and Claire

my very own

Christmas Crackers!

First published 2008

The History Press Ltd
The Mill, Brimscombe Port
Stroud, Gloucestershire, GL5 2QG
www.thehistorypress.co.uk

Reprinted 2009, 2013

British Library Cataloguing in Publication Data.
A catalogue record for this book is available from the British Library.

ISBN 978 0 7524 4818 3

Typesetting and origination by The History Press
Printed in Great Britain by CMP (uk) Limited

Contents

Foreword and Acknowledgements

As an archaeologist with a long-established interest in the megalithic monuments of ancient Europe, such as Stonehenge, I have long been aware that the winter solstice was an important annual event in the lives of our Neolithic ancestors. The solstice is the time at which the northern hemisphere finds itself, due to the axis of the earth's orbit, experiencing the shortest day of the year – according to our calendar on either the 21 or 22 December (in the southern hemisphere this is, of course, midsummer, and the longest day). To prehistoric people, this was a crucial time, when traditional ceremonies were held to ensure that the sun would begin to climb higher in the sky each day, and the days would gradually grow longer – if this did not happen then all life would soon end. Thousands of years after the construction of Stonehenge, I learned, as a child, to love Christmas. More recently, as a father, I have enjoyed experiencing my daughters' eager anticipation of Santa's arrival each Christmas Eve. My younger daughter announced with aplomb as she approached her fourth Christmas that 'Santa can't be real because it's stupid to think that he could go to everyone's house in one night'. Nevertheless, she and her sister, along with millions of other children, were delighted to discover on Christmas morning that he had been to see them! At first glance, Stonehenge and Santa Claus may appear to have little in common, but as we will see in this book, both owe their existence largely to the winter solstice, and today's Santa may well embody several characteristics of the priests who officiated at Stonehenge more than 4000 years ago.

A few Christmases ago, while out searching for presents for family and friends, I was struck by the lack of available books seeking to explain the development of Christmas further back than the Victorian era, through medieval and Roman times into the mists of prehistory. Yet I knew the evidence was there to attempt such an account. I can still recall the moment, as I drove home from my shopping expedition, when I realised it would be my job to write it. My plan was to research and present the definitive story of midwinter from the earliest times through to the present day, but this is an immense task that remains far from complete. Although this book covers all the main themes it should be considered as a summary of work still very much in progress.

Between the demands of my 'day job' and the long nights spent working on books such as this, I run an archaeological consultancy operating under the motto *Harnessing the spirit of our past – enhancing prospects for our future.* This neatly sums up the intended purpose of this book. Over the centuries, the spirit of Christmas has meant different things to different people, as it still does today. For some, it is primarily a religious occasion, celebrating the birth of Jesus Christ. I have much to say about this in Chapter 3, which I sincerely hope will not cause offence to any readers. I genuinely do believe in Christmas as a season of goodwill to all men (and women and children) but, although considering myself a very spiritual person, I must confess no allegiance to Christianity or any other conventional religion. Hence, I approach the Nativity as I would any other subject, with a critical and objective analysis of the available data. My conclusion, that the Nativity is but one version of the very ancient practice of celebrating the annual death and rebirth of the sun, has the potential to render the celebration of Christmas relevant to everyone within our modern, multi-cultural society. Many will choose to ignore the facts and continue to believe that Christmas is primarily about the birth of Christ – that is their prerogative. I prefer to regard it as a celebration of the wonder of being alive. It is a time, for those fortunate enough to be able to do so, to revel in the joys of the family, to forget about everyday routine and simply to enjoy. But it is also a time to be charitable, to remember those less fortunate than ourselves in so many ways. This book attempts to explain how we have arrived at our present-day 'traditional' Christmas through the analysis of thousands of years of our collective history. To paraphrase my consultancy's motto (and with apologies to Charles Dickens) it seeks to *harness the spirit of Christmas past*, and to *enhance prospects for Christmases yet to come.*

Many people have contributed, knowingly or otherwise, to the production of this book. I would like to thank my parents and grandparents for helping to provide me with so many happy Christmas memories, instilling within me a love of the festive season from an early age. Similarly, I must thank my two beautiful daughters,

Katie and Claire, for rejuvenating a love of Christmas within their old dad who at one time was threatening to develop some minor Scrooge-like characteristics. My ever suffering partner, Diane, has cheerfully endured too many lonely evenings while I have been hidden away on the computer, and when we have been together has had to put up with my incessant babbling about all manner of Christmas-related trivia. Although I know no apology is expected or required, I nevertheless offer one here.

Many of the examples and quotations cited in this volume are taken from secondary sources, and I am grateful to those authors who have included them within their own studies over the years. In the interests of readability, I have avoided littering the text with academic-type references, but sincerely hope that I have adequately acknowledged all sources (should this prove not to be the case, I will be pleased to make the necessary corrections in any future editions). In many places I have opted to provide direct quotations, rather than attempting to paraphrase original sources, as I feel this is the best way to present the views of others while reducing the possibility of misrepresentation. All publications consulted during my research, many of which will be of great interest to readers wishing to know more about specific aspects of the Christmas story, are listed in the references section at the back of the book.

I am grateful to my good friend Stan Beckensall for his perceptive comments on a draft of the text, and for help with illustrations I am indebted to Amanda Alcock, Keith Cooper, Javis Gurr, Vivian Krug, Yvonne Oliver, Tim Phillips, Tony Roche and Ronnie Scott. I owe an enormous debt of gratitude to Wendy Logue at The History Press who enthusiastically welcomed my initial proposal for this book, cheerfully accepted my hopeless inability to meet mutually agreed deadlines, skilfully edited my substantially over-size manuscript into publishable form, and generally played a crucial role in seeing the project through to publication. Without doubt, a few errors will have survived the editing process; as ever, responsibility for these must be mine and mine alone.

Finally, I hope people will forgive the present volume its many shortcomings and find it a positive addition to their festive season.

Merry Christmas!

P.F.
Weardale, County Durham

1

In the Bleak Midwinter.
An introduction to the history and prehistory of Christmas

Christmas is the feast, not only of man's redemption, but of man himself. It is the feast of humankind, because it releases – if only for a few days in every year – tendencies that a savage self-interest causes mankind, in the ordinary way, to repress.

At Christmas-tide tyrants grow benevolent – even merciful; misers spend, not only freely, but willingly; the fierce flames of religious and political prejudice die for a short while to a cold cinder; selfish memories are stirred by the recollection – tardy but intense – of the neglected and the outcast.

For a few days, once a year, the atrophied souls of the grown-ups are filled again with that spirit which inspires the wisdom of fools and children.

So the history of Christmas, unlike the history of so many other human things, is consistently a pleasant one.

Michael Harrison, *The Story Of Christmas* (1951)

I love Christmas. Not just Christmas Day itself, but the whole thing; the weeks of anticipation, the Day itself, and the extended holiday season extending into the New Year. Some of my earliest memories relate to childhood Christmases, and I now delight in watching my daughters take part in their school Nativity plays and opening their presents around the tree on Christmas morning. But what is it that makes Christmas so special? I am not a Christian, and the birth of Jesus means nothing to me. Yet, like millions of other non-believers, I still feel the power of Christmas every year. How can this be so? The answer, I suggest, lies in the fact that an annual midwinter festival has been celebrated by our ancestors for so long that it has become part of our collective psyche. What we refer to today as Christmas is a Christian (or perhaps in some ways a 'post-Christian') version of this ancient festival, the origins of which are lost in the mists of time.

In the pages that follow we will meet Stone Age shamans, Druids, Greek gods, Roman Emperors, Jesus Christ, Saint Nicholas, King

Arthur, St Francis of Assisi, assorted medieval monarchs, Oliver Cromwell, Santa Claus and Charles Dickens, all of whom have significant roles to play in our story alongside a host of relatively minor, but still far from insignificant characters. We will consider all the major Christmas traditions, including the Christmas tree, the holly and the ivy, mistletoe, the yule log, Christmas dinner, mince pies, presents, cards, crackers, pantomimes and carols. The emphasis throughout is on Britain, but our story will take us abroad on many occasions. However, before we can begin our journey to meet these fascinating characters and analyse these festive traditions, we must focus on the fundamental observation that Christmas occurs at midwinter.

The Science of the Solstice

Today, most of us live in towns and cities and pay increasingly little attention to the movement of the sun, moon, planets and stars in the sky. In our artificially lit world and heated buildings we can exist almost without reference to the changing seasons, but to ancient people the observation of the heavens was critical. This was for practical reasons – so they would know, for example, when to plant and harvest crops – but their observations also provided the framework for numerous ceremonies that occurred at particular times of year. After midsummer, as each day went by, people would have noticed the sun rising slightly further south on the eastern horizon, reaching a slightly lower point in the sky at noon, and setting correspondingly further south in the west. The days grew gradually shorter and the nights correspondingly longer until, at midwinter, the process was reversed. This slow but irreversible cycle was easily monitored by placing a post in the ground and measuring the maximum length of the shadow cast by it each day; there would be a small but noticeable change from day to day, except at midsummer and midwinter, at each of which the movements of the sun appeared identical for about six days. The sun thus appeared to 'stand still', hence the term 'solstice' (literally from the Latin *'sol stetit'*, meaning 'sun stands still'). In ancient times, midwinter was a particularly dangerous time, both practically due to the cold and the possible lack of food, and also ceremonially, as the gods had to be placated to ensure that the sun did indeed come 'back from the dead'. This is why midwinter became of such ritual importance to all communities, and ceremonies associated with it became bound up with cycles of death and rebirth.

Today, we know that the sun is not hauled across the sky by a god who would refuse to turn up for work a little earlier the next day if we failed to say the correct prayers or make the relevant sacrifice at midwinter. We understand that the sun doesn't move around the earth, and that the seasons are dictated by the earth's orbit around the sun, the key factor being the tilt of the earth's axis which ensures (for the northern hemisphere) midwinter on 21/22 December and midsummer on 20/21 June. The tilt of the earth on its axis also accounts for the fact that the sun, as seen by an observer on earth, appears to pass across the sky on a much lower trajectory in winter than it does in summer. This cycle of the earth's orbit around the sun, repeated year after year, century after century, underlies the complex cultural history of midwinter. We can use archaeology and ancient mythology to attempt some informed speculation as to the nature of prehistoric midwinter ceremonies, and thus to the ultimate origins of Christmas. Armed with an appreciation of the great time depth of midwinter celebrations, we will be better placed to ask why so many people continue to believe in the traditional story of the Nativity, and even why some of us, even though we know we shouldn't, would still very much like to believe in Father Christmas!

Before progressing any further we should offer a brief explanation as to why Christmas Day, according to our modern calendar, occurs three or four days after midwinter, rather than on the actual day of the solstice. We know very little for certain about the calendars employed by people in prehistoric Britain, although it would not be unreasonable to assume that the day of the winter solstice may have marked the beginning of the year. When the Romans began their occupation of Britain in the first century AD, they brought with them the calendar devised a century earlier by Julius Caesar. Known as the Julian calendar, this was based on an ancient Egyptian calendar that was already some 3000 years old by the time of Caesar. When the Julian calendar was originally adopted in Rome, 25 December actually *was* the shortest day of the year – the day of the winter solstice.

The Julian calendar consisted of 365 days, with an extra day inserted every fourth year. If the solar year (the exact time it takes the earth to orbit the sun) was exactly 365¼ days then no doubt we would still be using Caesar's calendar today, but the solar year is actually 365.242199 days long, meaning that discrepancies between the calendar and the seasons grew greater by 11 minutes and 14 seconds each year. Such a discrepancy was hardly significant over a single year, and not of great consequence over a lifetime, but over four centuries it added up to three days. This posed no great problem for Christmas, the date of which was fixed as 25 December, but began to cause serious problems for the Church's calculation of Easter which relied upon a complex formula relating to the sun and the moon within which the date of the vernal (spring) equinox was crucial.

In the fourth century AD, the Church tweaked the calendar so that the vernal equinox fell on 21 March, rather than 25 March as it had in the original Julian calendar. The four quarter-days within the calendar thus became 21 March (vernal equinox), 21 June (summer solstice), 21 September (autumnal equinox) and, crucially to our discussion, 21 December (winter solstice). Christmas Day was thus separated in the calendar from the day of winter solstice, as it is today.

While this decision helped to ensure that Easter Day fell at an appropriate time in the fourth century, it did not clear up the longer-term problem of the discrepancy between the seasons and the calendar, which continued to grow apart by 11 minutes 14 seconds each year. This issue would not be resolved by the Catholic Church until the introduction of the Gregorian calendar in the late sixteenth century; in Britain this calendar, which will be discussed further in Chapter 5, was not introduced until 1752. To cut a long story short, if Julius Caesar had got his calendar as accurate as Pope Gregory's then we would still be celebrating Christmas Day on the day of the winter solstice, but he didn't, so we don't.

A Brief History of Christmas

This book presents an overview of midwinter festivals from prehistoric times through to the present day. Its basic structure is chronological, but emphasis is placed throughout on continuity, demonstrating that while people occasionally introduced new elements into their festivities, many aspects of midwinter celebration have survived remarkably intact over thousands of years. Our story gets underway with a consideration of Stonehenge and a number of other spectacular Neolithic monuments, including the great tombs of Newgrange, Maes Howe and Clava, within which central chambers, containing the bones of the ancestors, were dramatically lit by shafts of sunlight at midwinter. Other great Neolithic monuments incorporating alignments with the midwinter sun include the wonderfully enigmatic stone circle of Long Meg and her Daughters in Cumbria, the bizarre Dorset Cursus which runs for 10km across the chalkland of Wessex, and henge monuments in Wessex, East Anglia and North Wales. Collectively, our great Neolithic monuments offer an intriguing insight into the minds of our ancestors of 5000 years ago and the significance they attached to the winter solstice.

The great Stone Age monuments fell out of favour during the second millennium BC, during which ceremonial practices seem to have become focused on smaller, more local monuments. There is little we can say about midwinter celebrations during this time, although they must surely have been held in some form. The first millennium BC witnesses the advent of the Celts, whose midwinter celebration would have been overseen by their Druids. Although we have little direct evidence of Celtic midwinter celebrations, we will examine a few ancient myths and legends that hint at the importance with which people in Britain may have regarded midwinter in the centuries prior to the Roman invasion.

From prehistoric Britain we travel to ancient Palestine and Rome to examine the story of the Nativity and the adoption of its celebration on 25 December by the Roman Church. Today, many Christians believe literally in the biblical story of the Nativity, while others accept that the story is simply representative of greater truths. Other people regard the whole story as nothing but fiction. Regardless of one's personal belief, it is crucial to examine the Nativity in some detail in order to set the scene for subsequent developments in our story. We will consider the traditional accounts provided by the Gospels of Luke and Matthew alongside a number of 'alternative gospels' that failed to make it into the Bible. We will discover that the story of the Nativity appears to have roots in earlier religious mythology, both in the Old Testament and elsewhere. Although not seeking to adopt an anti-Christian stance, this account will highlight a number of inconsistencies between the Nativity stories offered by Luke and Matthew, and question the extent to which these biblical accounts should be considered as reliable.

The greatest festival in the early Christian Church was Easter, and there seems to have been no widely practised celebration of the Nativity until the fourth century when the Bishop of Rome announced that it would be celebrated on 25 December – effectively replacing the pagan *Dies Natalis Solis Invicti*. To understand how this came about, we must spend some time analysing midwinter celebrations in ancient Rome prior to, and contemporary with, the development of Christianity. In the Roman world of the first three centuries AD, the traditional festivals of Saturnalia and the Kalends were popularly observed. Sandwiched between Saturnalia and the Kalends was the 'Festival of the Birthday of the Unconquered Sun' (*Dies Natalis Solis Invicti*) on the day of the winter solstice – 25 December. Although its history is not well known, this festival must have very ancient roots, possibly back in pre-Roman times, when religions such as those of ancient Egypt and Greece had their own fabulous myths relating to the rebirth of the sun at midwinter. *Dies Natalis Solis Invicti* was adopted as the main feast day of the Mithraic religion that was particularly popular amongst the legions – hence it was enthusiastically celebrated wherever the army was present, including the furthest corners of the Empire such as northern England. As will be seen, many ancient Roman midwinter traditions survive as ingredients of our modern Christmas, either through their incorporation into Christian doctrine or through the failure of the Church to wipe them out.

Returning to Britain, there is precious little information about Christmas prior to the Norman Conquest, but, amongst other things, the Arthurian legend of Sir Gawain and the Green Knight, the influence of the Roman Church and of Anglo-Saxon and Viking invaders on the festive season, and the introduction of the term 'Christmas' which only occurred in the eleventh century, will be outlined. We will also consider the frequency with which Christ is referred to, from early Christian times onwards, as the 'Sun' of Righteousness, implying a clear link with earlier, pagan sun worship.

After 1066 we are able to rely increasingly on contemporary accounts to tell the story of the medieval Christmas, though the reliability of these accounts cannot be taken for granted. In contrast to today, the medieval Christmas was not focussed so much on Christmas Day, but was celebrated throughout an extended festive season, reaching a grand finale on 'Twelfth Night' – the Christmas season's final invitation to over-indulge. Epiphany, an important Church festival commemorating the arrival of the Magi at Jesus' crib, was celebrated on 6 January with its own rituals, effectively bringing the Christmas season to a close. Sometimes, though, decorations were left up and festivities extended right through until Candlemas on 2 February, the Church festival commemorating the ritual purification of Mary 40 days after the Birth of Jesus. Although medieval sources focus very much on the Christmas celebrations of kings and nobles, we will also consider the season as it was enjoyed by the common man.

From the reign of Henry VIII, the Reformation saw the influence of the Catholic Church over the British Christmas much diminished, especially in Scotland. Despite his battle with the Catholic Church, however, Henry remained a great fan of Christmas; we will have much to say about his outrageously extravagant festive celebrations, and those of his successors. We will examine the earliest Christmases spent by British settlers in the New World, and the abolition of the festive season by the Cromwellian Parliament after the Civil War, followed by its subsequent restoration along with that of the monarchy. Following the Restoration, we will consider the story of Christmas through until the end of the eighteenth century. Included in this discussion will be a brief analysis of the introduction of the Gregorian calendar in 1752 and its effect on Christmas celebrations in this and subsequent years. Although a sizeable proportion of the population continued to celebrate Christmas with gusto, many commentators have written of a decline in the importance attached to the season by society in general towards the end of the eighteenth century and into the early nineteenth; we will seek to account for this, and thus to set the scene for the great Victorian 'revival' of Christmas covered in the following chapter.

Many aspects of our present-day 'traditional' Christmas were introduced during the nineteenth century. This was the time when Santa Claus became popular. Alongside Jesus Christ, Santa is one of our two great Christmas characters, and he is arguably even more of an enigma than Jesus. Santa as we know him today is an American invention of the early nineteenth century, although his origins can be traced back to the fourth-century St Nicholas. He also incorporates several characteristics normally associated with prehistoric shamans, and we will consider the extent to which his character may subconsciously embody very ancient traditions that would not have been entirely unfamiliar to our Neolithic ancestors. The nineteenth-century works of Charles Dickens and Washington Irving had immense influence over the development and popularity of Christmas in Victorian times, with Dickens particularly concerned with social conditions and the importance of festive charity. This period also saw the introduction of Christmas cards, trees and crackers, alongside a rise in popularity of the turkey, Christmas pudding, Christmas cake, presents, carols and pantomimes.

The twentieth century saw continuing emphasis on charity at Christmas, with much done to help the poor and the homeless over the festive season. Amidst the horrors of World War I, the extraordinary 'Christmas truce' of 1914 illustrates the unique power of Christmas to generate peace and harmony, however temporarily, in the most adverse of circumstances. Astounding technological advances during the twentieth century had a major impact on the nature of Christmas entertainment, but also worrying side effects that have contributed to global warming and the consequent reduction in the probability of a white Christmas. Within the family, children increasingly became the focus of Christmas Day celebrations, and their insatiable desire for presents had much to do with the continued rise in popularity of Santa Claus, while public sympathy for the traditional celebration of the Nativity waned and was accompanied by a general decline in churchgoing.

This introduction has outlined the complex, lengthy and fascinating history of Christmas, hopefully whetting the appetite for the chapters that follow. These chapters present elements of the story in more detail, eventually bringing our journey to a close with a brief analysis of the complexity of the modern Christmas.

But 'Christmas present' must await its turn. To begin our story we must travel back some 200 generations to visit our Neolithic ancestors as they celebrate the mysteries of the winter solstice at their magnificent tombs and temples. Imagine the scene: people gathering together on a frosty midwinter afternoon on Salisbury Plain, where a recently constructed edifice of spectacular proportions provides a new focus for the already ancient custom of watching the final rays of the dying midwinter sun before praying through the night for its return the following morning, marking the onset of a new year and the guarantee of slow but steady progress towards the long, warm days of summer.

2

Temples and Tombs.
Midwinter in prehistory

From about 3000 BC we begin to find indisputable evidence for the importance of the winter solstice to communities throughout the British Isles. This comes in the form of great monuments built during the Neolithic period, or New Stone Age, at the time when people were adopting agriculture in place of hunting and gathering. Exactly why these great monuments should have been built at this time will long continue to exercise the minds of archaeologists. Many different types of monument were built, including great enclosed tombs, like artificial caves, which contained the bones of the ancestors, and stone circles, open to the sky, within which communal ceremonies presumably took place. Their architectural sophistication is extraordinary, especially as many of them were designed to incorporate astronomical alignments. Over the years, many theories have been published about the astronomical interests of Neolithic people, but I don't believe that the astronomy of the time was particularly complex. People were not constructing deadly accurate monuments to record and predict the movements of the planets or stars, but alignments to particular solar events, such as the midwinter, midsummer or equinoctial sunrise or sunset, were clearly fundamental to the design of some structures. In addition, it seems fairly certain that some monuments were constructed in relation to the complex cycles of the moon, but these cannot concern us here. Rather, we will concentrate on a few spectacular examples that demonstrate beyond any reasonable doubt that the winter solstice, later to form the basis of our Christmas, was of monumental significance to the people who lived in Britain 5000 years ago. We will begin with arguably the most celebrated prehistoric monument in the world, Stonehenge.

Stonehenge

Wrecked in antiquity, chipped for mementoes in the eighteenth and nineteenth centuries, threatened with demolition in the 1914-18 war, sold at auction in 1915 for £6,600, the annual scene of mock-Druid midsummer masquerades, excavated by Cunnington in 1801, by Gowland in 1901, Hawley 1919-26, and, selectively, by Atkinson, Piggott and Stone since 1950, this ravaged colossus rests like a cage of sand-scoured ribs on the shores of eternity, its flesh forever lost. Stonehenge grudges its secrets. Each one explained – the date, source of the stones, the builders – leads to greater amazements, a spiralling complexity that even now eludes our understanding so that our studies remain two-dimensional and incomplete.

Thus, Aubrey Burl introduces Stonehenge in his book *The Stone Circle of the British Isles*, a bible for scholars of stone circles ever since its first publication in 1976. Described by Henry of Huntington in the twelfth century as one of the four wonders of Britain, it was christened *Stanenges* (which means the place of the hanging-stones or stone gallows) as its central trilithons resembled medieval gibbets. From this the term 'henge' has been applied to all manner of circular embanked enclosures of Neolithic date, the vast majority of which never actually contained any standing stones, and none of which had lintels and trilithons like the 'hanging stones' of Stonehenge. Although many henges and other spectacular monuments existed throughout Neolithic Britain, Stonehenge has a unique ability to fascinate and amaze some five millennia after its original foundation. Its unique appeal to the public is reflected in its appearance on the front cover of *National Geographic* magazine in June 2008. Within this magazine an article by Caroline Alexander entitled 'If stones could speak: searching for the meaning of Stonehenge' observes:

> There are no texts to explain Stonehenge. Secure in its wordless prehistory, it can thus absorb a multitude of 'meanings': temple to the sun – or the moon, for that matter; astronomical calendar; city of the ancestral dead; centre of healing; stone representation of the gods; symbol of status and power. The heart of its mystique is, surely, that it excites in equal measure both zealous certitude and utter bafflement.

We will return to this article shortly, but for now must concentrate on what we know of the history of Stonehenge, an exceedingly complex monument which, like a great medieval cathedral, evolved through several different phases over many generations. It began life (phase I) in about 3000 BC as a relatively unspectacular structure consisting of a 2m high circular bank of chalk around which ran an encircling ditch about 110m in overall diameter, with narrow gaps in the north-east and south providing easy access to the central area. A ring of 56 pits around the circumference of the interior probably held timber uprights. Over subsequent centuries (phase II) the enclosure seems to have been used as a cremation cemetery; at least 50 cremation burials have been excavated. More than 200 post-holes within the interior and immediately outside the north-east entrance probably also belong to this phase, but remain unexplained. Some may have held structural posts for buildings, while others may have held decorated posts that performed a ceremonial function rather like totem poles.

The first standing stones were introduced to the site only in phase III, in about 2500 BC. The earliest stone structure, of uncertain form, consisted of about 80 'bluestones', each some 2m in length and weighing about 4 tons, astonishingly transported here from the Preseli Hills in South Wales; the probable route is in excess of 400km. In addition to the bluestone structure, the 'Heelstone' (which may originally have had a partner) stood outside the north-east entrance, and four 'Station Stones' were set around the perimeter of the interior to form a large rectangle of unknown purpose. After standing for perhaps a century or two, the bluestones were removed, and a giant circle of 30 sarsen stones, standing nearly 5m high and dramatically topped with a ring of lintels, was built to surround five massive trilithons (the tallest, at the centre, standing to a height of 7.5m) that together formed a kind of cove, open to the north-east, at the centre of the site. For reasons we will never fully comprehend, these gigantic sarsen stones, weighing between 35 and 50 tons each, were dragged to the site from the Marlborough Downs about 35km away to enable the construction of a sophisticated and spectacular monument the like of which had never been seen before, at least not in stone. Although this magnificent new structure was unique, it may have had timber predecessors elsewhere as its huge lintels are held securely on their uprights by 'mortise-and-tenon' joints that would be familiar to any carpenter. Also in phase III, a further three massive stones were erected within the entrance, just one of which – the so-called 'Slaughter Stone' – survives today. In about 2200 BC, some 70 bluestones were re-introduced and erected on site to form a new circle between the great sarsen circle and the trilithons and also a horseshoe-shaped setting, open to the north-east, at the centre of the site. Within this central horseshoe, at the very heart of the structure, stood the 'Altar Stone', which may originally have been one of a pair. At some point towards the end of this sequence, the Avenue, a ceremonial way demarcated by linear banks and ditches, was constructed to run north-eastwards from the north-east entrance before turning east, then south-east to the River Avon some 3km away.

This is a much simplified overview of the main phases of Stonehenge's development; there are many more features than those discussed here and archaeologists continue to debate the detailed structural history of the site. What has long been recognised, though, is that the great sarsen structure in phase III was set with a north-east/ south-west axis that aligns with the midsummer sunrise, suggesting that this alignment was of crucial importance. However, as we will see shortly, this is by no means the only alignment at Stonehenge.

Several eminent authorities, in addition to many complete crackpots, have published accounts of the probable astronomical significance of this great monument. Some of the more 'scientific' theories see it as a giant eclipse predictor, a solar and lunar calendar, or even a supercomputer capable of calculating and predicting all sorts of earthly and supernatural events. We will not concern ourselves here with any such accounts, nor with those involving time-travel or alien invasions – the study of Stonehenge is fascinating enough without the need to introduce such nonsense. Of all the splendid books produced about Stonehenge over the years, one of the best, published in 1997, is entitled *Science and Stonehenge*. Edited by arguably the two greatest names in twentieth-century British prehistory, Barry Cunliffe and Colin Renfrew, this includes 15 contributions from acknowledged experts on different aspects of Stonehenge which collectively represent a summary of our understanding of the monument towards the end of the last century. Of particular interest to our story is the contribution on 'astronomy and Stonehenge' by the eminent archaeo-astronomer, Clive Ruggles. In this, he considers possible alignments with various phases of the sun, moon, planets and stars, making the crucial observation that the 'astronomy' of the Stonehenge people would have been very different from that of today's scientists. People at Stonehenge 5000 years ago may have witnessed the same phenomena as we do today, but their perception of them would have been very different from ours. As Ruggles puts it:

> Different groups or individuals may 'see' the same objects in the sky, but the significance that they attach to them will be influenced by their classification of the natural world and the various ways in which they interact with it.

Almost certainly, using today's terminology, the Neolithic interest in the heavens would be classified as 'astrology' rather than 'astronomy', but Neolithic people would have made no distinction between the two; more will be said later in this chapter about possible Neolithic beliefs as they relate to the heavens.

Ruggles' analysis of astronomical alignments at Stonehenge is very detailed, but his conclusions, perhaps not surprisingly given the nature of this most enigmatic of monuments, are far from certain. The site, especially during its early phases, seems to have incorporated alignments on the phases of the moon, but we cannot be certain of this. Ruggles is adamant, however, about one thing. By phase III, the main NE-SW axis of Stonehenge, respected by the great sarsen trilithons, the north-east entrance, the Avenue, the Heel Stone, the Altar Stone, and perhaps also the Slaughter Stone and its lost colleagues, lay on the line of the summer solstice sunrise.

This link with the summer solstice could certainly account for the axis of Stonehenge, but there is also an alternative explanation. While there is no doubt that the main axis of Stonehenge does lie on this alignment, could it have been the midwinter rather than the midsummer sun that was the key determining factor behind it? In his book *Astronomy in Prehistoric Britain and Ireland*, Ruggles provides data on astronomical alignments at Stonehenge and hundreds of other monuments. After considering the summer solstice alignment at Stonehenge, he states:

> … if the Altar Stone was the focus of attention and the Heel Stone and its companion marked the ceremonial entrance to the monument, it is certainly just as plausible, and arguably more so, that the alignment of particular symbolic value was that of the Altar Stone with the direction of midwinter sunset in the south-west.

Cambridge University prehistorian, Christopher Chippindale, develops this argument in *Stonehenge Complete* (2004):

> … the general rule is that religious buildings are organized so they are entered facing the sacred direction, the reverential way rather than with your back to the sacred. In their linked traditions, Jewish, Christian and Moslem sacred buildings show this: you enter a church at the other, western end and then advance towards the eastern, sacred altar.
>
> Apply these considerations at Stonehenge, in the elaborate form of the full final monument with its Avenue, and its sarsen and bluestone structures. The supplicant enters always facing towards the midwinter sunset and so with their back to the midsummer sunrise. They successively advance: up the gentle ascent of the straight

Avenue approach; by the Heel Stone and its vanished twin; through the major gap of the encircling ditch and banks; by the slaughter stone and its two vanished companions; across to the centre and through the extra-wide gap between uprights of the sarsen circle; through the uprights of the bluestone circle. Then they enter the central area – which in both scale and size is strikingly consistent with the common dimensions of an English church choir. Like a church choir, it is closed towards the sacred direction, open at the entrance opposite. It is defined by the horseshoe of sarsen trilithons, rising in their height and scale towards the sacred direction, and within them by the horseshoe of bluestones; at its south-western end, towards the sacred direction, stands the upright Altar Stone, largest of the exotic Welsh stones.

We should note that this is not an entirely new suggestion. Back in 1912, John Abercromby wrote:

> If Stonehenge has a sepulchral purpose it could hardly have been destined for any person less than a divinity – for one of those that was believed to die annually in winter and rise again in spring. As the position of the most sacred part of the cella lay at the south-west end, the faces of celebrants would be turned in the direction of sunset at the winter solstice. It may be supposed, then, that Stonehenge was erected after enormous labour to commemorate annually at midwinter the death of some great divinity, one who supplied grass for the cattle, who rendered the earth fecund, who multiplied the herds, and on whom the people depended for all supplies of food.

Abercromby believed that people gathered at Stonehenge 'at night with dramatic effect amid wild lamentation' to celebrate the death and burial of this great god, before gathering again in the spring when 'another festival of an orgiastic nature would celebrate the resurrection, with renewed life and vigour, of the divinity of Nature'. Whether or not two such celebrations (which would equate rather neatly with Christmas and Easter) were actually held at Stonehenge in Neolithic times can be no more than conjecture. Personally, I see no need for the spring festival; the midwinter celebration could commemorate both the death and rebirth of the sun simultaneously, and must surely have been the key annual event at Stonehenge. This argument receives support in *Solving Stonehenge: The New Key to an Ancient Enigma* (2008), in which Anthony Johnson provides a thorough analysis of the monument before concluding 'the pivotal event was indeed the winter solstice … heralding the birth of a new year.'

As we are about to discover, several other great Neolithic monuments were constructed with entrances facing *towards* the sunrise or sunset at the winter solstice. This, however, need not be a problem; Stonehenge is so very different from everything else that we shouldn't be surprised if the symbolism underlying its architecture is also uniquely complex. The problem at Stonehenge arises from the fact that it incorporates alignments on both summer and winter solstices, and possibly also on several other solar and lunar events, and it is not possible to say for sure which, if any, were the more important. Other monuments within the Stonehenge landscape are certainly aligned on the summer solstice, while the Stonehenge Cursus (a 3km-long linear earthwork) seems to have been designed in relation to the equinoctial sunrise and sunset. Timothy Darvill has considered all these monuments together in an ambitious yet convincing attempt to present a 'sacred geography' of the entire Stonehenge landscape, dividing it into different zones according to significant solar alignments and with Stonehenge at its heart. While agreeing that all these alignments are significant, I remain convinced that the single most important annual event at Stonehenge was the celebration of the winter solstice, when the sun died and was reborn.

Durrington Walls

This is not the place to consider the Stonehenge landscape in any detail, but we must spend a little time discussing the enormous, but relatively little-known, site of Durrington Walls, some 3km north-east of Stonehenge. Although very different in form and scale to Stonehenge, this is also classified by archaeologists as a 'henge' – one of a small number of so-called 'super henges' found in Wessex. Durrington Walls consists of an earthen bank originally some 3m in height, with an internal ditch, surrounding an internal area not far short of 0.5km in diameter. The site was little known to the general public prior to the broadcasting of a *Time Team* programme about it on Channel 4 in December 2005. This featured excavations undertaken during 2005 and also an ambitious project to reconstruct one of the massive timber circles known to have existed within the site. Two such circles had been discovered back in the 1960s when excavations were undertaken in association with a road improvement scheme (the busy A345 passes right through the site). The smaller of these, the so-called northern circle, consists of two concentric rings of standing timber uprights, while the larger must originally have been an altogether extraordinary structure, consisting of six concentric rings of massive posts standing to a height of about 6m.

It was the larger structure that was reconstructed by *Time Team* and which concerns us here. The excavated remains consist of concentric rings of postholes, into which the massive posts, probably all of oak, were set. The postholes towards the centre were larger than those towards the outer edge, suggesting that the posts may have formed the superstructure for a massive, circular building with a conical thatched roof – perhaps some sort of temple. However, most archaeologists who have studied timber circles conclude that they were probably open to the heavens, though possibly with lintels like Stonehenge. This of course does not preclude their use as temples; indeed a structure open to the heavens would probably have represented a more dramatic monument than one in which people participating in ceremonies were closed in beneath a roof. Evidence from the excavations suggests that ceremonies were indeed enacted at the Durrington Walls southern circle. By the entrance to the circle, archaeologists found evidence of extensive burning (suggesting the use of fire in rituals) along with flint tools, animal bone and much Grooved Ware pottery (a type of Neolithic pottery associated with many ceremonial sites throughout Britain). Further finds within the postholes of the structure are suggestive of ritual offerings, perhaps laid at the feet of some of the great timber uprights. While a few bones, flint tools and pieces of pottery may not seem much to us in our materialistic world, their deposition at an important place like Durrington Walls must have been of considerable symbolic significance to Neolithic people. The particular relevance of all this to the present discussion lies in the observation that the main axis of the southern circle is aligned on the winter solstice sunrise.

The recent excavations also targeted an area outside the east entrance to the henge, where evidence of Neolithic activity included pits, hearths, large quantities of animal bones, pottery and flint tools. The presence of many pig bones, along with the recovery of pig fat residues from fragments of pottery, suggest much cooking of pork on the site. Intriguingly, the analysis of pig teeth suggests that many of the beasts were about nine months old when slaughtered. Assuming they were born in the spring, this implies that the feasting was taking place at midwinter. Activities presumably took place at Durrington Walls on many different occasions throughout the year, but perhaps it was those held in the cold and dark of midwinter that were of paramount importance to the local people.

The aforementioned *National Geographic* article offers an intriguing interpretation of Durrington Walls in relation to Stonehenge. This is based on the work of Mike Parker-Pearson, who has spent much time living with native communities on Madagascar and observes that in traditional Malagasy culture, stone monuments, built to last 'forever', are associated with death and the ancestors, while wooden structures are associated with the transience of life. According to this model, Durrington Walls was a place for the living, while Stonehenge was primarily associated with the dead. Taking all the archaeological evidence into careful account, and adding just a small dash of artistic licence, we could perhaps envisage certain members of the community travelling to Stonehenge to join the ancestors in a special ceremony as the sun set on the shortest day of the year, then rejoining the rest of the community at Durrington Walls to enjoy an overnight feast before welcoming back the sun the following morning. To equate Durrington Walls with a banqueting house and Stonehenge with a cathedral would be going too far, but this general model may offer a clue as to the nature of midwinter festivities in the Stonehenge landscape four and a half thousand years ago.

Dorset Cursus

Although nowhere near as visually spectacular in today's landscape as Stonehenge, the Dorset Cursus is in its own way no less intriguing. Indeed, the prehistorian Christopher Tilley has recently stated that 'At the time of its initial use the Dorset Cursus was one of the two most spectacular monuments in Neolithic Britain, rivalled in the sheer scale of its construction only by the earthworks on Hambledon Hill just 12km to the west of its south-west terminal end.' Hambledon Hill is a vast hilltop enclosure, perhaps originally a necropolis, that by its nature cannot be expected to display any obvious astronomical alignments. An alignment on the midwinter sunset was fundamental , however, to the architecture of the Dorset Cursus.

Cursuses are curious monuments. The eminent eighteenth-century antiquary, William Stukeley, wrote in 1740 that the cursus near Stonehenge 'resembled a course suitable for the racing of chariots by the Ancient Britons'. They were thus christened 'cursuses', after the Latin for racetrack. Their original purpose remains obscure, although several archaeologists have recently attempted to interpret them as avenues for ritual processions. They generally consist of two parallel earthwork banks with external ditches enclosing a long, linear central area, with both terminals also closed off by banks. More than a hundred examples are known throughout Britain, with most ranging in length from 150m to 4km. A number of radiocarbon determinations from excavations over recent years suggest that they date from the middle Neolithic, with most probably constructed in the period 3500-3000 BC. Most have been damaged by ploughing and other subsequent activity over the millennia and few survive in good condition along much of their length; most have been discovered from the air as cropmarks or parchmarks rather than as upstanding earthworks.

The Dorset Cursus seems to date from a century or two either side of 3200 BC. It actually consists of two conjoined monuments and is by far the longest known cursus, travelling for some 10km across the gently undulating chalkland of Cranborne Chase. It is formed of parallel banks of chalk up to 2m in height, which seem originally to have been revetted walls rather than simple banks, and external ditches from which the chalk was quarried. The internal area averages 90m in width, making the entire monument approximately 10km long and 100m wide. This is architecture on a grand scale; at a steady walking pace it takes a little over two hours to traverse the entire length of the monument.

When the cursus was originally built, Cranborne Chase was considerably more wooded than it is today. The freshly constructed banks and ditches of the cursus would have appeared spectacular; artificial, straight white banks and ditches striding purposefully across the undulating, green landscape of woodland and pasture. Today, little of the original earthwork survives above ground, but air photography allows us to reconstruct its original form. The original phase ran 5.8km from Bottlebush Down to Thickthorn Down, while the later phase extended the monument a further 4.3km to the north-west to a new terminal on Martin Down.

It is important to realise that, although much natural woodland still survived in its vicinity, the Dorset Cursus was not built in a virgin landscape. Archaeologists have recovered evidence of human habitation here extending back to Mesolithic period well before 5000 BC, and several earlier Neolithic long barrows (burial mounds) were built here before the construction of the cursus. The cursus may, therefore, have been designed to reinforce pre-existing interpretations of the landscape and the place of people within it, rather than to herald the dramatic introduction of a new 'religion' or social structure. Indeed, the cursus seems to respect earlier long barrows in a way that suggests its route may have been of symbolic significance long before some half a million person-hours of labour were invested in its construction.

We have already noted that the general alignment of the cursus is north-east to south-west and have suggested that it was used for ceremonial processions. We have also observed that its architecture respects a number of earlier long barrows (probably regarded by people at the time as 'houses of the dead'). These are, I think, the critical factors in attempting an interpretation its purpose, and they all come neatly together at a point on Gussage Cow Down, about half-way along the original (south-west) length of the cursus. Here, an earlier long barrow is incorporated within the interior of the cursus in such a way that its profile appears on the horizon to anyone travelling along the monument from the north-east. This mound probably contained the bones of long-dead ancestors, and may already have been here for half a millennium by the time that the cursus was constructed. To fully appreciate its symbolic link with the cursus we must introduce the midwinter sunset; as seen by people within the cursus to the north-east, the midwinter sun appears to set directly behind (or within?) this ancient tomb.

There can be no doubt that the winter solstice was a key factor in the design and use of the Dorset Cursus. Perhaps a large proportion of the local population took part in processions along it to observe the midwinter sun setting behind the Gussage Cow Down long barrow. Alternatively, the apparent lack of any original entrances has led some archaeologists to believe that the Dorset Cursus was primarily a monument to and *for* the gods, and that it was only they, and not mere mortals, who observed the setting midwinter sun from within it. Perhaps the most likely scenario is that a select few individuals walked the route on the day of the winter solstice, communing with the gods on behalf of the wider community at this critical time of year. The cursus must have represented a sense of timeless order in the world, and the ceremonies undertaken within it would surely have created an unbreakable bond between past, present and future. Whatever the exact nature of these ceremonies (and the fine detail will forever elude us), the Dorset Cursus unambiguously incorporates relationships with the midwinter sun and with the ancestors. Richard Bradley, one of our most eminent prehistorians, observes that this link with the midwinter sun:

... strengthened the link between the Cursus and a monument built for the dead and made that very relationship seem part of nature itself. It ensured the permanence of this extraordinary monument and in doing so protected it from challenge. The ancestors who had been of such concern to the living were caught up in the forces of nature.

As at Stonehenge, the winter solstice was a key factor in the design of an extraordinary monument which, once built, served to reinforce peoples' views of themselves and their place in the cosmos.

Long Meg and her Daughters

We move now to north-west England, and the fringes of the Lake District, to visit one of my favourite archaeological sites, the stone circle of Long Meg and her Daughters. Located near the village of Little Salkeld, 8km east of the market town of Penrith, this is a place that can have a profound effect on visitors. William Wordsworth was here in 1833, observing that 'Though it will not bear a comparison with Stonehenge, I must say, I have not seen any other relique of those dark ages which can pretend to rival it in singularity and dignity of appearance'. Wordsworth penned the following verse, which perhaps comes closer to expressing the power of the place than any factual description can hope to do:

> A weight of awe not easy to be borne
> Fell suddenly upon my spirit, cast
> From the dread bosom of the unknown past,
> When first I saw that sisterhood forelorn;-
> And Her, whose strength and stature seemed to scorn
> The power of the years – pre-eminent, and placed
> Apart, to overlook the circle vast.
> Speak Giant-mother! Tell it to the Morn,
> While she dispels the cumbrous shades of night;
> Let the Moon hear, emerging from a cloud,
> When, how and wherefore, rose on British ground
> That wondrous Monument, whose mystic round
> Forth shadows, some have deemed, to mortal sight
> The inviolable God that tames the proud.

The site is indeed vast, consisting of an irregular ring, about 100m across, of enormous igneous boulders weighing an average of 9 tons each, with the heaviest weighing in at a hefty 30 tons. It has been estimated that the minimum size of the workforce needed to manipulate these mighty stones into place was in the order of 135 people, although it is possible that oxen may have been used to move the stones, probably on a system of rollers. Outside the circle, the massive red sandstone monolith of Long Meg stands guard over her 'daughters'.

The site was recorded by a local schoolmaster as 'meg with hir daughters' as long ago as 1600, but the origin of the name is obscure. A local legend tells that Long Meg was a witch, her Daughters being her coven, and all were turned to stone by a local magician. Linked to this is the belief that it is impossible to accurately count the number of stones in the circle, and that anyone who succeeds in doing so will bring the witches back to life! Today there are about 69 stones in the ring, of which 27 are still standing, several to a height of about 2m. However, without careful excavation of the entire site to count the original stone-holes it will be impossible to be sure of the original number of stones. Another story is that the stones were all girls, turned to stone for dancing on the Sabbath. Many stone circles have legends linked to dancing, and it is possible that these relate back to some ancient folk memory that dancing around them did indeed take place as part of prehistoric ceremonies.

At one time in the late eighteenth century, the landowner decided to blast some of the stones, presumably to clear the land for agriculture while also providing building stone. Fortunately, before it could proceed very far, this action was halted by an exceptionally violent thunder storm which scared off the labourers who refused to return and risk further incurring the wrath of the ancient gods. Later, in the nineteenth century, the local farmer shifted some of the stones, whereupon his crops failed, leading to their prompt return – though presumably not to their exact original positions. Other ancient accounts record the presence of two great piles of stone, some 3m in height, within the circle. These may have been burial cairns of Neolithic date, but could have been added during later times. There is no sign of them on the ground today. Intriguingly, air photography has recently revealed an enormous, but now flattened, embanked enclosure adjacent to the circle; this may have been used in association with, or have been superseded by, the stone monument.

We must now consider the outlying stone, Long Meg herself, in more detail. We have already noted that the circle consists of huge igneous boulders, laboriously manoeuvred into place some 5000 years ago by local people, having been dumped in the area by the retreating glaciers another 5000 years earlier. In contrast, Long Meg is of red sandstone and was presumably quarried from the nearby cliffs above the Eden before being brought a mile or so to the site. She stands 18m outside the circle's entrance. Why is she here? Some have speculated that she functioned as a kind of signpost, visible to people approaching the site from down by the river before the lower boulders of the circle came into view. She may indeed have performed this function, but the main reason for her presence here is rather more fascinating. When viewed from within the circle, Long Meg stands proudly against the sky, extending a line formed by the two western portals of the circle's south-east facing entrance. This alignment precisely marks the setting point of the midwinter sun.

Why should this single massive block of sandstone, which offers such a contrast to all the other stones in the circle, have been laboriously brought here and erected to accentuate this alignment? Surely the two portals of the entrance were sufficient on their own to incorporate this alignment into the architecture of the site, if that is what was required. Here we arrive at a discussion of the enigmatic carvings of spirals and circles that adorn Long Meg's eastern face. It is usually assumed that these were added to Long Meg after she had been erected on the site, but I consider this unlikely. There are a few places in Britain where red sandstone river cliffs are adorned with similar carvings (including one on the Coquet near Warkworth, Northumberland, and one at Hawthornden near Edinburgh). Given that the carvings on Long Meg occur only on one face, I believe they were probably produced when the stone still formed part of the river cliffs and may have been carved centuries before the stone was quarried and transported to the stone circle. Exactly why these carvings should have been carved on river cliffs must remain a mystery, as must their original significance. However, I have little doubt that they were regarded as sacred symbols by the people who built and used the stone circle and, having been positioned outside the circle in line with the midwinter sunset, they presumably assumed some kind of solar significance. I shall have a little more to say about such carvings later, as they occur in greater profusion at the Irish sites we will be visiting shortly. For now, we need only observe that Long Meg, with her carvings, marked the winter solstice sunset which must surely have been of very great significance to the people who designed, built and used this magnificent stone circle. We can imagine communities coming from far and wide to observe the midwinter sunset here, participating in ceremonies which may have included feasting, dancing, trading and the offering of gifts to the ancestors. Perhaps, if a programme of excavations can be mounted using modern techniques like that discussed above at Durrington Walls, then this 'wondrous monument' may yet reveal much about the lives and beliefs of the people who used it 5000 years ago.

In addition to Long Meg, Cumbria is endowed with many other fine stone circles. Swinside, described by Aubrey Burl as 'the loveliest of all the circles', lies well off the beaten track near the village of Broughton. It is sometimes referred to as 'Sunkenkirk', reflecting a local legend that the stones were set into the ground by the Devil to prevent their use as building material for a church. Swinside has a clear entrance incorporating portal stones like those at Long Meg, but whereas Long Meg's entrance faces towards the midwinter sunset, that at Swinside faces south-east, towards the winter solstice sunrise. Once again, it seems that the winter solstice was crucial to the builders of a great ceremonial monument, and we must assume that ceremonies were enacted here at midwinter.

Newgrange

The Neolithic passage tombs of the Bend of the Boyne, about 50km north of Dublin, represent one of the most amazing prehistoric complexes to be experienced anywhere in the world, easily justifying World Heritage Site status. About 40 substantial tombs are concentrated into an area of no more than 8 square kilometres. They are about 5000 years old and consist of mounds of earth and stone containing stone-built chambers accessible via long stone-lined passages; hence the term 'passage grave'. Over the years, 25 of these tombs have been either wholly or partially excavated, but the complex is dominated by the three truly huge monuments of Newgrange, Knowth and Dowth.

Here, for reasons that will come self-evident, we will concentrate largely on Newgrange. This magnificent monument was brought to the attention of the world in 1699 by the great Welsh antiquarian Edward Lhywd, who was touring Ireland and recorded in a letter dated 15 December that year that:

> The gentleman of the village observing that under the green turf this mount was wholly composed of stones, and having occasion for some, employed his servants to carry off a considerable parcel

of them; till they came at last to a very broad flat stone crudely carved, and placed edgewise at the bottom of the mount. This they discovered to be the door of a cave, which had a long entry into it.

From this moment, Newgrange attracted the attention of countless antiquarians and archaeologists, but its main secret would remain hidden for another three centuries. Its huge mound consists of some 200,000 tonnes of water-worn cobbles, presumably dug out of nearby river gravels, interspersed with layers of turf. It is sub-circular in plan and prior to its recent restoration still stood to a height of 13m. The mass of the cairn is retained by a contiguous kerb of 97 massive slabs, of which none weighs less than a tonne and several display mysterious carvings. The visual impact of the tomb exterior is enhanced by a vertical 'skin' of white quartz, the like of which is not recorded at any other Neolithic tomb and which, we should note, is somewhat controversial: the original exterior walls were probably not as sheer as they are today following consolidation in the 1970s. The entire tomb is surrounded by a stone circle, of which 12 large boulders remain from a probable original total of about 35. This circle has an average diameter of a little over 100m, and encloses about 1ha. The spectacular entrance to the tomb is in the south-east, from which a 19m long stone-lined passage leads to the hugely impressive cruciform-shaped central chamber. This chamber measures approximately 5 x 7m, and its great corbelled roof rises to a height of 6m.

An impressive programme of excavation and conservation was undertaken at Newgrange between 1962 and 1975, the results of which are presented in a splendid book by Michael O'Kelly. Prior to the excavation, a decorated slab, displaying a line of crosses carved in relief, could be seen protruding from the mound directly above the entrance. The purpose of this stone, described by O'Kelly as 'one of the most expertly executed designs found at Newgrange', was not known. The excavation demonstrated that it was the lintel of a box-like structure, a metre wide, forming a gap in the wall of the cairn leading into the passage directly above the entrance. Intriguingly, the slot at the time of its excavation was found to have been partially closed by two blocks of quartz, and scratches on the surrounding stones demonstrated that these blocks had apparently been removed and slotted back into position many times, the implication being that the roof-box had been opened and closed on many occasions. The entrance into the tomb could also be opened and closed using a large blocking stone found during the excavations, so there must have been some need for the roof-box to be opened or closed independently of the entrance. What possible purpose could this strange structure have served?

It was initially suggested that the box may have been for the placing of ritual offerings, perhaps at particular times of year, for the spirits of the ancestors that lay within the tomb. Or perhaps it was closed most of the time, but opened on specific occasions so that the spirits could enter or leave as they wished. The answer was altogether more spectacular. O'Kelly records that during the excavations he became aware that:

> a belief existed in the neighbourhood that the rising sun, at some unspecified time, used to light up the three-spiral stone in the end recess. No one could be found who had witnessed this but it continued to be mentioned and we assumed that some confusion existed between Newgrange and the midsummer phenomenon at Stonehenge.

It was clear from its alignment that there could be no link here with the midsummer sun, but due to the persistent nature of the local belief, O'Kelly decided to investigate a possible link with the winter solstice. From inside the tomb on 21 December 1969, he made the following astonishing observations:

> At exactly 8.54 hours GMT the top edge of the ball of the sun appeared above the local horizon and at 8.58 hours, the first pencil of direct sunlight shone through the roof-box and along the passage to reach across the tomb chamber floor as far as the basin stone in the end recess. As the thin line of light widened to a 17 cm-band and swung across the chamber floor, the tomb was dramatically illuminated and various details of the side and end recesses could be clearly seen in the light reflected from the floor. At 9.09 hours, the 17 cm-band of light began to narrow again and at exactly 9.15 hours, the direct beam was cut off from the tomb. For 17 minutes, therefore, at sunrise on the shortest day of the year, direct sunlight can enter Newgrange, not through the doorway, but through the specially contrived slit which lies under the roof-box at the outer end of the passage roof.

What an experience that must have been! The riddle of the roof-box was solved in the most spectacular fashion. Its purpose was to enable the midwinter sunlight to reach the mortal remains of the ancestors deep within the otherwise inaccessible tomb. Subsequent detailed survey demonstrated that, despite slight changes in the angle of the earth's orbit, this phenomenon would have occurred 5000 years ago (samples from O'Kelly's excavations provided a radiocarbon date of about 3200 BC for the construction of the tomb) and at every subsequent midwinter through until the present day. In fact the shaft of light would originally have been rather wider than at present, as it is restricted today by leaning stones in the passage that would originally have stood vertically. The complex planning and years, probably decades, of back-breaking construction work were all worth it to the people of Newgrange because they were building a house of the ancestors that would last forever, eternally linked to the annual death and rebirth of the sun.

The importance of the link with the midwinter sun is further demonstrated by spectacular carvings on the Newgrange kerbstones. The magnificent entrance stone and the kerbstone at the opposite side of the mound serve to reinforce the main axis of the site, towards the midwinter sunrise. The entrance stone displays a beautiful combination of spirals and lozenges, incorporating a very obvious vertical line that bisects the entrance and therefore marks the exact axis of the monument. The backstone (kerbstone 52) also incorporates spirals and lozenges, but is very different. It has an even more pronounced vertical groove down the centre which also lies exactly upon the main axis of the monument. None of the other kerbstones are as elaborately decorated as the entrance stone or kerbstone 52, though at least 29 others do display some decoration and many others have yet to be uncovered by excavation. At least 44 stones in the chamber and passage are also decorated, including the upright stone at the junction of chamber and passage with its beautiful and intricately executed triple spiral.

The meaning of all this art has exercised the minds of many archaeologists over the years, but remains obscure. A fascinating study of it was published in 1983 by Martin Brennan. He notes that in archaic astronomy the heavens were often viewed as spiralling, and quotes Ptolemy: 'I search with my mind into the multitudinous revolving spirals of the stars.' Brennan believes that spirals at Newgrange represent the sun, and suggests that anti-clockwise spirals relate specifically to the winter solstice. The riddle is far from solved, but much of Brennan's speculation is certainly very persuasive.

Newgrange should not really be discussed in isolation as it lies within a landscape of monuments, including the two other great passage graves of Dowth and Knowth. In 1769, Dowth was described as containing a 'cave' like the one at Newgrange. Human bones were recorded from this 'cave' in the early nineteenth century, but excavations undertaken in the mid nineteenth century uncovered little about the origins of the site. The passage to the 'cave' recorded in the eighteenth century leads into the mound from its western perimeter, but a little to the south of this a second passage has been discovered, leading to another chamber. This chamber, although not of the same architectural sophistication as that at Newgrange, does share with it an alignment on the midwinter sun. Whereas the Newgrange alignment is on the rising sun at the winter solstice, that at Dowth is on the setting sun; at the end of the shortest day of the year, the final rays of the setting sun illuminate the passage and chamber in a manner that would no doubt be much more widely known and appreciated were it not for the altogether more sophisticated and dramatic architecture of its near neighbour. Dowth also contains its own gallery of megalithic art, including decorated stones in its passages and chambers and at least fifteen decorated kerbstones that appear to incorporate solar symbols. This art, while still very impressive, does not appear to our eyes as of the same high quality as that of Newgrange, but there is something uniquely evocative about its character that renders it, to my mind at least, no less powerful than the masterpieces of Newgrange and Knowth.

The third great Boyne tomb, Knowth, contains two long passages, each leading to a chamber, and is surrounded by a further 19 satellite tombs. The main mound incorporates more than 300 decorated stones; a greater concentration of megalithic art than any other known site. This art is no less impressive than that of Newgrange, and includes one remarkable kerbstone that appears to incorporate a sundial, though its original significance remains unknown. While it would be fascinating to spend more time discussing Knowth, we cannot do so here as there is nothing to link the site clearly with the winter solstice. For our purposes, it shows that while the great tombs of Newgrange and Dowth demonstrate a clear interest in the midwinter sun, there were also other factors at work, something that should not surprise us given the architectural sophistication and undoubtedly complex cosmology of the Neolithic people of the Boyne Valley.

Maes Howe

We now travel to the Orkney Islands, another archaeological paradise containing the enigmatic remains of numerous stone tombs and other monuments of our Neolithic ancestors. It is possible to spend many days exploring these monuments, all of which have their own stories to tell, and in many ways it is bad practice to examine one site in isolation. However, there is one particular monument which, for reasons which will by now be familiar, is of great relevance to this discussion. In their inventory of Orkney's Neolithic tombs, James Davidson and Audrey Henshall note that 'the scale of its construction, the refinement of its design, and the quality of its masonry' make this 'one of the outstanding architectural achievements of prehistoric western Europe.' It has been estimated that, whereas most of Orkney's Neolithic tombs necessitated in the region of 2000 person-hours of labour, the construction of this site alone took some 100,000. If we allow an average working day of eight hours (which is not unreasonable, bearing in mind the winter weather and assuming that people didn't work after nightfall) then the construction of this site would have taken a team of 40 full-time workers nearly a year to complete. In practice, it was probably built over a longer time period on a part-time basis.

The monument in question is the passage tomb known to us as Maes Howe, half a kilometre from the Loch of Harray in a reasonably central and readily accessible location within the Orkney archipelago. Although in a lowland setting, Maes Howe appears prominent from all around due to the windblown and treeless nature of the Orkney landscape, which was as devoid of trees in Neolithic times as it is today. The tomb is not well dated, but a couple of radiocarbon dates suggest that it was originally built in about 2800 BC. This is quite late in the sequence of tomb-building on Orkney and some authorities regard Maes Howe as the culmination of this tradition. It consists of a large, oval mound which now measures about 38 x 32m in diameter and attains a height of just over 7m, but these dimensions owe much to archaeological excavations and conservation work during the nineteenth and twentieth centuries; the mound seems originally to have been much higher. Surrounding the mound is a level platform ranging from 15–20m in width, surrounded by a broad, shallow sub-circular ditch with an external bank.

Within the mound is an extraordinary square-shaped chamber, measuring 4.7m across with a corbelled roof which may originally have been 6m in height. We cannot be certain about its original height because the tomb was broken into through its roof by Vikings in the twelfth century. While we may regret the damage done, the Vikings did actually leave a record of their presence here which adds substantially to the archaeological value of the site. This is in the form of runic inscriptions and small engravings (of a dragon, walrus and serpent knot). Intriguingly, the runic inscriptions refer to the discovery of treasure within the mound, but the only finds made here by archaeologists are a fragment of a human skull and some bones and teeth of a horse. Presumably the Vikings, who may have taken temporary refuge within the site for shelter, removed any other bones and disposed of them outside the tomb. It is unlikely that any 'treasure' would actually have been found here and the runic inscriptions probably owe more to the desire to tell a good story than to any kind of historical authenticity (a theme we will encounter elsewhere in this volume).

The central chamber is floored with stone flags, and incorporates a large standing stone as a buttress in each corner. Such buttresses are not used in other Orkney tombs and their function may therefore have been symbolic rather than simply practical. The chamber's internal walls are of incredibly fine dry-stone masonry. Three of the four side-walls provide access to large, stone-built chambers which presumably once held the bones of the dead. The fourth side-wall provides access to the entrance passage, which is in itself an extraordinary piece of architecture. This leads south-west from the chamber, and was originally about 17m long. It seems to have been formed of two separate, linked sections – a higher, wider inner section, which survives intact, and a rather lower, narrower section towards the original entrance which has sadly been destroyed. The surviving side-walls of the passage consist largely of massive, single slabs laid lengthways, with a similarly sized slab forming the passage roof. At one point there is a large recess in one of the side walls. This is currently occupied by a large stone which archaeologists found in the passage and which appears to be an original blocking stone; it fits the width of the passage almost perfectly at the point where the original 'inner passage' gave way to the now lost outer passage, but leaves a slit a little over 10cm in height between it and the passage roof. Although not of the same architectural sophistication, this arrangement recalls the extraordinary roof-box structure at Newgrange; the monument could be closed to human visitors, but still allow sunlight to pass into the depths of the tomb.

Of what significance was this arrangement at Maes Howe? Well, we have already observed that the chamber faces south-west, and it will come as no surprise to readers who have read this far to learn that it faces precisely in the direction of the midwinter sunset. Sunlight

actually penetrates to the chamber of Maes Howe on several days
either side of the solstice, but any doubt as to the intended link
with the solstice is dismissed by the link with the nearby Barnhouse
Stone. This solitary standing stone stands in direct line with the
tomb entrance at a distance of some 720m, and the midwinter sun,
seen from the tomb, sets directly over the top of it. Observing the
midwinter sunset from within the chamber of the tomb in 1893,
local schoolmaster, Magnus Spence, recorded that:

> The view is very limited, not extending farther in breadth than a
> few yards. Strange to say, in the centre of this contracted view, and
> at a distance of forty-two chains stands the monolith at Barnhouse.
> The alignment formed with this long passage of Maeshowe and the
> Standing Stone of Barnhouse indicates directions too remarkable to
> be accidental.

The late great Orkney novelist and poet, George Mackay Brown, felt
the power of the midwinter sunset at Maes Howe:

> The winter sun just hangs over the ridge of the Coolags. Its setting
> will seal the shortest day of the year, the winter solstice. At this
> season the sun is a pale wick between two gulfs of darkness. Surely
> there could be no darker place in the be-wintered world than the
> interior of Maeshowe. One of the light rays is caught in this stone
> web of death. Through the long corridor it has found its way; it
> splashes the far wall of the chamber. The illumination lasts a few
> minutes, then is quenched. Winter after winter I never cease to
> wonder at the way primitive man arranged, in hewn stone, such
> powerful symbolism.

The Clava Cairns

We now return to the mainland to consider the group of
monuments near Inverness known as the Clava Cairns. It has long
been recognised that these monuments seem to have been designed
to align with the midwinter sunset, and experiments undertaken as
part of a fieldwork campaign by Richard Bradley in the 1980s have
confirmed this.

The Clava Cairns possess a peculiarly enigmatic quality which is
clearly felt by many modern visitors, some of whom are moved to
leave offerings such as coins, crystals, flowers and bones, several of

which were found in the recent excavations. In his report Richard Bradley observes that the popular local translation of 'Clava' is 'the Good Stones', noting that this eloquently 'evokes the distinctive character of the place'.

The site, at Balnuaran of Clava, seems originally to have consisted of five cairns, of which three are now consolidated and provided with interpretation panels for the benefit of visitors. These consist of two passage graves located either side of a central ring-cairn, with each individual monument surrounded by its own circle of standing stones. It is on these three monuments that we will concentrate.

The central ring cairn consists of an open central space surrounded by a circular wall of rubble with inner and outer retaining kerbs of large stones, the inner kerb being largely of slabs while the outer is of glacial erratics. There is no sign that an entrance passage through this bank ever existed. This cairn is surrounded by a stone circle of nine (probably originally 11) red sandstone slabs quarried from the banks of the adjacent River Nairn. There are three low rubble banks which radiate out from the outer kerb of the cairn to three of the circle stones in the east, west and south-east. The stones of the surrounding circle and of both the inner and outer kerbs of the ring cairn are graded so that the tallest are in the south-west, with the lowest in the north-east. The stones of the outer kerb are from different sources and seem to have been carefully arranged according to their colour; in some cases, for reasons which must have been of significance to the original builders, red stones are used to 'frame' others.

The south-west passage grave appears today as a circular cairn bounded by an outer kerb of massive boulders, surrounded by a circle of 11 standing stones (of a probable original 12). A rubble platform, now grass-covered but originally paved with sandstone slabs, occupies the space between the outer kerb and the stone circle. A well-preserved passage (crucial to the current discussion) leads into the cairn's central chamber from the south-west. This central chamber would originally have had a corbelled roof, sealed within the cairn – the only light reaching it would have been through the passage. The boulders forming the lower walls of the chamber are graded in height so that the highest two frame the entrance while the lowest are at the back of the chamber. Although their significance is unclear, several stones in the monument are decorated with cupmarks; one, at the junction of the passage and the chamber, has quite complex cup-and-ring decoration. As with the ring cairn, there must have been symbolism in the choice of red and white stones employed at particular places within the structure of this monument.

The north-east passage grave is very similar to the south-west one just described. It is also surrounded by a rubble platform and a stone circle which seems originally to have consisted of 12 uprights. Its entrance passage is on the same axis, and points towards the south-west cairn.

A series of radiocarbon dates suggests that the three monuments discussed here were initially constructed a century or two after 2000 BC, and that they saw re-use and modification as late as about 1000 BC when further monuments were added to the group. They are much later than the other great Neolithic monuments discussed in this chapter and, as Bradley notes in his report, 'seem to belong to a different world from the monuments of the third millennium BC.'

On first impression, the massive nature of the Clava Cairns suggests their construction must have necessitated an enormous amount of time and effort. In fact it has been estimated that they would each have taken about 3000 person-hours to construct, meaning that a team of 10 working full-time could have constructed one of the passage graves in about a month. Even if we double this and allow 20 men two months, then each cairn could still have been built in a relatively short period of time by the local community. In practice, the monuments were probably built on a part-time basis by people involved in other activities, perhaps over a year or two. It has been suggested that each may originally have been constructed to house a single burial, and that the tombs may have been closed after this burial and perhaps not originally intended for further burials or ceremonies, but alternatively the chambers may have remained accessible and used for regular ceremonies at particular times of year. This suggestion of regular ceremonies brings us to the reason why the Clava Cairns are included in this chapter. They are complex monuments, containing alignments on the midsummer sunrise and possibly also on lunar events, but the main axis of both the overall site and the individual monuments within it is undeniably on the midwinter sunset.

Despite a slight change in the sun's setting position since 2000 BC, due to a change in the earth's tilt over the intervening centuries, and the unfortunate planting of trees that restrict the view from the south-west cairn, the midwinter sunset can still be observed today from the chamber of the north-east cairn much as it could have been in 2000 BC. As part of Bradley's project, the chamber and passage of the north-east cairn were covered with a tarpaulin to mimic the original roof and, on the evening of 21 December 1998, two students settled down in the chamber to observe at first hand the midwinter sunset almost as it would have been seen from within the chamber 4000 years previously. As the sun began to set, the students observed that 'a narrow beam of light spread along the passage and across the chamber floor, striking the base of the rear wall'. The published report then notes how the beam of light seemed to emphasise particular architectural features of the chamber and passage, including stones of different colour and stones decorated with cupmarks. Four thousand years ago, the setting midwinter sun, when seen from within the north-east cairn, would have sunk out of view directly behind the south-west cairn at the point where its original roof would have intersected with the horizon; in other words, it would seem to have set down through the roof and into the chamber of the south-west cairn. The symbolic significance of these observations to people 4000 years ago must have been immense, though of course the actual witnessing of the sunset from within the monuments would have been restricted to a select few individuals deemed sufficiently important to be allowed access. Perhaps other members of the community performed ritual dances around the platform between the cairns and the stone circles while those inside undertook long-established but 'secret' rituals to encourage the sun to reappear in the morning and resume its slow journey back towards midsummer.

The few meagre finds from excavations at Clava and similar sites elsewhere suggest that human cremations were laid to rest within the chamber floors, and the knowledge that one or more ancestors lay buried within the chambers must surely have added to the power of the ceremonies that took place within them. This of course assumes that ceremonies actually did take place within the chambers; it is entirely possible that the alignment on the solstice was intended to be witnessed from within the chambers only by the dead who occupied them, and that no representative of the living could be present within the chambers at this crucial time. Either way, as Richard Bradley observes in his report:

> ... the fabric of the cemetery seems to have connected the dead inside their tombs with the movement of the sun that would remain constant across the generations. The emphasis on midwinter may have had a special significance too, for in such northern latitudes the shortest day of the year is a special time. Not only did the

winter solstice mark the moment when the hours of daylight began
to increase, it might also have signalled the rebirth of the natural
world. Perhaps the same ideas extended to the dead.

Arminghall

To complete our exploration of major monuments incorporating
alignments on the midwinter sun, we move down the east coast to
consider a site in East Anglia. This is not a region generally noted
for spectacular prehistoric monuments, and the site in question, the
Arminghall henge, is certainly not impressive today, consisting of a
very low, almost imperceptible circular bank in a far from spectacular
setting adjacent to an electricity pylon on the southern outskirts of
Norwich. The abandoned remains of the site had been gradually
eroding away, pretty much unnoticed for possibly 4000 years, when
Wing Commander Gilbert Insall, VC, noticed it from his plane at a
height of 600m on 18 June 1929. He observed a pattern in the grass
consisting of two concentric rings enclosing eight small, dark patches.

The site was excavated in the summer of 1935 by Graham Clark,
who contributed a fascinating report to the 1936 volume of the
Proceedings of the Prehistoric Society. Clark's excavation demonstrated
through the discovery of fragments of pottery and evidence of
flintworking that the monument was Neolithic. It consisted of an
outer V-shaped ditch, up to 3.6m wide and extending 1.4m beneath
the current ground surface (it may originally have been deeper and
wider, but we cannot be certain of this as the original Neolithic
ground surface has been destroyed by later ploughing). This ditch was
sub-circular in plan, and had an overall diameter of 80m. The much
more substantial inner ditch, also V-shaped in section, measured 8.4m
across and was 2.3m deep, with an overall diameter of 36m. It had a
causeway in the south-west, providing access to and from the central
area. Whether or not such a causeway also existed across the outer
ditch is not known as this portion of the site had been damaged,
but it is not unreasonable to assume that one did. Between the two
ditches was a low bank, about 15m wide, presumably consisting of
the material dug out of the ditches.

Within the central area, the 'dark patches' recorded on Wing
Commander Insall's photograph proved to be eight pits which had
originally held massive oak posts. In plan, these were arranged in a
horseshoe, open towards the entrance in the south-west. Two of the
post-holes were excavated. Each had a ramp which was used to slide

its massive post into position. The posts were presumably manoeuvred into place over these ramps, then pulled upright using ropes before gravel was rammed back into the holes to secure the posts into the ground. The posts were about a metre in diameter, suggesting that they were the trunks of large oaks at least 100 years old and would have stood possibly 6m or more above ground. The posts may well have been carved or painted, and may conceivably have supported lintels like the giant sarsens at Stonehenge. Charcoal recovered from one of the excavated post-holes was later submitted for radiocarbon dating, suggesting the monument was originally built within a few generations either side of 3000 BC. The excavation demonstrated that the posts had rotted *in situ* and were never replaced. They would have rotted away within a century or so, so the monument may have been abandoned after just two or three generations; alternatively, it may have retained significance long after the posts had disappeared.

The Armingall henge was interpreted by its excavator as an open-air temple, with the bank possibly functioning as a viewing area for spectators excluded from the ceremonies taking place in the interior. The excavations provided no evidence as to the nature of these ceremonies – there were no burials and no other features of note on the central platform. It is not at all clear why the Neolithic community chose this location for their henge. Although much older flints discovered during the excavation could be used to suggest that the site was of significance prior to the construction of the henge, it is perhaps more likely that they are representative of a simple campsite; they certainly do not demonstrate that earlier communities attached any special significance to this spot. The excavation also recovered later objects of Iron Age and Roman date, including some third-century AD coins, which could be interpreted as ritual offerings suggesting that the ancient henge retained some spiritual significance perhaps three millennia after its initial construction. Alternatively, they could represent nothing more than temporary occupation by 'squatters', taking advantage of the small degree of shelter offered by the remains of the bank and ditch.

So what are we left with in our attempt to interpret the site? Well, perhaps the single most significant fact is that the henge is orientated on the midwinter sunset, which when viewed from the centre of henge, sets down the slope of nearby Chapel Hill, its last rays neatly framed by the henge entrance. Although the weather would vary from one year to the next, we can imagine the huge East Anglian skies providing spectacular midwinter sunsets here. There are a number of round barrows (burial mounds) in the vicinity of the henge, including a group some 2.5km to the south-west, just about in line with the henge entrance. This might suggest a link with the ancestors, similar to that at several of the other sites discussed above, but the evidence here is much less certain. The Arminghall henge is not on the same scale as Newgrange, Maes Howe or Stonehenge, but in its prime it was a hugely impressive monument which must have been of enormous significance to the communities that built and used it. Given the alignment of their temple, we may conclude, I think without controversy, that the midwinter sunset was a key annual event for these people.

Celebrating the Solstice

The sites we have just considered are amongst the most spectacular Neolithic monuments surviving in Britain and Ireland today. There are also many others that could, and perhaps should, have been considered here in some detail. These include two henges at Llandegai, near Bangor in North Wales, set on a 15ha site that was hurriedly excavated in 1966-67 in advance of the construction of an industrial estate. Ritual activity at the henges was dated to between 3000 and 2000 BC, and both monuments seem to have been carefully designed to incorporate alignments on the winter solstice sunset. Beyond the British Isles, the great Neolithic tombs and standing stones clustered around Carnac in Brittany have long been celebrated as among the wonders of prehistoric Europe. Arguably the single most spectacular of these is the magnificent passage grave of Gavrinis, originally built on a low hill near the coast but now, due to today's higher sea level, preserved on its very own little island. In terms of its architecture and its extraordinary art Gavrinis rivals Newgrange, and it also has its entrance aligned on the midwinter sunrise. On Orkney, not far from the great passage tomb of Maes Howe, several houses at the recently excavated Neolithic settlement of Barnhouse were found to have central, stone-lined hearths, square in plan. It is a curious feature of Orkney's latitude that the directions of midwinter sunrise (in the south-east), midwinter sunset (south-west), summer sunset (north-west) and summer sunrise (north-east) intersect at exactly 90 degrees. This was clearly known to the inhabitants of Barnhouse, whose domestic hearths were carefully built so that their sides corresponded to these four directions. These people were so concerned with the summer and winter solstices that reference to them was incorporated within the symbolic architecture of their houses, visible to them not just at special ceremonial events but at every minute of every day.

There are many other Neolithic monuments where possible alignments on the winter solstice are not as clear-cut as those considered in this chapter, and I freely admit there are many others whose architecture does not indicate any specific interest in the sun, never mind a particular concern with the solstice. However, in my view, the sites we have discussed in this chapter demonstrate beyond doubt that many Neolithic people across Britain regarded the winter solstice as a special time. What, if anything, can we say of the ways in which these people may have understood and perhaps celebrated midwinter?

This is dangerous ground for the archaeologist; the desire to understand the nature of ancient religious practice can, and often does, result in wild and totally unjustifiable speculation. However, there is one potential avenue of enquiry that can at least provide some possibilities. Anthropology provides us with evidence about the religions of native societies from many places around the world, and while no such case studies provide exact parallels for the situation in prehistoric Britain, they can be used, albeit cautiously, to construct some possibilities which we might otherwise be unlikely to consider.

From the sixteenth century, European explorers and settlers increasingly came into contact with native societies in North America, and various aspects of native culture were recorded for posterity. These societies were effectively 'stone age' in nature, but all had complex cosmologies by which they sought to explain their place in the universe. The people lived in landscapes ripe with cultural symbolism, and told creation myths relating places on earth to the ancestors and the beginnings of time. In some cases, it was noted that the winter solstice was a key event. I certainly do not wish to suggest that people in Neolithic Britain would have celebrated the winter solstice in exactly the same way as Native Americans thousands of years later, but these accounts are potentially of some value to our story.

The Chumash people, whose population in the sixteenth century seems to have totalled about 18,000, occupied coastal areas of California. They were hunters and gatherers, and relied to large extent on marine resources such as fish, marine mammals and shellfish. Whereas many Native American societies were mobile, moving around the landscape to exploit different food sources at different times of year, the abundant natural resources in their territory enabled the Chumash to live in permanently occupied villages long before the introduction of farming. There was therefore no need to maintain a calendar to inform them of when to harvest or sow crops, and they built no great monuments like those of Neolithic Britain. Nevertheless, rituals based on the sun and its movement through the heavens played a major role in the Chumash year.

Chumash chiefs exercised power as 'officers of the people' rather than as 'rulers', sharing power as part of a group including other important individuals, collectively known as the *'antap*. Among the *'antap* were the shamans, who used a hallucinogenic drink prepared from the datura (jimsonweed) plant to enter drug-induced trances during which they had visions, interpreted as the result of contact with divine sources of power. The shamans undertook numerous tasks on behalf of the community, including officiating at many ceremonies and keeping the calendar. Some shamans had specific roles; one such was the *'alchuklash* or 'skywatcher' who recorded the movements of the sun, moon and stars and used this knowledge for various purposes including establishing the times of solstice celebrations and reading people's destinies. The role of the *'alchuklash* therefore combined elements of what we refer to today as 'astronomy' and 'astrology', but in the world of the Chumash these were as real as each other and certainly did not represent two separate subjects.

Spirits were everywhere in the Chumash universe and the shamans communicated with them on behalf of the community. Celestial beings, including the sun and the moon lived in an 'upper realm', while people lived in the 'middle world' and dangerous spirits occupied the 'underworld'. It was essential to keep everything in equilibrium by undertaking ceremonies at particular times of year. The winter solstice was one such time, and possibly the most important. It was the time when the sun and the 'sky coyote' tallied up the results of their gambling competition throughout the previous year, and the results were of crucial importance to the people. The *'antap* would try to intervene to ensure that the sky coyote was victorious, as he would ensure plentiful food in the year to come, whereas victory for the sun would result in food shortages and much loss of life. The *'antap* watched the sun each day as midwinter approached, and ensured that the people undertook the necessary activities at the correct times to honour the sun and seek to harness its power.

The Chumash midwinter solstice ceremony was known as *Kakunupmawa*, which can be translated as 'the radiance of the child born on the winter solstice', referring to the rebirth of the sun at this time. We owe most of what we know of *Kakunupmawa* to John Peabody Harrington, an ethnographer who interviewed Chumash people in the early twentieth century and made extensive notes of what he was told. The planning of the ceremony was overseen by 12 members of the *'antap* along with 13 'village captains'. One of the captains was elected as *slo'w* (eagle) and he supervised the ceremony, which involved the erection of poles decorated with feathers, the public clearing of all debts, and communal dancing. A key element was the placing of the 'sunstick', a stick about 50cm tall with a flat stone fixed to the top, into a hole in a ceremonial plaza. The sunstick represented the centre of the world and the associated rituals were intended to ensure that the sun would return for another year, thus enabling life in the world to continue as normal. The role of the *'antap* in ensuring the continuation of the status quo was crucial, and it was certainly not worth taking the risk of not performing the required time-honoured rituals, thus inviting the loss of the sun and consequent disaster for the world.

We could consider many other documented rituals associated with the winter solstice, from America and other places around the world, but this single example serves our purpose; to suggest that complex cosmologies must have existed in association with the observance of the winter solstice at Stonehenge and the other great Neolithic monuments. We may also note in passing that ceremonies such as those of the Chumash, though complex, may well leave no trace to be discovered later by archaeology; many similar such ceremonies, wholly invisible to the archaeologist, were probably conducted away from the great monuments that so dominate studies of the Neolithic.

The Winter Solstice in Later Prehistory

It is a curious fact that following the abandonment of the great Neolithic monuments considered in this chapter, which seems to have occurred in most cases during the second millennium BC, we have no clear evidence of the symbolic importance of the winter solstice in Britain until Roman times in the first to fourth centuries AD. During the first millennium BC, classified by archaeologists as the late Bronze Age and Iron Age, no great ritual monuments with alignments on the solstices or any other astronomical events were constructed. However, this lack of evidence must not be interpreted as implying that the sun did not retain great ceremonial significance, which it certainly did. One of the most iconic artefacts from the north European Bronze Age is the thirteenth-century BC Trundheim chariot, from Denmark, a small model of a horse-drawn cart on which sits a gilt disc that scholars agree must represent the sun. The Trundheim chariot probably relates to a myth in which the sun is hauled across the sky each day by horses, and, despite the current lack of evidence, similar beliefs may well have existed in Bronze Age Britain.

A few timber-built temples from Iron Age Britain, including one now entombed beneath Heathrow Airport, have been excavated. These tend to be of rectangular form with entrances facing between north-east and south-east, towards the sunrise, but this cannot be taken as evidence of any particular interest in the solstices. The late Bronze Age and early Iron Age saw the growth in popularity of a cult associated with wet places throughout Britain and Ireland. This seems to have developed in tandem with a decline in the climate which saw greater rainfall and less sunshine in the average year, apparently causing the abandonment of some long-established settlements in marginal settings. Evidence for this cult comes in the form of offerings of valuable metal objects, such as swords and spears, in bogs, marshes, lakes and rivers, many of which have been found over the years. These have been interpreted by archaeologists as offerings to the gods, representative of a shift in emphasis from the worship of a sun god to one associated with wet places; remnants of such beliefs survive to this day in the form of holy wells and wishing wells. Such a change would help to explain a lack of interest in the solstices at this time, but the development of ritual activity associated with wet places cannot have totally eclipsed the age-old veneration of the sun.

The Iron Age witnessed the construction of hillforts, of which many hundreds survive throughout Britain, ranging from the immense citadel of Maiden Castle in Dorset to numerous smaller examples which seem to have been little more than elaborately embellished homesteads. The construction of a large hillfort must have been a huge communal project no less complex than the building of the great Neolithic monuments some two or three thousand years earlier, but the end result was essentially a defended settlement rather than a tomb or a temple. That said, recent studies have demonstrated that many hillforts incorporated a large degree of symbolic architecture, and it is certainly possible that ceremonies were held within them to mark important events such as the winter solstice. In Ireland, large enclosures, such as that at Tara, have been interpreted in this way. By their nature, however, the hillforts do not incorporate neat solar alignments such as those recognisable at the Neolithic circles and passage tombs, and it is unlikely that we will ever be able to identify a specific relationship between hillfort architecture and the movements of the sun. Several scholars have commented on the general orientation of roundhouse entrances towards the rising sun, both within hillforts and elsewhere, and recent studies have claimed complex cosmological symbolism in the design and orientation of such houses, but nowhere is a specific link suggested between Iron Age architecture and the winter solstice.

Although we have a number of accounts of life in late Iron Age Britain, written by Romans, these make no mention of winter solstice celebrations. The Iron Age people of Europe are often referred to as 'Celts', although exactly what is meant by the term is a constant source of argument amongst archaeologists. We cannot enter into this debate here, but should note that whatever differences may have existed between different tribal groups during the Iron Age, the worship of the sun seems everywhere to have been an important element of Celtic religion. In her book, *The Gods of the Celts*, Miranda Green cites a wide range of archaeological and documentary evidence, concluding that 'The cult of sky and sun must be seen as integral part of Celtic society and culture.' Nowhere, however, does she mention the possible sacred significance of the winter solstice. Things may have varied from place to place within the vast area classified by classical writers as 'Celtic', but in Gaelic areas the calendar seems to have been constructed not around the movements of the sun, but around the four great quarter days of Samhain (1 November: New Year's Day in the pre-Christian Irish calendar), Imbolc (1 February), Beltaine (1 May) and Lughnasa (1 August). Although these great festival days all had their own religious significance, they were based primarily on significant stages in the agricultural calendar. Winter began at Samhain, which became associated with the dead (this tradition survives today as Hallowe'en), and ended at Imbolc when preparation for lambing got underway and people could again look forward to fresh natural produce as the days grew longer and gradually warmer. We must resist the temptation to discuss these festivals at any length as such discussion would be of little relevance to our story of the winter solstice. It is worth noting, however, that this period may have witnessed a dislocation of ancestor worship from midwinter celebrations. We have seen that in Neolithic times the rebirth of the sun at the winter solstice was inextricably linked with the worship of the ancestors, but by Iron Age times the 'day of the dead' had become Samhain. By the time that we again have clear evidence for midwinter celebrations, during the Roman era, there no longer seems to be an association between midwinter and the dead.

As already noted, there is very little evidence for a sun god in Iron Age Britain, still less as to how the winter solstice may have been celebrated. There are, however, some tantalising possibilities that we should briefly consider. Ronald Hutton, in *The Pagan Religions of the British Isles,* notes the potential importance of Belenus, perhaps the best candidate for a Celtic sun god, to whom occasional dedications have been found across Europe from Italy to Britain. However, there is little to suggest that Belenus was of any great importance away from his Austrian heartland, and no mention of him is made within the early Irish or Welsh literature which might be expected if he was of importance here. The great passage grave of Newgrange features in Celtic Irish mythology as a residence of gods, but there is nothing to suggest that the monument retained any of its original solar significance by Iron Age times, and the gods specifically associated with it should certainly not be considered in any way as 'sun gods'. However, a fascinating glimpse into sun worship in Iron Age Ireland is provided by St Patrick, who notes within his *Confession* in the mid fifth century AD:

> For the sun itself which we see rises every day for our sake at his bidding, but its splendour will never reign or abide, but all who worship it will come miserably and unhappily to punishment. We, on the other hand, who believe in and worship the true sun, Christ, who will never perish, nor will he who does his will but he will remain for ever even as Christ, too, remains for ever ...

St Patrick's *Confession* and his other surviving work, the *Epistle to the Soldiers of Coroticus,* are the only surviving Latin books known from the time of the Roman Empire that were written outside the Empire's margins. Their survival is altogether extraordinary, and they give a unique insight into many aspects of life in very early Christian Ireland. Ireland, of course, was never conquered by Rome, so it is reasonable to assume that the worshipping of the sun referred to Patrick was a tradition of the native Irish Iron Age, possibly with origins stretching back to the builders of Newgrange.

Patrick's condemnation of such practice sounds like a classic attempt to distract attention away from ancient sun worship towards the worship of Jesus; we will encounter further such attempts by the early Christian Church later in this book. Patrick makes no mention of the manner by which such sun worship was undertaken, nor how widespread or ancient the practice was, but the fact that he bothers to mention it suggests that it must have been an issue at the time, and we may reasonably suppose that if people were worshipping the sun then they would also have marked the winter solstice in some way. Patrick's description of Christ as 'the true sun' is fascinating, given that, as we will see in the next chapter, such links between Christ and the sun seem to have been commonplace in the early Church.

It has been suggested that Apollo, the Roman sun god who we will meet again in the next chapter, was worshipped in pre-Roman Britain. This arises chiefly from two sources. Firstly, the head of Apollo complete with radiant crown, sometimes in association with a wheel (a long established sun symbol throughout Celtic Europe), appears on several Iron Age coins from southern England. Some have claimed that this arose through the copying of Roman imagery without any real understanding of its significance, but this seems unlikely. We should also note that several coins from this period depict a sun symbol alongside a horse, perhaps indicative of beliefs similar to those symbolised by the Trundheim chariot. The second source linking Apollo with Britain is a curious ancient myth that he visited his temple in 'Hyperborean lands' every 19 years. This is contained within the so-called *Historical Library* compiled by Diodorus Siculus who lived on Sicily in the first century BC. Diodorus, giving his source as a now lost work of about 300 BC by Hecataeus of Abdera, tells us that:

> Opposite to the coast of Celtic Gaul there is an island in the ocean, not smaller than Sicily, lying to the north, which is inhabited by the Hyperboreans, who are so named because they dwell beyond the North Wind … In this island, there is a magnificent grove of Apollo, and a remarkable temple, of a round form, adorned with many consecrated gifts … It is also said that Apollo visits the island once in the course of nineteen years …

Diodorus further notes that Apollo's mother, Leto, was supposedly from the island of the Hyperboreans, and that for this reason Apollo is revered here above all other gods. The round temple has been identified in modern times as Stonehenge, and while this is not an unreasonable supposition it has to be admitted that there is no supporting evidence. By the time that Hecataeus and Diodorus were writing, Stonehenge had almost certainly been in ruins for centuries, although the ruins would have been spectacular and may well have been associated in folk-memory with the ancient worship of the sun; they may even have continued to provide a focus for solstice ceremonies of some kind. The 19-year cycle referred to by Diodorus seems to relate to the complex cycles of the moon, which cannot concern us here other than to note that such issues were crucial to the cosmologies of people in the ancient Greek world and probably also to the Celts; the visit of Apollo to Hyperborea related to complex astrological symbolism in which sun and moon both played key roles.

In parts of Gaul, Apollo seems to have been equated with the god Maponus, and John Matthews in his book *The Winter Solstice* suggests that Maponus can in turn be considered as a variation of Mabon, a god known from ancient Welsh literature. Matthews notes that the medieval Welsh myth-book known as the *Mabinogian* ('Tales of Youth') incorporates a compilation of ancient Celtic myths including the Arthurian legend of Mabon son of Modron. Although these myths are of uncertain date, they may include vestiges of very ancient tales and Matthews considers them to offer a valuable insight into pre-Christian times. Mabon (literally 'the Mother's Son') is the greatest hunter in the land, but had been stolen from his mother when only two days old and imprisoned within a dark cave. He is eventually discovered and released from the darkness of the cave by Culhwch, assisted by several wild animals as well as Arthur's warriors, at the time of the winter solstice. According to Matthews, Culhwch's quest to release Mabon from his dark prison relates to the returning sunlight at the winter solstice. The fabulous story of Mabon is complex, and its origins uncertain, but the symbolism contained within such stories certainly seems to draw on ancient awareness and celebration of the winter solstice, possibly dating back to Iron Age times if not beyond. We may also note the reference to Mabon as the best hunter in the land; hunting would almost certainly have been an activity associated with the Iron Age midwinter, and it is far from impossible that the medieval tradition of the boar's head was already underway in some form by Iron Age times when feasting would doubtless have been a main ingredient of any celebrations that did take place. Matthews also suggests that 'the figure of a smith god' was central to Celtic solsticial celebrations, but fails to elaborate on this. Given the known importance of smiths within Celtic society, and especially their 'magical' ability to create artefacts from raw materials using fire, it would come as no great surprise to find a 'smith god' associated in some way with midwinter, but given the available evidence (or rather the lack of it) this can be no more than conjecture at the present time.

Ancient writers inform us that religious ceremonies in Iron Age Britain were controlled by the Druids, who by this time had assumed the role undertaken by the Neolithic shamans. We should note that today's 'Druids', who flock to Stonehenge to celebrate the summer solstice each year, can trace their origins back no further than the seventeenth century. Modern druids have, however, adopted an interest in midwinter. Although many more flock to Stonehenge and other ancient monuments for the summer solstice, some 750 druids and pagans turned up at Stonehenge on 22 December 2006 to observe the midwinter sunrise (as we observed earlier in this chapter, it was the *setting* midwinter sun that was originally of most significance here, but never mind). *The Guardian* (23 December) quotes a member of the Druid Network who states that the celebrations were 'about the birth of the new growing cycle – the new sun is born in the depths of the darkness'. In its report, *The Guardian* notes that about 60 pagans had turned up 24 hours earlier in the belief that the solstice always occurs on 21 December – they were put right by English Heritage officials who explained that the actual moment of the solstice that year was at 22 minutes past midnight on the 22nd. It is possible that ancient Druids held similar ceremonies, perhaps even amongst the ruins of Stonehenge; they too may have occasionally got the wrong day but, in the absence of the heritage police to put them right, this would have posed them no problem.

Prehistoric druidical ceremonies were apparently performed in the open air, at sacred groves, lakes, rivers and other natural places, which might help to account for the lack of temples alluded to earlier in this section. In perhaps the best known passage about the Druids, Pliny describes the sacred importance of mistletoe in their rites:

> The Druids … held nothing more sacred than the mistletoe and the tree that bears it, always supposing that tree to be the oak. … They call the mistletoe by a name meaning in their own language, the all-healing. Having made preparation for sacrifice and a banquet beneath the trees, they bring thither two white bulls, whose horns

are bound then for the first time. Clad in a white robe, the priest ascends the tree and cuts the mistletoe with a golden sickle, and it is received by others in a white cloak. Then they kill the bulls, praying that God will render this gift of his propitious to those to whom he has granted it. They believe that the mistletoe, taken in drink, imparts fecundity to barren animals, and that it is an antidote for all poisons.

This is the classic image of the Druids, dressed in their white cloaks and armed with their golden sickles, recovering mistletoe from the sacred oak. We cannot be sure how accurate it is, but the importance of mistletoe seems unlikely to have been manufactured. We will encounter mistletoe much later in our journey through the history of Christmas – it is, of course, still associated with seasonal fecundity to this day. It is certainly tempting to envisage it being used in midwinter ceremonies in Iron Age times, but we have no evidence for this so must dwell on it no longer.

It is in some ways frustrating that we have no more than the above tantalising glimpses into the possible importance of sun worship and the winter solstice in Britain during the centuries prior to the Roman invasion. However, absence of evidence does not constitute evidence of absence. Personally, I have no doubt that the winter solstice, while perhaps not playing a key role in the structure of the Celtic calendar, would still have been of great importance to the people of Iron Age Britain, and that the Druids would have been out in force to welcome the first sunrise of each new solar year according to long established tradition.

During the first century AD, the Roman occupation of Britain began, and Roman midwinter celebrations were introduced along with the legions. Soon thereafter, the story of Jesus Christ would reach these shores for the first time, and the story of his birth would find itself intertwined with already ancient winter solstice celebrations. These Roman and Christian midwinter traditions form the subject of our next chapter.

3

The Nativity and the Festival of the Unconquered Sun

As a child, I took part in Nativity plays and sang Christmas carols without doubting that the story of Jesus' birth was historical fact. Millions of other children, in many cases alongside their parents, continue to do likewise every year. The traditional story of the Nativity is indeed immensely powerful and moving, but as I grew older I began to wonder about the extent to which it might be based on historical events. Is it rooted in historical reality, or should it perhaps be regarded as amongst mankind's most effective works of fiction – perhaps even as the most influential fantasy story ever told? In this chapter we will analyse the traditional story of the Nativity, concluding with an account of pagan midwinter festivities in pre-Christian Rome, thus providing a context into which the celebration of the Nativity was introduced by the early Christian Church. By the end of the chapter, 25 December will be firmly established as the day of the Nativity, merging a number of Christian and pagan traditions in a manner that still causes controversy today. For example, an article by Ian Drury on the front page of the *Daily Mail* (9 December 2006) under the banner headline 'Away with the Manger' reports:

> Religious images have been banished from almost all the Christmas cards on sale in High Street shops. Traditional Nativity pictures such as angels over a stable, Jesus in his manger and the three wise men appear on only one in 100. They have been replaced by a bizarre selection including Brussels sprouts, a shoe, a moonlit bridge and a line of meerkats. One card even carried the potentially offensive suggestion that shepherds saw an angel appear only because they had been smoking drugs. Religious groups and MPs were horrified. They said they feared the multi-million pound card industry was shunning religious images because of political correctness and the fear of offending other faiths.

Later in the article, a religious spokesman states:

The fact that so many cards barely allude to Christmas is very sad and disquieting. The card that suggests the shepherds had been smoking strange substances is not just unfunny, it is also deeply offensive. People should go out of their way to buy proper Christmas cards and help to bring pressure on manufacturers and those who sell them.

Such debates are nothing new as Christmas has always courted controversy. The same issue of the *Mail* contains a double-page spread entitled 'Who killed the Nativity play?' This observes that school Nativity plays now regularly feature characters such as grizzly bears, eskimos, even Elvis – with a baby Jesus often nowhere to be seen. Indeed, my most recent experience of a 'Nativity play' featured my youngest daughter and her classmates in a festive production about Doctor Who! Before we can comment with any authority on the relative merits of different cards and plays we must undertake an analysis of the traditional Nativity story.

The birth of Jesus Christ represents one of the most fundamental events in the history of mankind. Whether one chooses to believe in the word of the Bible or not, the influence of this event on humanity has been profound; even our calendar is based (albeit erroneously, as we will soon discover) upon it. But when exactly was Jesus born? Nowhere in the Bible is 25 December mentioned. Indeed, no mention whatsoever is made of the time of his birth. Why then does the Christian Church celebrate his birth on this day? The answer, as with so many Christian celebrations, is that the Church sought to appropriate pre-existing and already ancient festivals, putting a Christian gloss on them and adapting them as necessary to tie in with Christian orthodoxy. (There is one fundamental distinction that must be made at the outset in this discussion of Jesus. He can be studied as a historical figure or as the Son of God; the former is susceptible to historical analysis while the latter relies upon faith alone. In many ways, while it may appear odd to say so at this stage, whether or not he actually is the Son of God is something of an irrelevance to our story of the history of Christmas, as should soon become clear.)

Our evidence for the life of Jesus comes essentially from the New Testament, although there are other sources that we must also consider. Taken together, these sources leave little doubt that Jesus was indeed a real historical figure, but what they have to say about his birth is certainly not as clear-cut as the traditional Nativity play would have us believe. The traditional view has the Angel Gabriel appearing to Mary, a virgin, in Nazareth and informing her that she was to give to birth to a son and was to call him Jesus, meaning 'the Saviour'. Mary then travels with her betrothed, Joseph, to Bethlehem to take part in a census. When they arrive in Bethlehem, there is no room for them in 'the inn', so they are put up in a stable, where the infant is born, being laid in a manger. The birth is announced by angels to shepherds, watching over their flocks in nearby fields, who arrive to worship the infant. The event is also marked by the appearance of a great star in the sky, which leads three wise men, sometimes referred to as kings, to travel to Bethlehem from the East, bringing gifts of frankincense, gold and myrrh. This immensely moving story, of the Son of God being born into the world in poverty, is so powerful that it is often accepted without question.

But what is our evidence for it? The background is provided by the Gospels of Luke and Matthew. Nowhere else in the Bible is the birth of Jesus referred to at all, which, given its miraculous nature and critical importance to the whole of Christianity, might be considered by some as a trifle unusual. Nevertheless, let us begin our analysis by considering the accounts offered to us by Matthew and Luke.

The Gospel according to Luke, the third book of the New Testament, was probably written in about AD 80. The author is often thought to be 'the beloved physician' who accompanied Paul on his missions around the Mediterranean in the mid first century. Luke also wrote the book in the New Testament known to us as the 'Acts of the Apostles', in which he tells us much about the early development of Christianity in the decades following the execution of Jesus. This is a skilfully written account, but as it makes no reference to Jesus' birth we cannot delve into it here. It is perhaps worth noting in passing, however, that the Acts are regarded by many scholars as having been written earlier than Luke's Gospel. Could it therefore be that in writing his own Infancy Gospel Luke was to an extent trying to 'fill in the gaps' of Jesus' earlier life, about which few facts were known, perhaps enabling him to introduce an element of artistic licence into what appears as a historical account? As we will see, this may have been a factor in the accounts of Jesus' birth provided by Luke and Matthew.

The Gospel according to Matthew seems to have been written a few years after that of Luke, perhaps in about AD 90. It is not clear whether or not the author had access to Luke's Gospel, but both seem to have had access to an earlier unknown source, thus accounting for many similarities between the two while also allowing for a number of inconsistencies. Nothing is known for sure of the author, although he apparently lived in Antioch towards the end of the first century, spoke fluent Greek, and seems to have had some rabbinic training.

Both Luke and Matthew seem to have had access to the Gospel According to Mark, possibly written as early as AD 65, and have expanded on much of Mark's material. It might well be asked, therefore, why Mark had made no mention of Jesus' birth. It would not be unreasonable for us to conclude that he was unaware of the story, otherwise he would surely have included it in his account of Jesus' life which begins not with his birth, but with his baptism. This again might lead us to suggest that the accounts of Luke and Matthew incorporated legendary and perhaps unreliable accounts of the birth of Jesus that had begun to circulate after Mark had written his Gospel. The Gospel According to John, apparently written at the end of the first century using different source material from that available to Mark, Luke and Matthew, makes no mention of the Nativity. Perhaps John was unaware of the stories told by Luke and Matthew, or maybe he knew of them but thought them unreliable so made no mention of them. During his account of Jesus' preaching at the Feast of Tabernacles, John (7:42) implies that most people thought Jesus to be neither from Jerusalem nor from the line of David, although he does not state his own view on the matter. We may reasonably conclude that the Nativity was of no great significance to John, writing just a century or so after the great event had supposedly occurred.

The Evidence

Having established something of the biblical background, let us now examine the accounts of Jesus' birth offered by Luke and Matthew, before comparing and contrasting them with each other and also introducing some alternative accounts from ancient Christian sources that did not find their way into the Bible. The following biblical passages will be familiar to many readers, but as they represent the key sources for the entire Christian celebration of Christmas, which is fundamental to our story, they are provided here in full.

After outlining the miraculous conception of John the Baptist, Luke turns his attention to the conception of Jesus, which occurred six months after that of John:

1:26 Now in the sixth month the angel Gabriel was sent by God to a city of Galilee named Nazareth,

27   to a virgin betrothed to a man whose name was Joseph, of the house of David. The virgin's name was Mary.

28   And having come in, the angel said to her, "Rejoice, highly favoured one, the Lord is with you; blessed are you among women!"

29   But when she saw him, she was troubled at his saying, and considered what manner of greeting this was.

30   Then the angel said to her, "Do not be afraid, Mary, for you have found favour with God.

31   "And behold, you will conceive in your womb and bring forth a Son, and shall call His name JESUS.

32   "He will be great, and will be called the Son of the Highest; and the Lord God will give Him the throne of His father David.

33   "And He will reign over the house of Jacob forever, and of His kingdom there will be no end."

34   Then Mary said to the angel, "How can this be, since I do not know a man?"

35   And the angel answered and said to her, "The Holy Spirit will come upon you, and the power of the Highest will overshadow you; therefore, also, that Holy One who is to be born will be called the Son of God."

Then, after a discussion of the birth of John the Baptist, Luke describes the circumstances surrounding the birth of Jesus:

2:1   And it came to pass in those days that a decree went out from Caesar Augustus that all the world should be registered.

2   This census first took place while Quirinius was governing Syria.

3   So all went to be registered, everyone to his own city.

4   Joseph also went up from Galilee, out of the city of Nazareth, into Judea, to the city of David, which is called Bethlehem, because he was of the house and lineage of David,

5   to be registered with Mary, his betrothed wife, who was with child.

6   So it was, that while they were there, the days were completed for her to be delivered.

7   And she brought forth her firstborn Son, and wrapped Him in swaddling cloths, and laid Him in a manger, because there was no room for them in the inn.

8   Now there were in the same country shepherds living out in the fields, keeping watch over their flock by night.

9   And behold, an angel of the Lord stood before them, and the glory of the Lord shone around them, and they were greatly afraid.

10   Then the angel said to them, "Do not be afraid, for behold, I bring you good tidings of great joy which will be to all people.

11   "for there is born to you this day in the city of David a Saviour, who is Christ the Lord.

12   "and this will be the sign to you: You will find a Babe wrapped in swaddling cloths, lying in a manger."

13   And suddenly there was with the angel a multitude of the heavenly host praising God and saying:

14   "Glory to God in the highest, And on earth peace, goodwill toward men!"

15   So it was, when the angels had gone away from them into heaven, that the shepherds said to one another, "Let us now go to Bethlehem and see this thing that has come to pass, which the Lord has made known to us."

16   And they came with haste and found Mary and Joseph, and the Babe lying in a manger.

17   Now when they had seen Him, they made widely known the saying which was told them concerning this Child.

18   And all those who heard it marvelled at those things which were told by the shepherds.

19   But Mary kept all these things and pondered them in her heart.

20   Then the shepherds returned, glorifying and praising God for all the things that they had heard and seen, as it was told to them.

21   And when eight days were completed for the circumcision of the Child, His name was called JESUS, the name given by the angel before He was conceived in the womb.

Luke then explains how Jesus was then presented to God in the temple at Jerusalem, where an old man, Simeon, and an octogenarian prophetess, Anna, publicly praise God for sending Jesus to redeem Israel. Jesus, Mary and Joseph then return to their home in 'their own city', Nazareth.

This is all that Luke has to say about the conception, birth and early days of Jesus. We will now consider the account of the same events offered to us by Matthew. Matthew's Gospel opens with an account of the 'genealogy of Jesus Christ', tracing his ancestry back a total of forty-two generations through Joseph to King David and back to Abraham. Luke also offers such a genealogy which extends even further, all the way back to Adam! Such genealogies, tracing the family trees of important people back to famous ancestors and often ultimately to the gods are commonplace in the ancient world, but they are clearly fictitious and must surely have been recognised as such by writers such as Matthew and Luke. Their purpose is to provide a suitably grand 'historical' context for the individuals concerned, something that was certainly achieved in this case, although, if we are to believe in the virgin birth, we may legitimately question the relevance of Jesus' paternal ancestry. This is something to which we will return.

After detailing Jesus' genealogy, Matthew provides the following account:

1:18 Now the birth of Jesus Christ was as follows: After His mother Mary was betrothed to Joseph, before they came together, she was found with child of the Holy Spirit.

19 Then Joseph her husband, being a just man, and not wanting to make her a public example, was minded to put her away secretly.

20 But while he thought about these things, behold, an angel of the Lord appeared to him in a dream, saying, "Joseph, son of David, do not be afraid to take to you Mary your wife, for that which is conceived in her is of the Holy Spirit.

21 "And she will bring forth a Son, and you shall call His name JESUS, for He will save His people from their sins."

22 So all this was done that it might be fulfilled which was spoken by the Lord through the prophet, saying:

23 *"Behold, the virgin shall be with child, and bear a Son, and they shall call His name Immanuel,"* which is translated, "God with us."

24 Then Joseph, being aroused from sleep, did as the angel of the Lord commanded him and took to him his wife,

25 And did not know her until she had brought forth her firstborn Son. And he called His name JESUS.

1.1 Now after Jesus was born in Bethlehem of Judea in the days of Herod the king, behold, wise men from the East came to Jerusalem.

2 saying, "Where is He who has been born King of the Jews? For we have seen His star in the East and have come to worship Him."

3 When Herod the king heard this, he was troubled, and all Jerusalem with him.

4 And when he had gathered all the chief priests and scribes of the people together, he inquired of them where the Christ was to be born.

5 So they said to him, "In Bethlehem of Judea, for thus it is written by the prophet:

6 *'But you, Bethlehem, in the land of Judah,*
Are not the least among the rulers of Judah;
For out of you shall come a Ruler
Who will shepherd My people Israel.'"

7 Then Herod, when he had secretly called the wise men, determined from them what time the star appeared.

8 And he sent them to Bethlehem and said. "Go and search carefully for the young Child, and when you have found Him, bring back word to me, that I may come and worship Him also.

9   When they heard the king, they departed; and behold, the star which they has seen in the East went before them, till it came and stood over where the young Child was.

10 When they saw the star, they rejoiced with exceedingly great joy.

11 And when they had come into the house, they saw the young Child with Mary his mother, and fell down and worshipped Him. And when they had opened their treasures, they presented gifts to Him: gold, frankincense and myrrh.

12 Then, being divinely warned in a dream that they should not return to Herod, they departed for their own country another way.

13 Now when they had departed, behold, an angel of the Lord appeared to Joseph in a dream, saying "Arise, and take the young Child and His mother, flee to Egypt, and stay there until I bring you word; for Herod will seek the young Child to destroy Him."

14 When he arose, he took the young Child and His mother by night and departed for Egypt,

15 and was there until the death of Herod, that it might be fulfilled which was spoken by the Lord through the prophet, saying, *"Out of Egypt I called My Son."*

16 Then Herod, when he saw that he was deceived by the wise men, was exceedingly angry; and he sent forth and put to death all the male children who were in Bethlehem and in all its districts, from two years old and under, according to the time which he had determined from the wise men.

17 Then was fulfilled what was spoken by Jeremiah the prophet, saying:

18 *"A voice was heard in Ramah,*
    Lamentation, weeping, and great mourning,
    Rachel weeping for her children
    Refusing to be comforted,
    Because they are no more."

19 Now when Herod was dead, behold, an angel of the Lord appeared in a dream to Joseph in Egypt,

20 saying, "Arise, take the young Child and His mother, and go to the land of Israel, for those who sought the young Child's life are dead."

21 Then he arose, took the young Child and His mother, and came into the land of Israel.

22 But when he heard that Archelaus was reigning over Judea instead of his father Herod, he was afraid to go there. And being warned by God in a dream, he turned aside into the region of Galilee.

23 And he came and dwelt in a city called Nazareth, that it might be fulfilled which was spoken by the prophets, "He shall be called a Nazarene."

In addition to the accounts provided by Luke and Matthew, we must also consider a number of other accounts of the Nativity which are undeniably of ancient origin and should not be discarded as in any way less 'genuine' than those included within the Bible. The New Testament was not finalised without much debate, as it was always known that many further scriptures had legitimate claim to be included within it alongside the 27 that eventually made it. The first few centuries of Christianity saw much heated controversy between different sects, including arguments over the nature of God, whether Jesus could be considered as both human and divine, and the relationship between Judaism and Christianity (and hence between the Old and New Testaments). Eventually, by the fourth century, one group prevailed, and this group collated a collection of sacred texts that it regarded as authentic, leaving others by the wayside. It is not known exactly when the New Testament as we know it was collated, but in the AD 367 Athanasius, Bishop of Alexandria sent out what has become a famous letter stating that the 27 books in the New Testament, and only those 27 books, should be regarded as Scripture. Of those that were excluded, some will sadly have been lost for all time, a few are known through extraordinary archaeological discoveries, having been lost for centuries, while others survived, at least in part, through having been used by some sectors of the medieval Church or through incorporation into later documents.

The most relevant of the non-canonical books to the present discussion is the so-called 'Proto-Gospel of James', referred to here simply as 'The Gospel of James'. It is sometimes termed a 'proto-gospel' because it covers events prior to the appearance of Jesus in addition to stories about him. It is presented as having been written by James, a son of Joseph and step-brother of Jesus, but careful analysis of the text suggests that it was not actually written until the mid to late second century; it seems to be a classic example of a pseudepigraphical work, claiming to be written by a particular author but actually written by someone else. The author clearly had access to the Gospels of Luke and Matthew, but also uses other ancient sources which are now lost to us. The Gospel of James was extremely popular in ancient and medieval times. It was translated into numerous languages and about 130 ancient Greek manuscripts containing versions of it still survive (all quotations provided here are from Ehrman 2003).

The Gospel of James focuses on Mary, providing accounts of her own miraculous birth, her childhood in the Jerusalem temple, her marriage at the age of 12 to Joseph, the immaculate conception and the birth of Jesus in a cave outside Jerusalem. The details of Mary's background are fascinating, but here we must focus on the accounts of the conception and birth of Jesus. When Mary reached the age of 12, the priests decided that they must find her a husband. The chief priest was informed by an angel of the Lord to 'go out and gather the widowers of the people, and have each of them bring a rod: she will become the wife of the one to whom the Lord God gives a sign.' After some praying on the part of the chief priest, a dove flew out of Joseph's rod and landed on his head. This was the sign, and the priest said to Joseph, 'You have been called to take the Lord's virgin into your safe-keeping.' Joseph initially refused, stating that he was an old man with sons of his own whereas Mary was but a child. However, the priest convinced him not to incur the wrath of God by refusing, and he begrudgingly took Mary 'into his safe-keeping', leaving her at home while he left to continue his trade as a carpenter.

At the age of 16, Mary was approached by an angel of the Lord, saying 'Do not fear, Mary. For you have found favour before the Master of all, and you will conceive a child by his Word.' When she was six months pregnant, Joseph returned from his work and was dismayed to find his betrothed heavily pregnant, asking 'How can I look upon the Lord God? How can I utter a prayer for this young girl? For I received her from the temple of the Lord God as a virgin, but I did not watch over her. Who has preyed upon me? Who has done this wicked deed in my home and defiled the virgin?' Joseph then turned on Mary, asking her 'You who have been cared for by God: why did you do this? Have you forgotten the Lord your God? Why have you humiliated your soul – you who were brought up in the Holy of Holies and received your food from the hand of an angel?' But Mary wept bitterly and replied 'I am pure and have not had sex with any man', saying that she did not understand how she had become pregnant. On becoming aware of this situation, the priest (not unreasonably, under the circumstances) found himself unable to believe either Joseph or Mary, so subjected them to the biblical equivalent of the polygraph. Both were forced to take a mysterious lie-detecting potion and to the surprise of the priest, both passed the test. The priest announced 'If the Lord God has not revealed your sins, neither do I judge you', and the couple returned home 'rejoicing and glorying the God of Israel'.

We then encounter the census of Augustus (as told by Luke) and Joseph is obliged to take Mary to Jerusalem. When they were half-way there, the time came for Mary to give birth. They found a cave in which Mary was left, to be looked after by Joseph's sons while

Joseph himself went in search of a midwife. Before long, while he is out searching, we are told of 'time standing still' at the moment of Jesus' birth:

> But I, Joseph, was walking, and I was not walking. I looked up into the air, and I saw that it was greatly disturbed. I looked up to the vault of the sky, and I saw it standing still; and the birds of the sky were at rest. I looked back to the earth and saw a bowl laid out for some workers who were reclining to eat. Their hands were in the bowl, but those who were chewing were not chewing; and those who were bringing their hands to their mouths were not bringing them to their mouths. Everyone was looking up. And I saw a flock of sheep being herded, but they were standing still. And the shepherd raised his hand to strike them, but his hand remained in the air. I looked down at the torrential stream, and I saw some goats whose mouths were over the water, but they were not drinking. Then suddenly everything returned to its normal course.

(This powerful passage raises the mystical nature of 'mythic time' – something to which we will briefly return later in this chapter and which, as we will eventually discover, is not entirely unfamiliar to Santa Claus.) Once time had returned to normal, Joseph found a midwife 'coming down from the mountains'. They went together to the cave which was hidden within a bright cloud. The cloud lifted, but the cave was full of a bright light, so bright that nothing could be seen within it. Soon, this light, too, departed, and Joseph and the midwife then saw the infant Jesus with Mary. The midwife and another character named Salome, who appeared outside the cave at the time, then examined Mary and found her to be still a virgin, even after the birth.

The Gospel of James then tells the story of the wise men and the star of Bethlehem, presenting it in a similar style to that of Matthew, but does not mention the flight to Egypt, saying only that 'When Mary heard that the infants were being killed, out of fear she took her child and wrapped him in swaddling clothes and placed him in a cattle manger.' There is an account of Herod's search for John the Baptist, and the murder of John's father, Zacharias, but no further discussion of Jesus. The account ends with the death of Herod.

Two further accounts that we should mention in passing are those known to us as the 'Questions of Bartholomew' and the 'Epistle of the Apostles'. The former, probably of third-century date, includes an account of the Annunciation supposedly given by Mary herself, in response to questioning by the Apostles. This dramatic story includes references to an angel, a great earthquake, a sprinkling from a cloud of dew, a very great loaf of bread, a great cup of wine and a statement that three years hence Mary would find herself pregnant with the Son of God. The Epistle of the Apostles, possibly of mid second-century date, records Jesus claiming that he himself appeared as the angel Gabriel before passing into Mary's womb, an intriguing variation on the conventional theme, but one which would, I fear, refuse to repay any kind of modern analysis.

We have mentioned the sheep, but what of 'the ox and the ass' that appear in all Nativity scenes? Perhaps we are to assume that the ass was the beast on which Mary had travelled to Bethlehem, but the ox does not get a mention anywhere other than in the Gospel of Pseudo-Matthew which informs us that:

> … on the third day after the birth of our Lord Jesus Christ, the most blessed Mary went forth out of the cave, and entering a stable, placed the child in the stall, and the ox and the ass adored Him. Then was fulfilled that which was said by Isaiah the prophet, saying: 'the ox knoweth his owner, and the ass his master's crib. The very animals, therefore, the ox and the ass, having Him in their midst, incessantly adored Him.' Then was fulfilled that which was said by Abacuc the prophet, saying: 'Between two animals thou art made manifest.'
>
> *Quotation from Ridge 2006*

So this story manages to combine both a cave and a stable, while apparently seeking to demonstrate how the birth of Jesus fulfils ancient prophecies. (A stable, it is worth noting, is not mentioned by Matthew or Luke; it is Luke's reference to the manger, in which the infant Jesus was placed, that has led to the assumption that the birth took place in a stable.) The Gospel of Pseudo-Matthew is not well known, but two key characters in its Nativity scene, the ox and the ass, have made it through into our contemporary celebrations.

This brief survey has presented the main themes of the Nativity as discussed in various ancient sources. We will now analyse a number of these themes in detail before attempting to arrive at something of a conclusion regarding their authenticity.

A Note on the Christian Calendar

A.N. Wilson warns us in his excellent biography of Jesus that the gospels 'were not written as source-material for modern biographers', and that 'the story of Christ invades history, but this does not mean that it is "historical".' Bearing these warnings in mind, are there any clues in the available accounts of Jesus' birth to enable us to date this momentous event according to our calendar? The first thing to establish is that our modern calendar, measuring years as either BC (Before Christ) or AD (*Anno Dominae*, 'after Christ') with the two separated by the birth of Jesus, is fundamentally flawed. This system was invented by a Scythian monk, Dionysius Exiguus while living in Rome in about AD 530. Prior to this, years were measured in relation to founding of Rome. Dionysius calculated that Jesus was born 754 years after the founding of Rome, and the year of Jesus' birth became AD 1. Although the expert of his day in this field, he somehow managed to incorporate a number of fundamental errors into his new system. For example, he omitted from his calculations the four years during which the Emperor Augustus had ruled under his own name, Octavian, and also failed to insert a year 'zero' between 1 BC and AD 1. All scholars would now agree that Jesus was not born in AD 1, but a few years earlier.

The Census

During the course of this chapter we will note that Matthew relies upon several 'fulfilment texts', whereby elements of his story represent the fulfilment of specified Old Testament prophecies. Luke does not do this so blatantly, but one key element of his story may well originate from such a prophecy. Matthew does not specify the location of Joseph and Mary's home prior to the birth of Jesus, and we are left to assume that it is Bethlehem. Luke, by contrast, is clear that they lived in Nazareth, but had to travel to Bethlehem to fulfil the demands of a census, and Jesus was born while they were there. If we can establish the date of this census then we will know once and for all the year of Jesus' birth.

Luke tells us that Jesus was born during the reign of King Herod, and there is no reason to doubt this. Herod ruled Judea from 40 BC to 4 BC, making 4 BC the latest possible date for Jesus' birth. Luke also tells us that the census which caused Joseph to return to Bethlehem was ordered by Caesar Augustus, Roman Emperor at the time, and that Quirinius was Governor of Syria. This reads like well-researched history, but there is a major problem. Quirinius did not become Governor of Syria until AD 6, 10 years after the death of Herod. It has been suggested that Luke may have made a mistake due to Quirinius having been present in a military capacity (but not as Governor) in Syria during the first half of the last decade BC, and some scholars have pleaded that Luke may have been referring to a census 'before that of Quirinius', with the original meaning having been lost in translation. However, both these scenarios are considered unlikely by most experts, and it seems that Luke's account, despite reading as history, cannot actually be considered as historically reliable.

We might reasonably expect some historical record of a 'universal' census such as that alluded to by Luke, but no such record exists. The Romans were keen on censuses, which provided information for levying taxes and enlisting men into the army. But Herod was a client king and as the Romans did not generally collect taxes from the citizens of client kings it is hard to see why such a census would have been ordered here by Augustus. The generally reliable Jewish historian, Josephus, records that Quirinius did oversee a census of sorts in Judea in AD 6, when direct Roman rule was imposed here, but this is obviously much too late to provide a context for Joseph and Mary's journey to Bethlehem.

Luke, who was writing nearly a century after the event, may have made a genuine mistake with his dates, leading him to believe that Jesus' birth and Quirinius' census had occurred at the same time, allowing him to use the census as a convenient mechanism by which to get Mary to Bethlehem in time for Jesus' birth. However, even if a census had occurred at the time of the birth, it is hard to understand why it would have necessitated Joseph and his heavily pregnant wife travelling the 70 miles from Nazareth to Bethlehem. Only the head of the household was required to register with the censor, so Joseph could have done so on his own. Another problem is that he would only have been required to register in Bethlehem if he owned property there. If he owned property, we may reasonably assume that he would have stayed in it, in which case Jesus would presumably not have ended up being born in a stable.

Why did Luke invoke this implausible story rather than simply allow Jesus to be born in Nazareth? The answer is, of course, that the Messiah could only be born in one place: David's 'Royal City' of Bethlehem. Bethlehem, a small village in the hills about 5 miles outside Jerusalem, was the birthplace of David, the shepherd boy who had killed Goliath and became Israel's second king in about 1000 BC, founding the royal line from which it was believed by Jews that the Messiah would be born. This belief was rooted in the words of Micah, a Judean prophet from the late eighth century BC, a time when much of the Middle East was threatened by the expanding kingdom of Assyria. In fact, what Micah actually seems to have prophesied was that a Judean ruler, born in King David's village would eventually conquer the Assyrians; there is nothing in his prophecy to suggest a direct or indirect link with the birth of Jesus seven centuries later.

The discussion of real places like Bethlehem, Nazareth and Jerusalem, along with historical figures such as Augustus, Herod and Quirinius, lends the biblical Nativity an aura of geographical and historical credibility, inviting us to believe that the events themselves were no less 'real'. However, Luke's account of the census, conveniently forcing Joseph and Mary to travel from their home in Nazareth to Bethlehem so that Jesus could be born there, is most unlikely to be historically accurate. Rather, it should be regarded as an exquisite piece of storytelling that owes its origin more to a desire to fulfil an Old Testament prophecy than to any kind of historical authenticity.

The Virgin Birth

In contrast to the conventional accounts, the Gospel of Philip offers an alternative interpretation of the story of the Virgin birth that may appeal to many Christians in the modern world. The Gospel of Philip seems to have been virtually unknown from Late Antiquity until its spectacular discovery, along with 51 other ancient texts, in an earthenware jar unearthed by an Egyptian peasant near the village of Nag Hammadi in 1945. It is probably of third-century date, but clearly draws on earlier sources. It is a difficult document to interpret, but collates a series of reflections on life, presenting them under the name of Philip, Jesus' disciple, even though he must have been long dead by the time that it was written. Bart D. Ehrman in his fascinating book, *Lost Scriptures*, notes that it invites those 'in the know' to regard the virgin birth, and other key events such as the resurrection, not as literal statements of historical fact, but rather as 'symbolic expressions of deeper truths'.

The earliest surviving accounts of Jesus' life (those of Mark and Paul) make no mention of a virgin birth; this might reasonably be considered something of a major omission if the story was true and widely known at the time. Later accounts, however, stress its prime importance in the story of the Nativity, so we must consider it in some detail. There are two important facts that we must bear in mind when considering the virgin birth. First, Matthew claims that it was prophesied in Isaiah (7:14), but there is doubt as to whether Isaiah's original Hebrew referred to a 'virgin' or just a 'young woman'. Second, it is perfectly possible to read Luke in such a way that no virgin birth is implied. We will consider both of these ideas shortly.

There have been some pseudo-scientific claims that Mary may have become pregnant through some natural process of spontaneous conception (parthenogenesis), but such claims are nonsense as medical science regards such conception in human beings as biologically impossible. We may note, however, that the eminent Jesus scholar, Geza Vermes, has made the intriguing observation that, due to a quirk in the ancient Jewish concept of virginity, a virgin birth may indeed be biologically possible. This is because in the ancient Jewish world there were two types of virginity. On the one hand, a girl is a virgin until she has had sexual intercourse. On the other, a girl is a virgin until she achieves puberty (that is, until her first menstruation), but ceases to be a virgin at this point regardless of whether or not she has intercourse. Given that it was common practice in New Testament times for girls to be betrothed and married at the age of 12, it is certainly possible, though statistically unlikely, that a girl could conceive after her first ovulation, but prior to her first menstruation. On this basis, it is biologically possible for a 'virgin' to give birth. However, this is a semantic argument and is most unlikely to have any relevance to the Nativity. Basically there are two possibilities regarding Jesus' conception; either it was truly immaculate or he was illegitimate. History can throw no light on the matter. Readers must make up their own minds.

It is important to remember that the biology of reproduction was not well understood in biblical times, and issues of fertility and conception were very much associated with religious belief. In ancient Judaism, God had the power to 'open' or 'close' a womb and could therefore dictate in every case of intercourse whether or not a woman would conceive. However, a woman could not become pregnant without the active participation of a male, thus the virgin birth has no clear parallel in the Old Testament. That said, virgin births are well attested in numerous miraculous birth stories from around the ancient world, several of which involve liaisons between male gods and mortal women. According to various myths, Alexander the Great was fathered by Zeus, Romulus' father was Mars, and both the Greek philosopher Plato and Augustus,

Roman Emperor at the time of Jesus' birth, were fathered by Apollo. Augustus also derived divine status from his relationship to the deified Julius Caesar – just like Jesus he was directly a 'Son of God' and also of royal, divine stock by virtue of his family links on earth.

We have noted the detailed, though clearly fictitious, genealogies of Jesus which Matthew and Luke use to stress the importance of his Davidic descent through Joseph. Both Luke and Matthew trace Jesus' ancestors back through King David to Abraham and in Luke's case, to Adam. Clearly, this is nonsense, but it serves an important purpose, underlining Jesus' royal Messianic claim and providing a context enabling him to fulfil a number of Old Testament prophesies. It is legitimate to ask, however, how this lineage relates to the virginal conception. Surely, if Mary conceived Jesus through the Holy Spirit, with no intervention from Joseph, then Joseph's genealogy becomes irrelevant to the story of Jesus? Some authorities have tried to claim that as Joseph accepted Jesus as his son then Jesus, regardless of his actual paternity, became legally able to claim direct descent from David. This smacks of rather feeble and desperate pleading; to claim that Jesus was not the biological son of Joseph, but is nevertheless entitled to claim descent from David *through* Joseph is clearly nonsense.

Be that as it may, Joseph undeniably plays a key role in the Nativity story. On finding herself pregnant other than by her fiancée, Mary became, in the eyes of the law, an adulteress. Joseph could have taken the matter to the courts, as a result of which both Mary and the father of her unborn child (if he could be identified) could have been hideously but legally executed by stoning. Joseph, according to Matthew, opted instead to nullify the betrothal quietly, but in any case such nullification became unnecessary once the 'real' nature of Mary's pregnancy had been revealed to him by an angel. (What useful creations those angels were!) Presumably, Isaiah's ancient prophecy was known to Joseph and had much to do with his acceptance of this extraordinary situation, providing something of a context (whether in reality or just in the story) within which he could believe the words of the angel.

There seems little point in attempting any further historical analysis of the virgin birth story, but we must consider one potentially major flaw in its genesis. We have already noted that the Gospel according to Matthew bases some aspects of its Nativity story on the fulfilment of Old Testament prophecies, one of which is that provided by Isaiah. Matthew (1:23) quotes Isaiah (7:14): 'Behold, a virgin shall conceive and bear a son, and his name shall be Emmanuel'. But (and it is a very big 'but'), in the original Hebrew, Isaiah does *not* refer to a virgin, but more generally to a 'young woman' who may or may not have been a virgin. At some point the original Hebrew word *'almah* was translated into the Greek *parthenos* which unambiguously does mean virgin. Quite simply, the original version of Isaiah's prophecy did not necessitate a virgin birth, stating merely that 'a young woman shall conceive and bear a son'. Only after this had been translated into Greek did the virgin birth become an issue. So Matthew's story (at least in its surviving Greek) appears to have been designed to fulfil an ancient prophecy that didn't even exist! To be fair to Matthew, we should note that contemporary folklore may well have come to accept the concept of the virgin birth by the time that he was writing, so we are not accusing him of necessarily having made it up. As we have seen, the account of pseudo–James further embellishes the myth of the virgin birth, stating that Mary remained demonstrably a virgin even after giving birth to Jesus; other than by reference to the traditional biblical method, the miracle, this is plainly ludicrous.

We should note at this point that a careful reading of Luke does not necessitate Mary's having been a virgin at the time of Jesus' conception or birth. She was indeed a virgin at the time of the annunciation, but nowhere does Luke imply that she did not have intercourse with Joseph between the annunciation and the birth. There is, therefore, the possibility that Jesus' conception was rather like some Old Testament conceptions (or indeed that of John the Baptist in the New Testament) whereby a special child results from normal intercourse between a mother and father, but also involved the miraculous intervention of God in some unspecified way.

On balance, it seems very much as though the whole notion of the virgin birth may owe its origin to an early case of the key facts having been lost (or at least misinterpreted) in translation. It was probably made up some time after Jesus' death in a retrospective attempt to tie in with Isaiah's prophecy, even though Isaiah, whose original prophecy was made in the mid eighth century BC, surely did not have such events in mind. It also ties in neatly with a number of more ancient pagan myths that account for the birth of gods through intercourse between 'senior' gods and mortal virgins. Almost certainly, there was no virgin birth. The story was invented to fulfil an ancient (and misunderstood) prophecy, while attempting to make the conception of Jesus appear suitably special and wholly unique in a biblical context.

The Star of David

Many scholars believe that the most likely year of Jesus' birth is either 7 or 6 BC, and much effort has been spent on searching for possible explanations of the 'Star of David' at about this time. In his bestseller, *The Bible as History*, Werner Keller makes a convincing case for 7 BC, arguing that the explanation of the bright star followed by the wise men could have been a conjunction of the planets Jupiter and Saturn. Astronomers have calculated that these two planets appeared to merge together, and therefore would have shone exceptionally brightly in the Mediterranean night sky on three separate occasions during that year. This conjunction took place within the constellation of Pisces, which was considered in Jewish astrology to be the sign of the Messiah. These events occurred on 29 May, 3 October and 4 December. Keller argues that the wise men may have observed the first conjunction (perhaps marking the birth) from their base in Babylon in May, and using the astronomical techniques of the day would have been able to predict the two subsequent occurrences. They could have set off on their journey at the time of the October conjunction, arriving in Jerusalem some six weeks later in time to observe the third conjunction, which occurred due south (and therefore over Bethlehem when seen from Jerusalem) in the evening sky on 4 December. This theory sounds very plausible, but there have also been many others.

David Hughes, in *The Star of Bethlehem Mystery*, considers many possible explanations of the star, ranging from a genuine miracle, through various forms of lightning to a whole range of possible astronomical phenomena. After more than 200 pages of scholarly analysis and speculation, he also concludes that the explanation lies in the conjunction of Jupiter and Saturn in 7 BC. He cautiously concludes that Jesus was probably born on the occasion of the acronychal rising of Jupiter and Saturn (meaning the occasion on which they rose in the east just as the sun set in the west, staying visible all night until the following sunrise). On this basis, Jesus would have been born on the evening of Tuesday 15 September, 7 BC.

When seeking to account for the Star of David we must remember that the 'wise men' or 'Magi' were primarily astrologer-priests, so the answer may lie in 'astrological' rather than astronomical phenomena. Despite Matthew's apparent reference to a single bright star, we should perhaps be searching for what would have been regarded as significant relative positions of the sun, moon, planets and stars rather than for one particularly bright object. Whatever we might think of astrology today, at the time of Jesus it was regarded as a complex science and was used to predict important events. The astronomer Michael Molnar, an expert on astral symbolism, notes that Aries was thought to be especially important in influencing human activity in Judea at the time of Herod. He also notes that the 'Star of Zeus' (Jupiter) was of particular importance to the birth of kings, especially when it was rising as a morning star (which is what 'in the east' means in astrological terms). This offers an intriguing possibility with regard to the date of Jesus' birth. On 17 April in the year 6 BC, Jupiter emerged as a 'morning star' in Aries. At the time the sun, the moon and Saturn were also all in Aries, all of which would have been of great significance to astrologers looking for possible signs of the birth of a great king. Molnar records that a Christian Roman astrologer, Firmicus Maternus, observed in about AD 334 that these conditions marked the birth of 'a divine and immortal person'. They may well have provided sufficient impetus for the Magi to set off on their journey to Judea in search of the newborn Son of God. Molnar also notes that later in 6 BC, after having left Aries, Jupiter returned there and, due to the illusion we refer to today as 'retrograde motion', appeared to become stationary against the background of the stars for several days. Could this relate to Matthew's observation that the star 'stood over' the place where Jesus was at the time? If so, then it could imply that the Magi visited some time after the birth, by which time Joseph, Mary and Jesus were living somewhere other than the site of the birth; it will be recalled that while Matthew makes no mention of a stable or cave as the birth site, he states unambiguously that the Magi found Jesus 'in a house'.

Astronomers, astrologers and theologians may continue to debate the Star of Bethlehem until the ends of time, but may never reach final agreement on its nature or date. Indeed, such work may well be futile, as the star may well never have existed in any form or at any time! It may have been invented, perhaps by Matthew, to fulfil another Old Testament prophecy. There are many recorded examples in the ancient world of stars signalling the birth of great leaders, so the fact that Jesus' birth was signalled in this way should come as no great surprise. It is recorded in the Old Testament (*Numbers* 24:17) that the prophet Balaam, who lived at the time of Moses, prophesied that 'a star shall come forth out of Jacob and a sceptre shall rise out of Israel'. It may have been simply to tally with this prophecy that the story of the star was invented. It may have become part of the traditional story of Jesus' birth prior to Matthew, who simply wrote it down, or it may have been invented by Matthew as part of his apparent grand plan to present the Nativity as the fulfilment of Old Testament prophecies. Either way, there can be no proof that the star actually existed at all, never mind whether or not it rose at the time of Jesus' birth. It is much more likely that the story was concocted in retrospect; perhaps someone with astrological knowledge realised, long after the event and probably some time after Jesus' death, that the aforementioned conjunction of Jupiter and Saturn had occurred at about the time of Jesus' birth, and that it 'predicted' perfectly the birth of the Saviour. The story of the star thus became part of Nativity mythology, and was recorded as such by Matthew.

We have seen that the Star of David has been used by scholars to provide convincing cases for Jesus having been born on or around 29 May and 15 September 7 BC, and 17 April 6 BC. There is certainly no suggestion that the birth occurred in December. Luke records that at the time of the birth 'there were in the same country shepherds abiding in the field, keeping watch over their flock by night' (2:8). Then, as now, shepherds would not be out with their flocks in December, when the weather can be very wet and freezing cold. The practice of the time was for shepherds to move out to summer grazing grounds in the hills with their sheep and cattle in the spring, returning back to the shelter of their villages by November where they would stay until the following spring. This was a common way of life amongst agricultural communities throughout much of Europe and Asia until very recent times, and indeed is still practised in some rural areas. Therefore, we may assume that Jesus was born at some point between March and November; certainly not in December. The reasons why we celebrate his birthday on 25 December will become clear shortly; for now we need note only that they bear no relation whatsoever to his actual birthday, whatever that may have been.

The Flight into Egypt and the Return to Nazareth

According to Matthew's Gospel, at some point after his birth in Bethlehem and presentation to God at the Temple in Jerusalem, the infant Jesus and his parents were forced to flee to Egypt. This was because the Magi had returned home without informing Herod of the whereabouts of the infant Messiah, causing Herod to order the 'massacre of the innocents'. With the vast resources at his disposal, Herod could surely have located and disposed of Jesus with minimal difficulty – Bethlehem, as we have seen, was but a small village. Instead, he opted for the absurd alternative of murdering all infant boys in the district aged two years or under. He may have been an evil tyrant, but why, when a small-scale investigation would surely have sufficed, did he order such wholesale slaughter, which must inevitably have caused enormous resentment and hatred amongst his people? I would suggest that we should be asking 'whether' rather than 'why' he did so. The explanation, as with so many aspects of the Nativity, may be found in the pages of the Old Testament.

In some ways, the story of the flight into Egypt bears an uncanny resemblance to the Old Testament tale of Moses as told in the Book of Exodus. In this, Pharaoh ordered Jewish parents to drown their newborn sons in the Nile, but the baby Moses survived, having been placed by his parents in a reed basket which floated away down river. Jesus was taken to Egypt by his parents to escape Herod's murderous intent, while we must assume that other infants perished. In both cases we have an evil tyrant ordering the murder of infants, and the survival of a single baby boy, each of whom would come to be regarded in due course as a 'saviour'. There are also other similarities between the early lives of Moses and Jesus – at the birth of Moses the house was 'filled with light', which brings strongly to mind the pseudo-James account of the birth of Jesus.

It certainly seems that the story of the infant Jesus and Herod was heavily influenced by that of Moses and Pharaoh. It also cleverly enabled the fulfilment of two further important Old Testament prophecies. Can you think of a better story than the flight into Egypt to enable the Messiah to have been born in 'David's royal city' of Bethlehem, yet also fulfil the ancient prophecy that the Lord would call his son 'Out of Egypt'? Not only that, but there is a further link with the massacre of the innocents. Matthew (2:17-18) tells us that the event:

> … fulfilled what was spoken by Jeremiah the prophet, saying: 'A voice was heard in Ramah, Lamentation, weeping, and great mourning, Rachel weeping for her children. Refusing to be comforted, Because they are no more.'

This is another clever use of an Old Testament prophecy to demonstrate the preordained nature of certain aspects of the Nativity.

Jeremiah was writing with reference to events at Ramah, not far from Bethlehem, a place which figured prominently in the Babylonian conquest of Jerusalem in the sixth century BC. Matthew presents Rachel as weeping for the little boys of Bethlehem some half a millennium after she had first wept for 'her children'. Once again, this is powerful narrative, but it is surely not possible that Jeremiah had Herod in mind when he wrote of Rachel. Nevertheless, this was perfect material for Matthew in his mission to present the Nativity in the context of Old Testament prophecies. I would go so far as to suggest that the entire story of Herod's murder of the innocents was manufactured (though not necessarily by Matthew, who may simply have written down what was already accepted oral tradition) to fit this intended pattern.

According to Matthew, after the death of Herod, Mary, Joseph and Jesus were unable to return to Bethlehem as this was now under the control of Herod's equally bloodthirsty son, Archelaus. Instead, they headed north to Nazareth, a small town in a valley about 15 miles west of the Sea of Galilee, where we know that Jesus spent most of his life (and actually where, in all probability, he was born). This sounds reasonable, until we realise that Nazareth was under the control of another of Herod's sons, Antipas, who would have been no less of a threat than Archelaus back in Judea. In short, this seems to be another example of 'history' being used effectively, but selectively and inaccurately, to provide a context for the Nativity story. Matthew (2:23) relates the fact that Jesus lived in Nazareth to an ancient but sadly unspecified ancient prophecy that 'He shall be called a Nazarene'. We know nothing of the source of this; it may well have been invented, but does, nevertheless, provide another example of Jesus having apparently fulfilled an ancient prophecy.

The Infancy Gospels as Fiction

It is tempting to try and collate the accounts offered by Matthew and Luke, along with snippets obtained from other ancient sources, to tell the 'complete' story of the birth of Jesus. Indeed, this is precisely what our conventional Nativity play attempts to do, and does to great effect. Sadly, such a composite account cannot be considered as in any way historically reliable. Indeed, Luke and Matthew tell stories which, while not necessarily conflicting with each other, are certainly very different in nature. Luke's account is low-key. Other than the parents and the baby, presented as a simple, rural family, the only participants (other than the heavenly band of angels) are a few local shepherds from nearby fields. This may have been intended as a suitable introduction into the world for one who would later preach about the 'blessedness of the poor', but Matthew, in contrast, paints a much more grandiose scene involving the star of Bethlehem, the Magi and gifts of gold, frankincense and myrrh, and includes the dramatic episode of Herod's 'massacre of the innocents', of which Luke makes no mention. In Luke, Joseph and Mary were natives of Nazareth, only travelling to Bethlehem to comply with the demands of Augustus' census. They returned to Nazareth, apparently uneventfully, some 40 days after the birth of Jesus; there is no suggestion of a threat to Jesus' life in Bethlehem. Matthew, in complete contrast, has the family settling in Nazareth, after the flight into Egypt, because it was too dangerous to return to Bethlehem. Luke and Matthew actually face opposing dilemmas in presenting Jesus as having been in Bethlehem but living in Nazareth. Luke has to get Mary *to Bethlehem* in time for the birth before moving back home to Nazareth. Matthew has to account for the move to Nazareth after the escape, via Egypt, *from Bethlehem*. Either way, there was no alternative other than for Jesus to end up in Nazareth, as it is probable that most of the Gospels, telling of his life in and around Nazareth, were already written some time before the Nativity episodes were added to the Gospels of Luke and Matthew.

There is a tendency in the modern mind to seek to place the fabulous story of the Nativity in both geographical and chronological frameworks, so that we can understand it according to western 'scientific' thought. But perhaps it was never intended to be understood in this way. The stories of Jesus' birth in the gospels read as though they are history, and tell of places that are familiar to us today, but in reality they should be regarded as mythical rather than historical. This is not to question their importance; indeed myths have arguably been of greater significance to the development of humanity than has history. Myths have been crucial to human development since people first looked up at the heavens and sought to explain those aspects of existence which were otherwise inexplicable to them, and in many cases remain inexplicable to us today. They transcend time, travelling outside the world of everyday experience to provide a framework within which such everyday experience can occur. Only in recent times has the western mind begun to alienate itself from myth, demanding scientific or historical explanations for everything. Hence we subject the myth of the Star of Bethlehem to all manner of complex computerised analyses in the desperate but probably futile attempt to calculate the exact date of Jesus' birth, when it is actually the *story* of the star that matters, not the star itself.

Karen Armstrong in her book, *A Short History of Myth*, tells us that:

> unless a historical event is mythologised, it cannot become a source of religious inspiration. A myth … is an event that – in some sense – happened once, but which also happens all the time. An occurrence needs to be liberated, as it were, from the confines of a specific period and brought into the lives of contemporary worshippers, or it will remain a unique, unrepeatable incident, or even a historical freak that cannot really touch the lives of others.

St Paul was largely responsible for transforming Jesus from a historical figure to a mythical hero. In the words of Armstrong, everyone who was baptised 'entered into Jesus' death and would share his life. Jesus was no longer a mere historical figure but a spiritual reality in the lives of Christians by means of ritual and the ethical discipline of living the same selfless life as Jesus himself.' People know the myth to be 'true' not because of historical facts, but because they themselves participate in the religious events associated with it. The Nativity has become part of the myth of Jesus. In many ways, the 'historical facts' simply do not matter to Christians, which is probably just as well because, as we have seen, these 'facts' are largely, if not entirely, made up.

Perhaps all we can say with certainty about the traditional story of Jesus' birth, whether in a stable or a cave, with its virgin mother, its astrologer-priests and shepherds, its ox and its ass, all overseen by the magnificent Star of David, is that it is a beautiful story. Over the years, folklore has impacted upon this story. It has for example, created three kings out the Magi whereas in fact there is no suggestion in the Bible that they were kings. The Bible does not even specify there were three of them; this has simply been inferred from the fact that they brought three gifts (which, incidentally, could have been readily obtained at trading posts along the route from Babylon to Jerusalem in what we could perhaps regard as the first instance of Christmas shopping). Nowhere in the Bible does it state that Jesus was born in a stable, but folklore has now established this as the scene of the Nativity. Despite having been embellished over the centuries, the story of the Nativity remains compellingly simple. Its simplicity contributes much to its potency, but, sadly, does not make it any more believable. It is clearly not history, and even if we chose to believe it, we cannot say with any certainty when it happened. On balance, I believe it was invented, probably some time after Jesus' death, when those writing about his life had to find some way to account for his entry into the world. Under the circumstances, and with no available 'facts' to hand, it was natural to search for clues in the Old Testament and to build a story around the ancient prophecies found therein. The Nativity scenes are effectively standalone documents; they make no reference to anything else in the New Testament, and are themselves referred to nowhere else within the New Testament. If those portions of the Gospels of Luke and Matthew dealing with the Nativity are simply deleted, then the two gospels still read perfectly well without them. It may well be that they were inserted, perhaps by the original authors or perhaps by others, some time after Luke and Matthew had completed the rest of their gospels.

Some Christians may have difficulty coming to terms with the fact that the Nativity is little more than a fairy story, but according to *The Times* (20 December 2007) no lesser authority than Rowan Williams, Archbishop of Canterbury, regards the three wise men as 'legend', has a good deal of scepticism about other aspects of the story, and does not consider Jesus to have been born in December. He does, however, retain belief in the Virgin Birth (it would, of course, be scandalous if he were ever to deny this, given the importance of it to Christian doctrine). *The Times* article also states:

> In spite of his scepticism about the aspects of the Christmas story, as told in infant Nativity plays up and down the land, he denied that believing in God was equivalent to believing in Santa Claus or the tooth fairy … Dr Williams was not saying anything that is not taught as a matter of course in even the most conservative theological colleges. His supporters would argue that it is a sign of a true man of faith that he can hold on an orthodox faith while permitting honest intellectual scrutiny of fundamental biblical texts.

Many Christians never attend theological college and will find Dr Williams' views on the Nativity awkward to say the least. Still, at least they should be reassured to hear that their belief in God is not exactly equivalent to my younger daughter's affection for the tooth fairy.

In attempting to uncover the 'truth' from the gospels of Luke and Matthew, Geza Vermes observes that 'this truth … belongs only very slightly to history and mostly derives from man's hopeful and creative religious imagination.' He further observes that 'with the benefit of hindsight, the ultimate purpose of the Infancy Gospels seems to be in the creation of a prologue, enveloping the newborn Jesus with an aura of marvel and enigma … This prologue forms the appropriate counterpart of the equally wondrous epilogue of the Gospels – also replete with angels, visions and apparitions — the resurrection of Jesus.' In short, despite its acceptance as 'history' throughout much of the Christian world and its celebration by millions of people every year, our traditional story of the Nativity is complete fiction, cobbled together largely from fragments of ancient prophecies to provide a suitably grand entrance into the world for the Son of God.

The Roman Midwinter and the Invention of Christmas

It is beyond the remit of this volume to explain in any detail how Christianity rose from its humble beginnings as a Jewish sect to effectively take over the western world, but it was in AD 325 that the Emperor Constantine adopted Christianity as the official religion of the Roman Empire, and it is largely on account of this decision that we celebrate Christmas today rather than the pagan equivalents enjoyed by people in earlier times. However, given that we have established that Jesus was certainly not born in December, how is that we now celebrate his birthday at midwinter? The explanation is both simple and, I think, beyond dispute. To find it we must visit Ancient Rome, where festivities had been associated with the time of the winter solstice since long before the advent of Christianity. We must consider three separate, but interrelated, elements of Roman tradition which are relevant to the adoption and subsequent history of Christmas: the festivals of Saturnalia (17-23 December) and the Kalends (1-3 January), and the day of the winter solstice (25 December) which came to be known as the 'Birthday of the Unconquered Sun'.

Saturnalia was originally a single-day festival in honour of Saturn, the god of agriculture and time, held on 17 December. It involved ritual sacrifices, and the symbolic liberation of the god through the ceremonial untying of the ropes that bound his statue within his temple throughout the rest of the year. The festival was very popular and expanded into a week-long public holiday, lasting until 23 December, during which many normal patterns of social behaviour were reversed; slaves dined and played dice with their masters, and senators abandoned their togas in favour of colourful, informal clothing. Schools, law courts and businesses were all closed, and most people seem to have engaged in an orgy of feasting, drinking and gambling, greeting each other with cries of '*Io, Saturnalia!*' (which might translate as 'Ho, Praise to Saturn!' – a Roman precursor to our 'Merry Christmas!'). Gifts of various types were exchanged, with wax candles (*cerei*), symbolic of the sun, and small terracotta figures (*sigillaria*) especially popular. It seems that the festival was imbued with the thought of a distant golden age, when the just and benevolent Saturn ruled the world and all people were happy. A mock king, probably representing Saturn, was chosen by lot each year to preside over the revelry; within reason, this mock king was able to order people, including those normally considered his social superiors, to do silly things in the name of festive entertainment. The festivities could certainly be rowdy. Pliny wrote in the early second century that he had a special area set aside in his villa where he could hide in peace 'especially during the Saturnalia when the rest of the house is noisy with the licence of the holiday and festive cries.'

After a few days to recover from the excesses of Saturnalia, the Romans embarked on the festival of the Kalends. This officially lasted three days from 1 January, but in practice seems to have lasted for five. Clement Miles, in *Christmas Customs and Traditions*, discusses the Kalends at some length, providing two lengthy quotations from ancient sources. The first is from the fourth-century Greek philosopher, Libanius, who provides an extraordinarily detailed first-hand account of the Kalends celebrations:

> The festival of the Kalends is celebrated everywhere as far as the limits of the Roman Empire extend …Everywhere may be seen carousals and well-laden tables; luxurious abundance is found in the houses of the rich, but also in the houses of the poor better food than usual is put upon the table. The impulse to spend seizes everyone. He who the whole year through has taken pleasure in saving and piling up his pence, becomes suddenly extravagant. He who erstwhile was accustomed and preferred to live poorly, now at this feast enjoys himself as much as his means will allow … People are not only generous towards themselves, but also towards their fellow-men. A stream of presents pours itself out on all sides … The highroads and footpaths are covered with whole processions of laden men and beasts … As the thousand flowers which burst forth everywhere are the adornment of Spring, so are the thousand presents poured out on

all sides, the decoration of the Kalends feast. It may justly be said that it is the fairest time of the year ... The Kalends festival banishes all that is connected with toil, and allows men to give themselves up to undisturbed enjoyment. From the minds of young people it removes two kinds of dread: the dread of the schoolmaster and the dread of the stern pedagogue. The slave also it allows, so far as possible, to breathe the air of freedom ... Another great quality of the festival is that it teaches men not to hold too fast to their money, but to part with it and let it pass into other hands.

Libanius also describes processions on New Year's Eve, after which people went about leaping and singing in the streets rather than sleeping, going to bed only at daybreak. He further records that houses were decorated with evergreens, gifts (known as *strenae*) were exchanged, masters and slaves drank and played dice together, and the festivities lasted for up to five days (which, we might note in passing, takes us through to 5 January, the day that would later become known as Twelfth Night, the traditional end of the Christmas season in medieval times).

The second quotation is rather later in date and gives a Christian perspective on the Kalends. Miles notes that it is often ascribed to St Augustine of Hippo, but that is more likely to be the work of the sixth-century Caesarius of Arles. He also makes the interesting suggestion that some of the practices described, rather than being strictly Roman in origin, may have been introduced to Rome from peoples conquered by the legions. Either way, and whoever its author, the passage demonstrates that the traditional Kalends revelries were still very much in full swing well into the Christian era.

On those days the heathen, reversing the order of all things, dress themselves up in indecent deformities ... These miserable men, and what is worse, some who have been baptized, put on counterfeit forms and monstrous faces, at which one should rather be ashamed and sad ... Some are clothed in the hides of cattle; others put on the heads of beasts, rejoicing and exalting that they have so transformed themselves into the shapes of animals that they no longer appear to be men ... How vile, further, it is that those who have been born men are clothed in women's dresses, and by the vilest change effeminate their manly strength by taking on the forms of girls, blushing not to clothe their warlike arms in women's garments; they have bearded faces, and yet they wish to appear women ... There are some who on the Kalends of January practise auguries, and do not allow fire out of their houses or any other favour to

anyone who asks. Also they both receive and give diabolical
presents. Some country people, moreover, lay tables with plenty of
things necessary for eating ... thinking that thus the Kalends of
January will be a warranty that all through the year their feasting
will be in like measure abundant. Now as for them who on those
days observe any heathen customs, it is to be feared that the name
of Christian will avail them nought. And therefore our holy fathers
of old, considering that the majority of men on those days became
slaves to gluttony and riotous living and raved in drunkenness and
impious dancing, determined for the whole world that throughout
the Churches a public fast should be proclaimed ... let us therefore
fast, beloved brethren, on those days ... For he who on the Kalends
shows any civility to foolish men who are wantonly sporting, is
undoubtedly a partaker of their sin.

Many similar Christian denunciations of pagan practice are recorded
from sources ranging from Britain to Africa, and from Spain to Syria,
during the latter half of the first millennium AD. It is notable that they
focus on the Kalends rather than Saturnalia, although the revelry
associated with both festivals seems to have been of equal intensity.
The term 'Saturnalian' would later be used as a general adjective to
describe Roman midwinter excesses, but we may reasonably assume
that Saturnalia itself, as a 'pagan' religious festival, had fallen out of
favour following Theodosius' banning of pagan religions in 391,
with midwinter celebrations focused largely on the Kalends (as an
essentially secular festival) by the early fifth century. Whatever the
explanation, as we will see in subsequent chapters of this book, the
desire for midwinter revelry had no qualms about attaching itself
to the new religion and re-labelling itself the 'Christmas season'
– a season that would extend over 12 days to encompass both the
Nativity and New Year.

Sandwiched between Saturnalia and the Kalends was the actual
day of the winter solstice; 25 December according to the Julian
calendar. Roman religion typically borrowed deities from earlier
traditions throughout the ancient world, several of which were
associated with the winter solstice. Attempts to establish exactly how
these different deities were regarded by the people within ancient
societies is fraught with difficulty, especially as numerous different
myths and legends provide sometimes conflicting accounts. The
myths, which can be fantastically complex, are rarely done justice by
attempts to summarise them; nevertheless we must briefly consider
a few examples which relate to the concept of the winter solstice.

In ancient Egypt, at a time when some of the great Neolithic monuments discussed in Chapter 2 were still in regular use, Osiris was worshipped as one of the chief gods, variously described as the god of life, death and fertility. In one of the greatest of all Egyptian myths, Osiris was killed by his brother, Set, and his remains scattered to all corners of the kingdom. Osiris' wife, Isis, recovered all the parts of his body, reassembling them and bringing him briefly back to life; an event that was traditionally believed to have occurred at the time of the winter solstice. While Osiris was briefly revived, Isis, who according to one version of the story was still a virgin at the time, became pregnant with Horus, who was thought to have been born at the time of the solstice (when considering such accounts we must remember that they took place in 'mythic time' and were not governed by time constraints as experienced by mere mortals). Horus became the god of the sky and patron of the pharaohs; often represented as a falcon, his eyes were said to represent the sun and the moon. The Osiris-Horus combination represents a classic life-death-rebirth legend which was closely associated with the sun at the time of the winter solstice.

Two ancient Greek gods have particular associations with the winter solstice. The first is Apollo, the god of many things including light and the sun, whose cult seems to have been widespread throughout the Greek world by 1000 BC and was adopted in Rome by the fifth century BC. (Although Helios was originally the god of the sun, and Apollo that of light, the two become merged in later mythology.) Apollo was the son of Zeus, king of the Greek gods, and the goddess Leto. Accounts of his birth vary, but according to some he was born on the island of Delos at the time of the winter solstice. Another of the major Greek gods, Dionysus, son of Zeus and Semele (a mortal), was also born at the winter solstice. Dionysus was the god of wine, agriculture and the theatre, and was adopted in Rome as Bacchus. To some extent, Apollo, representing harmony and reason as well as light and the sun, was regarded as complementary to Dionysus, who stood for ecstasy and disorder. It is not difficult to see how both could be of relevance to Roman and later midwinter festivities.

Although the evidence is often ambiguous, several other important gods of the ancient world are also said to have been born at the winter solstice. Examples known to the Romans include Heracles (the greatest of the Greek heroes, later adopted in Rome as Hercules), Attis (an Anatolian life-death-rebirth deity mythically linked with the evergreen pine tree, introduced to Greece and thence to Rome by the time of Christ) and Tammuz (a Babylonian sun god whose origins may stretch back to Osiris, and who seems to have found his way into the Greek pantheon as Adonis in the mid first millennium BC). Another example, over which we must linger a while for reasons that will become apparent, is Mithras.

For three centuries after its introduction in the late first century AD, Mithraism was perhaps the single most popular religion in the entire Roman Empire. This coincided with the time when Christianity was founded and grew from a minor cult into a position from which it would dominate the western world throughout medieval times. Many scholars suggest that had Jesus not appeared on the scene then we would all be living in a 'Mithraic' rather than a 'Christian' society, and Ernest Renan famously observes in *The History of the Origins of Christianity* (1882) that 'if Christianity had been impeded in its growth by some mortal malady, the world would be Mithraic'. There are certainly many uncanny parallels between the two religions, including the special importance attached by both to 25 December, and there is some evidence for direct conflict between them until the Theodosian decree of 391 banned all pagan practices, thus sounding the death knell for Mithras.

Mithraism was a 'mystery religion', its secrets passed from initiate to initiate without the need for a body of scripture such as the Bible. Consequently, its rituals are poorly understood. Our knowledge of Mithraic philosophy and practice is largely speculative, based on the archaeological investigation of temples, known as Mithraea. It is thought that several hundred Mithraea were built in Rome and in Britain good examples can be visited in London and at Brocolitia on Hadrian's Wall. The origins of Mithraism, like its system of worship, are shrouded in mystery. It is usually thought to have been introduced to Rome from the east by soldiers who had served in Persia, but recent studies suggest that it may have been founded within Rome. Either way, it developed in popularity through the second and third centuries, being especially popular within the army and counting several emperors among its devotees.

The central event of Mithraism was the 'tauroctony', the slaying by Mithras of the sacred bull that probably represented all the animal and plant life in the world. Sculptures and wall paintings depicting this were present in all mithraea. As the sacred bull dies, grain and blood emerge from its body; these were represented by bread and wine consumed during ritual re-enactments at Mithraic services.

While the symbolism is complex, the key focus is undoubtedly on death and rebirth; the sacred bull dies and in doing so provides food for mankind. The event must also have had transcendental meaning of relevance to personal salvation; in death, it poured new life into the soul, triggering spiritual rebirth. We don't know exactly when in the year the tauroctony was celebrated, but astrological symbolism and the concern with rebirth combine to suggest that it was during the spring, perhaps at the time of the spring equinox; it is tempting to link its symbolism with that of Easter in the Christian Church. From this point of view, Mithraism might legitimately be regarded as of limited relevance to our discussion of Christmas, but its midwinter festival could not be more relevant.

The birth of Mithras was celebrated at the time of the winter solstice. Details of his birth are uncertain, but he seems to have been born in a cave from which he emerged as a youth, equipped with a torch to provide light and the knife with which he would perform the tauroctony. His emergence from the cave (which we should probably regard as synonymous with his birth) was witnessed by two shepherds who are invariably depicted alongside images of Mithras and must have been of great significance, though sadly this significance is now lost to us. After a fight, the sun is said to have pledged his loyalty to Mithras and the two became close allies. Mithras was never actually regarded as the sun, but was very closely associated with it. Rudyard Kipling's *A Song to Mithras* (from *Puck of Pook's Hill*) reflects the relationship between the two, its third verse being of particular relevance:

> Mithras, God of the Sunset, low on the Western Main,
> Thou descending immortal, immortal to rise again!
> Now when the watch is ended, now when the wine is drawn,
> Mithras, also a soldier, keep us pure till the dawn!

Mithras' close relationship with the sun is reflected in the fact that he was one of the Gods celebrated at the *Dies Natalis Solis Invicti* (the 'Birthday of the Unconquered Sun') which, despite the undoubted importance of the tauroctony, is usually regarded as the most significant event in the Mithraic calendar. *Dies Natalis Solis Invicti* was celebrated on the day of the winter solstice, 25 December. Although it must have had very ancient origins, perhaps dating back to the worship of the sun god, Sol, in pre-Roman times, it became particularly prominent within the cult of *Sol Invictus Elagabal*, introduced from Syria during the first century AD. In 218, a high priest of *Sol Invictus Elagabal* became emperor; known as Elagabalus, he took every opportunity to further promote the cult of *Sol Invictus*. After Elagabalus' assassination in 222 the cult declined somewhat, but was reborn half a century later under Aurelian who, in 274, made *Sol Invictus* the primary god of the Roman Empire and *Dies Natalis Solis Invicti* his chief festival. It is interesting to note that by the year 274 the solstice (for reasons explained in Chapter 1) had receded two and a half days from its traditional date in the Julian calendar; a situation of which Roman astronomers at the time must surely have been aware. Nevertheless, the symbolic importance of 25 December was already so great that the festival of *Dies Natalis Solis Invicti* continued to be celebrated then, rather than at the actual time of the solstice a couple of days earlier.

Emperors up to and including Constantine portrayed *Sol Invictus* on their coinage, thus identifying themselves with the god who many regarded as synonymous with Mithras. Thus, although we have little information as to the nature of festivals held on 25 December during the third and fourth centuries, there can be no doubt that this day was of great religious importance throughout the Roman Empire.

The Birthday of the Unconquered Sun and the Nativity

The early Christian Church wisely adopted a policy of seeking to adapt and tweak pagan festivals rather than suppress them outright. Given the importance of 25 December in pagan Roman religion, it was therefore obvious that something dramatic had to be done about this date, both to encourage people to embrace Christianity and to deter them from following the old long-established pagan customs. The solution could not have been simpler or more dramatic: 25 December became Jesus' birthday!

That said, there is little evidence that the birth of Jesus was celebrated in any way during the first three centuries of the Christian era. Indeed, birthdays seem to have been regarded as pagan and were not apparently celebrated by early Christians. Origen, writing in the third century AD, observed that Pharaoh and Herod (not exactly Christian role models) are the only biblical characters recorded as having commemorated their birthdays. The evidence is obscure to say the least, but it does appear that some elements of the early Christian Church, perhaps as early as the second century, celebrated the birth of Christ on 6 January as part of the feast of the Epiphany. Epiphany thus combined celebration of both Christ's baptism and his birth. It is probable that, in the early Church, Christ's Baptism was regarded as the moment at which he became truly the Son of God, while his actual birthday was considered as relatively insignificant. Given that a passage in Luke's Gospel was once thought to imply that Jesus was baptised on his thirtieth birthday, it was natural to assume that the birth and the Baptism should be celebrated together. Indeed, the Eastern Church continued to celebrate the Nativity on 6 January long after 25 December had become the accepted date in the West.

The earliest recorded evidence for the celebration of the Nativity on 25 December comes from a Roman document known as the Philocalian Calendar. This dates from AD 354 but incorporates an earlier document dating from AD 336; it is not clear to which of these dates the reference to the Nativity originally belonged. Either way, it seems to have been Julius I, Bishop of Rome from AD 337-352, who decreed once and for all that the great event should be celebrated on this date. Despite the shaky evidence for its nature and its date, the birth of Christ was, from the mid-fourth century, accepted by the Roman Church as having taken place on 25 December, where it has remained ever since and presumably will remain forever. As noted by Michael Harrison:

> To select 25 December … as the official date of the Nativity was to adapt, to the service of Christianity, a feast of immemorially ancient origins and world-wide observance … correctly or incorrectly, the date of the Nativity has been fixed for ever. Even if scholars' research should establish, beyond a shadow of doubt, that Christ was born on some other day of the year, it is unthinkable that 25 December – a date so hallowed by centuries of worship – should be abandoned in favour of another date.

This chapter has demonstrated that the Nativity incorporates a large amount of symbolism from earlier sources, and that its celebration was assimilated into an already complex midwinter season within the Roman world. The following chapters will discuss how Christian and pagan practices merged to form the basis of Christmas throughout medieval and post-medieval Britain.

4

Christmas Sacred and Profane.
Aspects of the medieval midwinter

With the date of the Nativity established as 25 December, the Church did all it could to encourage Christian worship over pagan midwinter tradition. In a message that would be echoed countless times over subsequent centuries, Gregory of Nanzianus, the highly influential fourth-century Bishop of Constantinople, warned people against feasting and dancing to excess and urged 'the celebration of the festival after a heavenly and not after an earthly manner'. There was actually much debate in the early Church as to the nature of Jesus (was he 'man' or 'God', or a bit of both?) and whether or not he could ever have been 'born' in a conventional sense. These arguments cannot concern us here, but it is worth at this point stressing the link many early Christian writers made between Christ and the sun, and in particular between his birth and the 'rebirth' of the sun at the winter solstice. Of particular interest to our story is the use of the term 'Sun of Righteousness', the earliest known use of which is by the prophet, Malachi, in the final book of the Old Testament:

> But to you who fear My name
> The Sun of Righteousness shall arise
> With healing in His wings.

Within the New Testament, several passages use solar imagery when describing Jesus, but nowhere within it is he directly associated with the sun. By the third and fourth centuries, however, he is referred to as the 'Sun of Righteousness' by several writers. Joseph Kelly in *The Origins of Christmas* suggests that this term (*Sol Iustitiae* in the original Latin) may have been adopted by early Christians in a third-century propaganda war between them and followers of the pagan 'Unconquered Sun' (*Sol Invictus*) as the two cults fought for supremacy. Whatever the explanation, the worship of Jesus was clearly linked with the sun in the minds of many Christians during the fifth century, as is clear from this statement from a Christmas sermon given by Leo the Great (Pope from 440-461):

> Simple minds are deceived by some who hold the pernicious belief that our celebration today seems to derive its high position, not from the birth of Christ, but from, as they say, the rising of the 'new sun'.

Several Christmas hymns and carols demonstrate this perceived link between Christmas and the winter solstice. For example, the Spanish composer Aurelius Prudentius Clemens (*c.*348-413) includes the following verse within his popular 'Hymn for Christmas Day':

> Now let the sky more brightly shine
> And joyful earth keep holiday!
> The radiant sun mounts high again,
> Rejoicing in his former course.

Today, millions of people each Christmas enjoy 'Hark the Herald Angels Sing', but few give much thought to the ancient symbolism behind the words of its third verse:

> Hail the heaven-born Prince of Peace!
> Hail the Sun of Righteousness!
> Light and life to all He brings
> Risen with healing in His wings.

We will consider further Christmas songs linking Christ with the sun later in this book, but for now must return to ancient Britain. The period covered by this chapter includes more than a thousand Christmases, from the end of the Roman occupation, in the fifth century, through Anglo-Saxon and medieval times to the reign of King Henry VIII in the sixteenth century. While we have very little information relating to midwinter celebration in immediate post-Roman times, by the sixteenth and seventeenth centuries we have so much authentic source material that we run the risk of becoming bogged down in the detail of, for example, the fantastic menus available at royal Christmas feasts.

This chapter, and the one that follows, have been built up from many sources, but their basic framework owes much to two early twentieth-century publications and one of the mid nineteenth that collate a vast amount of material from wide-ranging sources and represent essential reading for anyone wishing to find out more. The earliest of these is William Sandys' *Christmastide – its History, Festivities and Carols*, published in 1852 and much used for source material by later writers. The second is W.F. Dawson's *Christmas: Its Origin and Associations*, published in 1902 and the third, by far the most polished of the three, is Clement Miles' *Christmas Customs and Traditions: Their History and Significance,* originally published in 1912.

Waess haell! Christmas with Anglo-Saxons and Vikings

Although it is unlikely that clear evidence will ever be found, the Nativity must surely have been celebrated in some way by early Christians in Roman Britain. However, the Romans abandoned Britain in the early fifth century, and while Christianity may have survived in some form in some places, Britain descended into the so-called 'Dark Ages' which saw much conflict between native British tribes and pagan Germanic incomers from across the North Sea. This was the time of the legendary King Arthur, about whom we know virtually nothing for certain; the earliest written reference to him dates from some four centuries after his supposed lifetime. Geoffrey of Monmouth, the famous twelfth-century chronicler who was largely responsible for the subsequent popularity of Arthurian legend throughout Europe, tells us that Arthur kept Christmas with the greatest joy and festivity – in one case, following a great military victory over the invading Saxons, hosting a fine Christmas feast in the recaptured 'city' of York. Christmas features strongly in the fabulous, if bizarre, legend of Sir Gawain and the Green Knight, arguably the most fascinating of all Arthurian legends. The legend is known to us through a single late fourteenth-century document, though it may be considerably older, and incorporates much pagan and Christian symbolism. It opens with the arrival of the mysterious Green Knight at a Christmas feast within Arthur's great hall. The Green Knight challenges any of Arthur's assembled knights to a duel, which Gawain accepts. Gawain chops off the Green Knight's head, only for the Green Knight to retrieve and replace it and politely leave, reminding Gawain that the second part of the challenge involves a return meeting the following Christmas at the Green Chapel. To cut a long and fascinating story outrageously short, the Green Knight spares Gawain during the second encounter, informing him that he is a man of honour and inviting him back to his house to celebrate the rest of the festive season. The fact that this fabulous tale begins and ends at Christmas is certainly no coincidence, but sadly speaks more of medieval times, when it was written, than of the time of Sir Gawain and King Arthur.

Sir Thomas Malory reworked a lot of Arthurian legend in the mid fifteenth century, merging material from English and French sources. He records that Arthur's Christmas festivities included a number of special jousting tournaments, with the winner of each receiving a diamond, and that this jousting took place amidst 'all manner of hunting and hawking and jousts and tourneys between many great lords'. Sadly, the authenticity of this account is thrown into some doubt by the fact that diamonds, although recognised as symbols of kingship by the time Malory was writing, were all but unheard of in Arthur's Britain. Similarly, jousting was very popular in Malory's time, but unknown in Britain prior to the Norman Conquest.

In addition to the military and political conflict between native Briton and invading Anglo-Saxon, the early seventh century saw a degree of dispute between the British (Celtic) Church, based on Iona in Scotland, and the Church of Rome, introduced initially to the Kingdom of Kent by Augustine in 597. The two Churches squabbled over the method of calculating the date of Easter; after the Roman Church won the debate in the mid seventh century, influence of the Celtic Church declined. Although there was great debate over the correct date of Easter, no such dispute seems to have existed with regard to the celebration of the Nativity, which from the moment of its introduction to Britain seems always to have been celebrated on 25 December. Indeed, the date had been confirmed as one of the Christian Church's three major annual festivals at the Council of Tours in 567, when it was also decreed that the entire 12 days between the Nativity and the Epiphany should be kept as a sacred season.

The success of Roman Christianity in Britain owes much to the mission begun by Augustine in 597. Four years after arriving in England, Augustine received a letter from Pope Gregory the Great suggesting that rather than seek to destroy pagan religions, he should, wherever possible, attempt to integrate existing pagan beliefs into Christian worship. In Gregory's own words:

> Because they [the pagan Anglo-Saxons] are accustomed to slay many oxen in sacrifices to demons, some solemnity should be put in place of this, so that on the day of the dedication of the churches, or the nativities of the holy martyres whose relics are placed there,

they may make for themselves bowers of branches of trees around those churches which have been changed from heathen temples, and may celebrate the solemnity with religious feasting.

Nor let them now sacrifice animals to the Devil, but to the praise of God kill animals for their own eating, and render thanks to the Giver of all things for their abundance; so that while some outward joys are retained for them, they may the more easily respond to inward joys. For from obdurate minds it is undoubtedly impossible to cut off everything at once, because he who strives to ascend to the highest places rises by degrees or steps and not by leaps.

Gregory further advised Augustine to 'accommodate the ceremonies of the Christian worship as much as possible to those of the heathen, that the people might not be much startled at the change'. Thus, people were encouraged to kill and consume a large number of oxen at the Christmas festival, but to do so to the glory of God rather than in the name of any pagan deities. We know very little of the nature of pagan belief at the time of Augustine's mission, although the Venerable Bede, the 'Father of English History', wrote in the early eighth century that:

The ancient peoples of the Angli began the year on the 25th December when we now celebrate the birthday of the Lord; and the very night which is now so holy to us, they called in their tongue, 'modranecht'. That is, the mother's night, by reason we suspect of the ceremonies which that night-long vigil they performed.

While we do not know how 'modranecht' was celebrated, it would appear that 25 December was of great significance to the pagan Anglo-Saxons.

The earliest recorded event in the story of the English Christmas dates from just one year after the beginning of Augustine's mission. King Aethelbehrt of Kent, having apparently been recently converted himself, arranged a mass baptism on Christmas Day 598, at which some 10,000 of his people were baptised by Augustine into the Roman Church (the numbers in such stories are invariably exaggerated). These people may have accepted the new religion for a variety of reasons; in some cases perhaps out of genuine enthusiasm for the new God, in others primarily out of loyalty to their King, and in some cases simply in the hope of political self-advancement. What cannot be doubted, however, is that the Christian Church was gaining in power, and Christmas was already one of its key annual events.

Whether the common man in early medieval England really understood much about the Christian Christmas must be open to doubt. During the first couple of centuries of early medieval Christianity there were very few priests in England, and most religious activity took place within the confines of monasteries in ceremonies unintelligible to all but the educated elite. It is possible that some in Britain heard renditions of the very earliest Christmas hymns but few would have understood them as they were sung in Latin. The earliest known Christmas hymn, *Veni Redemptor Gentium* ('Redeemer of our Nations, Come') was written by St Ambrose, Bishop of Milan from 374-397, and Aurelius Prudentius Clemens followed this with *Corde Natus Ex Parentis* ('Of the Father's Love Begotten') which was by all accounts rather more popular. These, and other early hymns about the Nativity, are very much of and for the Church; written in Latin by churchmen, they were sung only within churches. They are very much doctrinal in nature and display none of the tenderness of the later medieval carols.

In practice, most people would never have heard or sung these songs, and probably held their own midwinter festivities firmly rooted in ancient tradition, influenced by the Yule celebrations of the incoming Anglo-Saxons. These festivities may have acquired something of a Christian gloss, but must have remained stubbornly pagan, almost certainly including eating and drinking to excess and probably also song, dance and gambling. Theodore of Tarsus, a Greek priest who was Archbishop of Canterbury between 668 and 690, stated that it was not unacceptable for a man to eat too freely at Christmas as long as he did not overstep the limits allowed by the Church – unfortunately we have no record of exactly what these limits were.

Wassailing may have featured at this time. The word 'wassail', seems to derive from the Old English *waess haell!*, meaning 'be healthy!' or 'good health!', but it is not clear when the phrase was first used in England. In later times, two different types of wassailing are recorded. The first involved groups of wassailers visiting houses and offering the owners a drink and a song, in exchange for which a small gift was often expected (in effect, an early form of door-to-door carol singing). The second type of wassailing, popular in rural areas, was the offering of alcoholic drinks to trees in orchards; this 'wassailing of the trees' was intended to ensure a good harvest in the following year.

The Yule log is another custom that almost certainly featured in the Anglo-Saxon Christmas. Today, few of us enjoy open fires in our homes and the term 'Yule log' is more likely to conjure up an image of a log-shaped chocolate cake (such cakes seem initially to have become popular in France in the early nineteenth century) than an actual log to be placed on the fire. However, the real Yule log, the origins of which must lie in Anglo-Saxon or perhaps even earlier times, was a hugely symbolic element of the medieval European midwinter. It was natural for fire to feature prominently during the long, cold, dark nights of midwinter in northern Europe, but the tradition of the Yule log was about much more than the basic provision of warmth and light, incorporating a large degree of symbolism rooted in ancient pagan belief. Ideas that seem to be particularly popular, from many locations around Europe, include the need for each year's log to be kindled using a brand from the previous year's, and the requirement for it to burn from Christmas Eve, throughout Christmas Day and perhaps for several days thereafter. Clement Miles includes a chapter specifically about the Yule log in *Christmas Customs and Traditions,* noting that it is possible 'to see in its burning the solemn annual rekindling of the sacred hearth-fire, the centre of the family life and the dwelling place of the ancestors.' It may also, of course, symbolise the sun and possibly also gods or spirits associated with trees and woodland, or perhaps more general cycles of fertility and the seasons.

We have no references to Yule logs from Anglo-Saxon sources, but it is perhaps worth quoting a few lines penned by Robert Herrick in 1648:

Come, bring, with a noise,	With the last year's Brand
My merry, merry boys,	Light the new Block, and
The Christmas Log to the firing:	For good success in his spending,
While my good Dame she	On your psaltries play,
Bids ye all be free,	That sweet luck may
And drink to your hearts' desiring.	Come while the log is a-tending.

Although Herrick is writing more than half a millennium after the end of Anglo-Saxon England, he is probably writing of a long-established tradition that must surely extend back to Anglo-Saxon times. His words are interesting in that they clearly state the need to 'light the new block' with 'last year's brand', and also link the log with general revelry including the invitation to 'drink to your heart's desiring.' The lack of any reference to the Nativity is also telling; the Yule log is very much a pagan tradition.

Alfred the Great, King of Wessex between 871 and 899 and arguably the first 'King of England', decreed that the 12 days of Christmas-tide should be set aside for celebration, with no work done and all legal proceedings put on hold. There is a legend that Alfred lost the Battle of Chippenham (878) to the Danes because he refused to fight during the Christmas season. This must be doubted, although it is true that the Danes captured Chippenham during the night of 6-7 January and, according to a contemporary source, Alfred was forced to retreat 'with a small force into the wilderness'. A legend that Alfred spied on the Danish army by wandering around its camp disguised as a Christmas minstrel must be taken with a large pinch of salt, but again it is interesting that such a legend should link him with Christmas.

The Vikings seem to have had no great influence on the development of the English Christmas, probably because their midwinter celebrations did not differ greatly from those of the Anglo-Saxons. We know that the Vikings did celebrate a great midwinter festival, known to them as Yule, incorporating traditions from various earlier sources, including the Teutonic 'Feast of the Dead' that coincided with the winter solstice. In the year 960, King Hakon of Norway decreed that 'Jul' was to be celebrated on 25 December to align it with the Christian Feast of the Nativity. We know that some of the Norse Vikings lit Yule logs to honour Thor, their God of Thunder. Once the log was lit, feasting would continue for several days until it burned out.

Odin, the chief Norse god, is associated with midwinter (and as Odin is generally regarded as having evolved from the rather earlier Anglo-Saxon god, Woden, such a link may well have pre-Viking origins). He was god of many things, including wisdom, magic, prophecy, hunting, war and death. He rode a magnificent eight-legged horse named Sleipnir on which he could travel across the sky and move between the worlds of the living and the dead. At the winter solstice, Odin led a great hunting party of gods and slain warriors, and it became the custom for children to stuff their boots with carrots, straw and sugar and leave them out at night as food for Sleipnir. Some scholars believe that this is the ultimate origin of Santa Claus; Odin, always depicted as a bearded old man, would reward the children for their kind actions by replacing Sleipnir's food with gifts. Whether or not there is any truth in such folklore, we can be sure that Odin would have featured in the midwinter celebrations of the Norse Vikings at the time they were invading

England. It is interesting to note the link with the dead at mid-winter, in the form of Odin's great hunting party of slain warriors; in Britain by this time the day of the dead had become Samhain (Hallowe'en), and the links between the ancestors and midwinter, although clearly crucial back in Neolithic times, seems to have faded, never to return.

By 1042, the Crown had reverted from the Vikings back to the English in the person of Edward the Confessor. Edward ruled through challenging times, and despite becoming known as 'the Confessor' and eventually being canonised, his alleged piety seems to owe more to legend than historical fact. Edward desired to build a great new symbol of royal authority, and to this end ordered the construction, just outside London, of the West Minster of St Peter (known today as Westminster Abbey). This was consecrated on Christmas Day, 1065, just in time for him to be buried within it following his death a few days later. It hosted the coronation of Harold II, the last of England's English kings, on 6 January 1066, and that of William the Conqueror on Christmas Day that same, momentous year. Over subsequent centuries, this magnificent building has continued to play a key role in the political and religious life of the nation.

During the Anglo-Saxon centuries, the pagan midwinter traditions of the native British, influenced in turn by those of Rome and of incoming Anglo-Saxons and Vikings, were merged with the Christian Feast of the Nativity. While the Church celebrated the birth of Christ, many of the people must have perpetuated age-old traditions without any specific understanding of, or perhaps even interest in, the new religion. However, the power and influence of Christianity continued to grow, and the ancient midwinter feast gradually became known by a new name; for centuries it had been referred to by the Church as the 'Nativity' or the 'Midwinter-mass', but in 1043 the *Anglo-Saxon Chronicle* records the first historical reference to 'Christmas'. Even those who saw the festival as an opportunity for revelry rather than for worship would, from this time on, refer to the 25 December as 'Christmas Day'.

Unto us a Child is Born. The Nativity and the medieval Church

We will now consider some religious aspects of the medieval Christmas between 1066 and the Reformation of the mid sixteenth century. We will not attempt to trace in detail the development of the Christmas liturgy, as this is a vast and complex subject, but rather to touch on a number of themes relating to the celebration of the Nativity by Church and people.

Advent, covering the four weeks leading up to Christmas, seems to have been kept as a fast by monks in the Roman Church as early as the sixth century. The Advent season within the medieval Church was all about anticipation of Christmas, and services made great play of Old Testament prophesies relating to the birth of Jesus. When the great day eventually arrived, there were three masses on Christmas morning, the first of which was the Midnight Mass, followed by one at dawn and another in full daylight. This tradition seems to have begun in Jerusalem and Bethlehem as early as the fourth century, being adopted within Rome during the fifth century when the three masses were celebrated by the Pope at different churches throughout the city. Various suggestions were offered by medieval writers regarding the symbolism of these three masses. Clement Miles notes that:

> The midnight celebration was supposed to represent mankind's condition before the Law of Moses, when thick darkness covered the earth; the second, at dawn, the time of the Law and the Prophets with its growing light; the third, in full daylight, the Christian era of light and grace. Another interpretation, adopted by St Thomas Aquinas, is more mystical; the three Masses stand for the threefold birth of Christ, the first typifying the dark mystery of the eternal generation of the Son, the second the birth of Christ the morning-star within the hearts of men, the third the bodily birth of the Son of Mary.

Other days in the Christmas season were also of religious significance, either as saint's days (St Stephen on 26 December, St John the Evangelist on 27) or as days on which to commemorate particular elements of the Nativity story (Holy Innocents' Day, 28 December). Specific services were held by the Church to celebrate each day of the Christmas season, and while space precludes any detailed discussion of these we must briefly consider Epiphany. The word 'Epiphany' comes from the Greek for 'revelation' and the Feast of Epiphany is said to commemorate the revelation of God in human form though Jesus Christ. There are several references to the Feast of Epiphany, which seems always to have been celebrated on 6 January, from as early as the fourth century, but there is a degree of confusion as to exactly what is being commemorated. We may summarise the situation by stating that within the Western Church the Feast of Epiphany commemorates the coming of the Magi, while for eastern Christians it commemorates the baptism of Christ in the River Jordan. Either way, its basic purpose is to celebrate the mystery of the incarnation and the manifestation of Christ to the world. Within Britain, Epiphany has also come to represent the close of the Christmas season, marking the end of the Twelve Days of Christmas. (Some readers may have calculated that if 25 December is the first day of Christmas, then 6 January is the thirteenth, rather than the twelfth; the explanation lies in the ancient custom of treating sunset, rather than midnight, as the beginning of the following day. Hence the Twelve Days of Christmas actually run from the evening of Christmas Day through until the day of 6 January, with Twelfth Night being the night of January 5/6.) There was also a wider Christmas season that started as early as Hallowe'en and ran through until Candlemas (2 February), an important feast commemorating the presentation of Jesus in the Temple and the Purification of Mary after the birth of Jesus. Just like Christmas, the date of Candlemas, half-way between the winter solstice and spring equinox, may well have been fixed to equate with a pre-existing pagan festival, but this is not known for certain.

Evidence from fourteenth-century accounts (which must also be relevant to earlier times) provides some background to the symbolism of Christmas services. We have seen that the tradition of the Midnight Mass on Christmas Eve extends back beyond medieval times; this reflected and reinforced a popular belief that Jesus was born at midnight. The Mass was preceded by the tolling of a single bell symbolising the funeral of the Devil, and was followed by a great peal of the bells to celebrate the arrival of Christmas Day. The brightly lit church contrasted vividly with the cold, dark conditions outside, and the candles symbolised the Light of the World, with a single particularly large candle often lit to represent the Star of Bethlehem. Churches were decorated with evergreens, long-established pagan symbols of eternal life, and particular evergreens took on new meanings. The laurel and bay became symbols of triumph, while holly took on several new symbolic associations; its prickly leaves came to represent Christ's crown of thorns and his eternal life, its bright red holly berries the blood of Christ and its white flowers the Virgin's Immaculate Conception and her milk with which she fed Jesus. The Christian significance of ivy is not clear. In pagan tradition it has always been considered as female, and some have suggested that this relates to its 'feebleness' and the fact that it can only grow when supported by others! Perhaps its Christian symbolism developed this idea to represent the feebleness of mankind generally and the idea that the support of God is needed for people to thrive. Ivy also has links with death in pagan tradition, perhaps because it thrives in shade, and this may be why it never gained a specific role in Christian tradition. Mistletoe was always frowned upon by the Church, presumably because its well-established and ancient association with pagan fertility rites rendered the task of ascribing it a new identity all but impossible. There was a medieval legend that the cross on which Christ was crucified was of mistletoe, but that the mistletoe 'tree' was so ashamed of its role that it subsequently shrank to the parasitic plant it is today, forever doomed to have no contact with the ground. This rather dubious tale never really caught on and mistletoe's Christmas associations have remained firmly pagan, though far from unpopular!

The Church encouraged belief in several Christmas legends, such as the belief that cattle fell to their knees at midnight on Christmas Eve to worship the Lord, and that bees awoke from their hibernation to hum their praises. A popular legend tells of Joseph of Arimathea (the owner of Christ's tomb) visiting England bearing a staff grown from a shoot taken from the crown of thorns worn by Christ on the cross. While at Glastonbury on Christmas Day, Joseph placed this staff on the ground, whereupon it miraculously grew into a bush which from that day forth began to blossom on Christmas Day every year. The story of the Glastonbury Thorn blooming out of season represented the power of God, and we should remember with regard to such tales that medieval people lived in a very superstitious world; they did not have the benefits of modern science to explain natural phenomena and the power of God was the only available explanation for a whole variety of things.

Christmas sermons during the thirteenth and fourteenth centuries concentrated on the Nativity, stressing the poverty of Joseph and Mary and (of particular interest to rural congregations) the key role played by the shepherds. The slaughter of the innocents was also a popular theme, bringing a degree of horror to the otherwise joyous celebrations. Nativity plays became popular during medieval times, apparently developing out of the 'tropes' which had been introduced into the liturgy in England by the tenth century. According to Ethelwold, Bishop of Winchester in the tenth century, the tropes were intended to strengthen the faith of the vulgar and the illiterate, although it is difficult to envisage them being of great effect for as long as they were performed in Latin. The tropes generally consisted of questions and answers sung by church choirs. Clement Miles discusses two examples from the Abbey of St Gall, Switzerland, one of the most important Benedictine abbeys in medieval Europe. The first example dates from the ninth century and was sung immediately preceding the third Mass of Christmas Day. The original Latin can be translated as:

Today we sing of a Child, whom in unspeakable wise His Father begat before all times, and whom, within time, a glorious mother brought forth.

Question: *Who is this Child whom ye proclaim worthy of so great laudations? Tell us that we also may praise Him.*

Reply: *This is He whose coming to earth the prophetic and chosen initiate into the mysteries of God foresaw and pointed out long before, and thus foretold.*

A second example, slightly later in date, uses the shepherds as its theme:

On the Nativity of the Lord at Mass let there be ready two deacons having on dalmatics, behind the altar, saying:

Whom seek ye in the manger, say, ye shepherds?

Let two cantors in the choir answer:

The Saviour, Christ the Lord, a child wrapped in swaddling clothes, according to the angelic word.

And the deacons:

Present here is the little one with Mary, His Mother, of whom Isaiah the prophet foretold: Behold, a virgin shall conceive, and shall bring forth a son; and do ye say and announce that He is born.

Then shall the cantor lift up his voice and say:

Alleluia, alleluia. Now we know indeed that Christ is born on earth, of whom sing ye all, saying with the Prophet: Unto us a child is born.

It is easy to see how these tropes could develop into more dramatic presentations, which could be effectively and powerfully enacted within church services.

The earliest known record of what might reasonably be termed a 'Nativity play' comes from the famous Abbey of St Martial at Limoges, a very important centre for medieval church music and a great pilgrimage centre during medieval times. Here, a trope about the shepherds, referred to as the 'Officium Pastorum' was traditionally performed at High Mass on Christmas Day; by the eleventh century this had evolved into a dramatic production. A little later, it was merged with an Epiphany play involving the Wise Men, Herod, the slaughter of the innocents, and the flight into Egypt – the ingredients of all those school Nativity plays were clearly now in place. It is unclear when such performances were first enacted within churches in Britain, but documentary sources demonstrate that they had become part of Christmas services by the late twelfth century.

Several Christmas hymns were available for church services by the late twelfth century, some of which were sung all over Europe. The best known of these is attributed to St Bernard (1090-1153), founder and abbot of Clairvaux Abbey in north-east France and a key figure in the development of the cult of the Virgin Mary during the twelfth century. The original Latin of its opening verses can be translated as:

Come rejoicing,	Angel of the Counsel here,
Faithful men, with rapture singing	Sun from star, he doth appear,
Alleluya!	Born of maiden:
Monarch's monarch,	He a sun who knows no night,
From a holy maiden springing,	She a star whose paler light
Mighty wonder!	Fadeth never.

Note in particular the reference to 'a sun who knows no night' – another solar reference to Jesus to add to those mentioned earlier.

All the known early Nativity hymns, from the fourth to the thirteenth century, are essentially theological in nature. In the words of Clement Miles, they dwell 'on the Incarnation and the Nativity as part of the process of man's redemption … There is little attempt to imagine the scene in the stable at Bethlehem, little interest in the Child as a child, little sense of the human pathos of the Nativity.' In contrast to the monks who wrote and performed such works, the vast majority of people in medieval Europe were illiterate peasants, living subsistence lives in little villages spread throughout the countryside. When these people went to church, they could not understand the services which, through until the thirteenth century, were held in Latin regardless of the local language. People attending

Latin Christmas services may have had a general understanding of what was going on, but they would not have been able to follow the details of a sermon or understand the words of hymns. This would change with the intervention of St Francis of Assisi.

St Francis (1181-1226) was born into a wealthy family, but became disillusioned with material wealth, living as a beggar for a while before becoming a friar. He founded the Order of Friars Minor, commonly known as the Franciscans, and is renowned today as the Patron Saint of animals, birds, the environment and Italy. If there was ever to be a 'patron saint of Christmas' then this would have to be St Nicholas; Francis, however, would make an appropriate deputy. St Francis and the Franciscan missionaries who spread his word throughout thirteenth-century Europe brought about fundamental changes in the way that Christmas was celebrated by the Church. Clement Miles observes that these changes were not solely down to Francis, who was:

> rather the supreme embodiment of the ideals and tendencies of his day than their actual creator; but he was the spark that kindled a mighty flame. In him we reach so important a turning-point in the history of Christmas that we must linger a while at his side.

So why exactly was St Francis' role so crucial to the history of Christmas? The neatest way of describing the importance of St Francis to our story is to borrow a further passage from Clement Miles:

> Early Franciscanism meant above all the democratising, the humanizing of Christianity; with it begins that 'carol spirit' which is the most winning part of the Christian Christmas, the spirit which, while not forgetting the divine side of the Nativity, yet delights in its simple humanity, the spirit that links the Incarnation to the common life of the people, that brings human tenderness into religion. The faithful no longer contemplate merely a theological mystery, they are moved by affectionate devotion to the Babe of Bethlehem, realized as an actual living child, God indeed, yet feeling the cold of winter, the roughness of the manger bed.

The Franciscan message stressed the humanity of Christ and his accessibility to the common man, expressed graphically in the form of the baby in the manger. In December 1223, in a cave near the monastery at Greccio, near Assisi, and with the blessing of the Pope, Francis famously set up his Christmas crib: a model of the Nativity complete with straw-filled manger and real live ox and ass. According to his contemporary biographer, Thomas of Celano, the crib was beautiful in appearance, and the manger served as the altar for the Christmas Mass during which Francis sang with such inspiration that many who heard him were moved to tears. While Francis was by no means solely responsible for the cult of the crib (legend has it that Pope Theodore had relics from the original crib transported to Rome and set up in the Church of Sancta Maria and Praesepe in the seventh century) it is to him that the widespread medieval interest in it can be traced.

By the fifteenth century, the setting up of a crib was a major element of Christmas celebrations throughout much of Western Europe. Peasants would have readily associated with the very human image, and indeed the poverty, of the babe in the manger within the agricultural setting of the stable. Epiphany services incorporating a degree of re-enactment were also popular in the fifteenth century. In a play known as the Feast of the Star, three priests played the roles of the Magi (or Three Kings as they increasingly became known), entering the church and pointing at a star which, thanks to an elaborate system of ropes and pulleys, actually moved along the church to the altar, where a curtain was drawn back revealing a child in a crib. The Magi worshipped the child and left their gifts, after which prayers were said. Such performances must have been enacted at many churches, with the star propelled by devices of varying degrees of sophistication; the accounts of St Mary's, Cambridge for 1557-58 include the spending of 40*d* for the manufacture, painting and gilding of a star which was presumably used in slightly later versions of the same play. Although we can never be sure how much the Christmas story meant to people throughout medieval times, the introduction of the crib and the Feast of the Star must have had a profound effect on rural congregations, contrasting the power and the glory of the infant Jesus with the poverty of an everyday stable, and the simple lives of the shepherds with the grandeur of the Three Kings.

Following the intervention of the Franciscans, Nativity plays were increasingly performed in local languages rather than Latin, and, rather than being exclusively controlled by the clergy within the church, were performed by ordinary people in the streets and at various public venues. Exactly why this occurred is not clear, but J.A.R. Pimlott suggests that it might be because 'as they became more popular they acquired comic and other material from folklore and everyday life which would not have been suitable for use in church.' Regardless of the explanation, it seems that Nativity plays were widely performed in cities, towns and villages throughout much of Europe from the thirteenth century onwards.

In England, Christmas did not provide ideal conditions for open-air plays and the Nativity found itself subsumed within vast outdoor productions known to us as miracle or mystery plays. Well-known examples include the York, Chester, Townley and Coventry plays, which told of everything from the Creation through to the Last Judgement and were generally performed in the warmer months. These performances merged biblical themes with aspects of contemporary life, often containing a degree of humour that a modern audience might consider irreverent, though it was certainly not considered so at the time. In the York and Chester scripts, aspects of the shepherds' scene appear hilarious and must have generated considerable mirth within what were essentially rather serious productions. Sadly, these great plays did not thrive under Protestantism and were performed less and less frequently after the Reformation, dying out by the end of the sixteenth century.

Having considered the early history of the Nativity play, we must now examine another great tradition of the medieval Christmas – the carol. Whereas the Nativity play developed within the Church and moved out into the streets, the reverse is true of the carol. It seems that the origin of the Christmas carol is to be sought in popular French dance songs which owe their origin in turn to ancient pagan rites, hence the Church's condemnation of them as obscene and lustful and its encouragement of more appropriate alternatives.

St Francis, a keen musician and composer, wrote what were effectively devotional poems set to popular folk tunes. Crucially, he wrote in the vernacular rather than in Latin so that anyone could understand and sing his songs. We don't know how many songs he wrote himself, though he is traditionally credited with 'The Canticle of Brother Sun'. This beautiful work (which loses something in translation) is not about Christmas but does include the following verse which intriguingly mirrors the words by St Bernard of Clairvaux in suggesting a link between the Lord and the sun:

> All praise be yours, my Lord, through all that you have made,
> And first my lord Brother Sun,
> Who brings the day; and light you give to us through him.
> How beautiful is he, how radiant in all his splendour!

Francis presumably wrote many verses in similar vein, including some about the Nativity. Sadly, no such works survive, although we do have a 'psalm' for Christmas Day vespers, which is attributed to him:

> … For the most holy Father of heaven,
> Our King, before ages sent His Beloved Son from on high,
> and He was born of the Blessed Virgin, holy Mary.
>
> This is the day which the Lord hath made: let us rejoice and be glad
>   in it.
> For the beloved and most holy Child has been given to us and born
>   for us by the wayside.
> And laid in a manger because He had no room in the inn.
> Glory to God in the highest: and on earth peace to men of good will.

Although little of his own work survives, many Franciscans followed Francis' example and composed popular songs about the Nativity that we may reasonably regard as amongst the earliest Christmas carols. The best known of these composers is Jacoponi da Todi, a fascinating character who turned his back on his noble background to become a wandering ascetic. He is credited with having written more than a hundred songs, both in Italian and in Latin, towards the end of the thirteenth century. A flavour of his work is provided by the following example:

> Come and look upon her child
> Nestling in the hay!
> See his fair arms opened wide,
> On her lap to play!
> And she tucks him by her side,
> Cloaks him as she may!
> Gives her paps unto his mouth,
> Where his lips are laid.

Hundreds of Christmas verses, that we may reasonably refer to as 'carols', were written in all the major western European languages in the centuries between 1300 and 1800; here we must restrict ourselves to a brief consideration of early carols written in English. The Franciscans arrived in Britain in 1224 and began composing religious songs in English for the benefit of the population at large. The term 'carol' first appears in England in about 1300, and seems gradually to have become associated specifically with religious songs. The earliest known English 'Christmas carol', recorded in the mid fourteenth century but conceivably written several decades earlier, contains the following verse:

> A child is boren amonges man,
> And in that child was no wam:
> That child is God, that child is man,
> And in that child, our lif bygan.

Several early carols are included in a book written in the 1420s by John Awdley, a Shropshire chaplain, who introduces them with the words:

> I pray, sirus, boothe moore and lase,
> Sing these caroles in Cristemas.

The songs he provides are intended for use by wassailers, and possibly also by professional musicians who toured the towns and cities at Christmas. Clement Miles makes the observation that many such carols tend to be 'somewhat external in [their] religion ... there is little deep inner feeling ... salvation is rather an objective external thing than an inward and spiritual process'. Some examples present Christmas as a kind of cure for evil influences within humanity:

> It was dark, it was dim
> For men that leved in great sin;
> Lucifer was all within,
> Till on the Cristmes day.
> There was weeping, there was wo,
> For every man to hell can go.
> It was litel mery tho,
> Till on the Cristmes day.

Other examples owe little to the conventions of religious devotion, being more like folk-songs that we can imagine being sung with great gusto in taverns and at other non-religious gatherings:

> The shepherd upon a hill he sat;
> He had on him his tabard and his hat,
> His tarbox, his pipe, and his flagat;

His name was called Joly Joly Wat,
For he was a gud herdes boy.
Ut hoy!
For in his pipe he made such joy.

Whan Wat to Bedlem cum was,
He swet, he had faster than a pace;
He found Jesu in a simpell place,
Between an ox and an asse.
Ut hoy!
For in his pipe he made such joy.

'Jesu, I offer to thee here my pipe,
My skirt, my tar-box, and my scripe;
Home to my felowes now I will skipe,
And also look unto my shepe.'
Ut hoy!
For in his pipe he made so much joy.

In contrast, some early English carols are very gentle songs, almost lullabies, portraying Mary as an ordinary mother and Jesus as a feeble baby in many ways just like any other. This example is of early fifteenth-century date:

I saw a sweet and seemly sight,
A blissful bird, a blossom bright,
That morning made and mirth among,
A maiden mother meek and mild,
In cradle kept a knave child,
That softly slept; she sat and sung.

Some fifteenth-century carols concentrate on the Annunciation and stress the humanity of Mary, while others focus on the Wise Men or Magi, or on tales about the later life of Jesus rather than just his birth. In addition to all these works dealing with biblical themes, many medieval carols concentrate more generally on the nature of the world and of our place within it, sometimes incorporating references to the Nativity and sometimes not. These are often clearly rooted in pagan tradition. The holly and the ivy represented a particularly popular theme and seem to have accompanied dances in which men were associated with holly and women with ivy. These songs may have had a religious theme but were certainly not restricted to church, being more commonly sung for fun by people at home and in the street. The ancient symbolism within them is sometimes very hard to comprehend, but clearly must relate back to ancient pagan tradition.

Nearly a hundred carols specifically associated with the Nativity are known to have been in existence in England by the mid sixteenth century, and there must have been many more of which no record survives. Those that do survive present us with a fascinating insight into contemporary attitudes to the religious aspects of Christmas. They tend to dwell on the relationship between Mary and the baby Jesus, and to stress the sheer joy of the occasion. In many ways it is this emphasis on joy and merriment that provides the link between the religious and secular aspects of Christmas celebrations even though, as we will see in the following section, the latter can appear wholly incompatible with the serenity, and indeed the poverty, of the Nativity scene.

We must now consider the curious phenomenon of the 'boy bishop'. Boy bishops are first recorded in the thirteenth century when, for example, St Paul's Cathedral appointed one to fulfil various duties including the preaching of a Christmas sermon. There was considerable variation in boy bishop traditions from place to place, but the basic idea was that a young and relatively insignificant individual, such as a choirboy, was temporarily appointed as a bishop and empowered to preach sermons and undertake other duties in full bishop's regalia, after which he might lead a procession with a 'mock' retinue and receive gifts from the public. The election of the boy bishop often occurred on St Nicholas' Day (6 December) and he remained in post through until Holy Innocents' Day (28 December). The tradition had many opponents within the Church, but remained stubbornly in place throughout most of the medieval period and was regarded as important by many senior figures and important institutions. In 1299, while on campaign near Newcastle upon Tyne, Edward I allowed a boy bishop to sing vespers (evening prayers) in his presence, and a few years later in 1316, it is recorded that Edward II rewarded a boy bishop in Nottingham for his services with a handsome payment of 10 shillings. In the mid fifteenth century, the statutes of several prestigious institutions, including Eton and King's College, Cambridge, made specific provision for the election of a boy bishop to preside over the Christmas season. Boy bishops were also appointed at many parish churches throughout the land.

In France and some other areas of Europe the concept of the boy bishop was taken to bizarre extremes within the so-called 'Feast of Fools', for which a 'Lord' (sometimes referred to as 'Bishop', 'Archbishop', or even 'Pope') was appointed to oversee seasonal festivities within a church, a custom that can appear outrageous and even in some respects blasphemous. A letter, dated 1445, from the Paris Faculty of Theology to the bishops and chapters of France includes this astonishing passage:

> Priests and clerks may be seen wearing masks and monstrous visages at the hours of office. They dance in the choir dressed as women, panders or minstrels. They sing wanton songs. They eat black puddings at the horn of the altar while the celebrant is saying Mass. They play at dice there. They cense with stinking smoke from the soles of old shoes. They run and leap through the church, without a blush at their own shame. Finally they drive about the town and its theatres in shabby traps and carts, and rouse the laughter of their fellows and the bystanders in infamous performances, with indecent gesture and verses scurrilous and unchaste.

The Feast of Fools was forbidden by the Council of Basel (1431–1445), but took quite some time to die out. In England it was finally suppressed by the Catholic Queen Mary in 1555 and elsewhere it was seen off by early Protestants; in France, however, it lingered into the seventeenth century. While there are some references to the 'Feast of Fools' within British churches (in Scotland the presiding 'official' was known as the 'Abbot of Unreason'), it does not seem ever to have been as wildly celebrated as in France. In comparison, the English 'boy bishop' appears rather quaint and altogether less threatening. The boy bishop clearly recalls elements of Roman Saturnalia, when people temporarily took on false identities, mock kings were temporarily installed to oversee festivities, and masters waited on their slaves. Exactly why the tradition should have become so popular at this time within the conservative institution of the Church, opposed at it was to 'pagan customs', remains something of a mystery, although it seems to have been justified by some on the grounds that it demonstrated how the lowly and the meek could legitimately gain power and respect, as Jesus had done. J.A.R Pimlott makes the interesting observation that however the boy bishops may have originated,

> … it is evident that they filled a psychological need, whether it was as an outlet for youthful high spirits constrained by the normally

severe discipline of medieval religious and educational institutions, or as an assertion of human equality at the season when universal goodwill was supposed to prevail.

There are other aspects of the medieval celebration of the Nativity that lack of space precludes detailed discussion of here, perhaps most notably the extent to which it provided inspiration for artists. In medieval times vast numbers of murals, panel paintings, stained glass windows, sculptures, oil paintings and manuscript illustrations were produced featuring the Nativity. Popular themes included the Nativity itself, featuring the newborn Jesus along with Mary and sometimes assorted other characters, the annunciation to the shepherds, the adoration of the Magi, the flight into Egypt and the slaughter of the innocents. Such works were produced by many of the great masters, alongside countless others by lesser, often anonymous, artists and craftsmen such as those who designed stained glass windows in churches throughout Europe.

The influence of the Nativity on life in medieval England was without doubt profound, especially once church services were held in English rather than Latin and theatrical performances moved out from the church into the wider community. Whereas the subject matter of most medieval church feasts was to a large extent intangible, relying largely on fear of the unknown amongst the people for support, the appeal of Christmas is first and foremost about celebrating the birth of a human child, something accessible to most people and recognisable to all as a time of great joy. It is also the supreme example of the appropriation of existing pagan tradition by the Church; the people welcomed Christianity, but never completely gave up their ancient, pagan midwinter practices. Key elements of the medieval Nativity reflect such ancient tradition; for example the boy bishops and the worshipping of the humble baby in the manger by the Three Kings call to mind the role reversal characteristic of Roman Saturnalia. Nevertheless, the Nativity does have a power all of its own, and that power must have been even more apparent to people in the superstitious and illiterate medieval world than it is to most of us today.

Although the Church embraced much of pagan practice, there must have been many occasions when aspects of pagan and Christian belief came into conflict. For example, the following strange story, recorded by the famous twelfth-century chronicler William of Malmesbury, describes the rather severe punishment of some youths who, while engaged in presumably unchristian dancing, disturbed a priest who was performing mass on Christmas Eve. The story is powerfully reflective of the medieval mind games that must have been constantly played between pagan and Christian:

> I, Othbert, a sinner, have lived to tell the tale. It was the vigil of the Blessed Virgin, in a town where there was a church of St. Magnus. The priest, Rathbertus, had just begun the mass, and I, with my comrades, fifteen young women and seventeen young men, were dancing outside the church. We were singing so loud that our songs were distinctly heard inside the building, and interrupted the service of the mass. The priest came out and told us to desist; and when we did not, he prayed to God and St. Magnus that we might dance as our punishment for a year to come. A youth, whose sister was dancing with us, seized her by the arm to drag her away, but it came off in his hand, and she danced on. For a whole year we continued. No rain fell on us; cold, nor heat, nor hunger, nor thirst, nor fatigue affected us; neither our shoes nor our clothes wore out; but still we went on dancing. We trod the earth down to our knees, next to our middles, and at last were dancing in a pit. At the end of the year release came.

Despite such horror stories, there is one very noticeable and altogether more positive trend that seems to apply equally to both the sacred and profane aspects of the festive season: the desire to celebrate and be happy during the shortest days of the year. The Church stressed the joy that all should feel at the birth of Jesus, while kings and peasants did their utmost to enjoy the season through the most extravagant feasting and entertainment that their means would allow. For several centuries, despite concern on the part of the Church over certain excesses, this was the story of the medieval Christmas, the great annual holiday season for everyone in Europe from pontiff to peasant.

Grete plente of mete and drink! Secular aspects of the medieval Christmas

The story of the Nativity as told by the medieval Church represents an important episode in our history of Christmas, but there were also many other festive traditions that had precious little to do with the birth of Jesus. William Sandys, writing in 1852, notes that 'It would be easy to give a list of the different places where our monarchs kept their Christmases, from the time of the Conquest, in nearly, if not quite, an unbroken series; but as this would be scarcely as amusing as a few pages in a well conducted dictionary, it will no doubt be considered to have been wisely omitted.' This account follows Sandys in omitting any such detailed chronology of the royal Christmas, concentrating instead on a few examples of relevance to our story.

The medieval history of England effectively began on Christmas Day 1066, with the coronation in Westminster Abbey of King William I, destined forever to be known as William the Conqueror. Whilst a time of great triumph for William and his loyal Norman barons, who would benefit hugely as the new king allocated the lands of his new kingdom among them, the coronation was a time of great sadness and humiliation for the English. For centuries, the tradition had been that the crown should placed upon a new king's head by the Archbishop of Canterbury, but Stigand, Archbishop in 1066, refused to crown William, apparently stating that he refused 'to crown one who was covered with the blood of men and the invader of others' rights.' The coronation was instead overseen by Ealdred, Archbishop of York – it did not exactly go smoothly. A contemporary account is provided by the Anglo-French chronicler Orderic Vitalis:

> But at the prompting of the devil, who hates everything good, a sudden disaster and portent of future catastrophes occurred. For when Archbishop Ealdred asked the English, and Geoffrey bishop of Coutances asked the Normans, if they would accept William as their king, all of them gladly shouted out with one voice if not in one language that they would. The armed guard outside, hearing the tumult of the joyful crowd in the church and the harsh accents of a foreign tongue, imagined that some treachery was afoot, and rashly set fire to some of the buildings. The fire spread rapidly from house to house; the crowd who had been rejoicing in the church took fright and throngs of men and women of every rank and condition rushed out of the church in frantic haste. Only the bishops and a few clergy and monks remained, terrified, in the sanctuary, and with difficulty completed the consecration of the king who was trembling from head to foot. Almost all the rest made for the scene of conflagration, some to fight the flames and many others hoping to find loot for themselves in the general confusion.

Not exactly a good start for medieval England, and hardly the kind of 'goodwill to all men' expected on Christmas Day!

At Christmas 1067, William sent a Christmas present to the Pope. This consisted of a large proportion of the booty captured during the conquering and plundering of England – a generous Christmas present indeed, although William's real motive behind it must surely have been more to do with the salvation of his own soul than a desire to present the Pope with seasonal gift out of the goodness of his heart. He was apparently not in such a generous frame of mind at Christmas 1069, spending it in royal splendour at York while his army was engaged in the 'harrying of the north', brutally laying waste towns and villages where any hint of threat was perceived, and many others besides.

Although Henry II will be forever tainted by having, perhaps inadvertently, ordered the murder of Thomas à Becket, Archbishop of Canterbury, he is generally regarded as having been a good king, and certainly upheld the tradition of celebrating Christmas to excess. It is recorded that Irish kings and princes were astonished and overawed by the scale of the celebrations at his Christmas feast of 1171, when guests had to be persuaded to eat the flesh of cranes which none had apparently tasted before. The range of alcoholic drinks available at such Christmas feasts was impressive. In addition to various kinds of wine there was morat (mead made from honey and mulberries), hypocras (wine mixed with honey), claret (wine mixed with various spices), cider, perry and ale. Overindulgence was clearly a problem, even amongst monks; there is a record of monks at Canterbury complaining to the king that their abbot was reducing their options at Christmas Day from the standard 17 dishes (plus dessert) which were generally 'dressed with spices and sauces which excited the appetite as well as pleased the taste'.

Richard I, known to history as 'the Lionheart', spoke little English and during his decade on the throne spent only six months (and not one Christmas) in the country. His main interest in England was as a source of funds for his Crusade; on one occasion he is said to have remarked that he would have sold London if only he could have found a buyer! He was, though, a big fan of Christmas, holding great feasts each year at which it is recorded that 'all his clerkes and barouns were ... served with grete plente of mete and drink'. At Christmas 1190, spent with the French King Philippe II in Messina, Sicily, en route to the Third Crusade in the Holy Land, Richard was so generous in bestowing gifts upon his men that 'it was thought he spent more in a moneth than anie of his predecessors ever spent in a whole yeare'.

Henry III was a devout man and ploughed vast sums into church-building, including the extravagant rebuilding of Westminster Abbey. He also kept outrageously extravagant Christmases. At Christmas 1252, his daughter, Margaret, was married to Alexander, King of Scots, at York. The accompanying celebrations, attended by a thousand English knights and a further 60 from north of the border, necessitated the slaughter of 600 fat oxen, all apparently paid for by the Archbishop of York who further provided the then astronomical sum of 4000 marks (about £2700) towards the feast. It is not clear who paid for the alcohol consumed at this gargantuan feast, but it is known that Henry ordered at least 'two tuns of white wine' (a 'tun' is roughly equivalent to 950 litres) for the manufacture of garhiofilac (wine flavoured with cloves), along with an unspecified quantity of claret. It was not only the wealthy that benefited from Henry's festive goodwill – at Christmas 1248 he commanded that Westminster Hall be filled with poor people for a week, all of whom were to be exceptionally well fed. A couple of decades later he ordered all shops to remain closed in London throughout his 15-day Christmas festival.

Edward I was the first genuinely English King since the Conquest. Although his military ambitions ensured that he was thoroughly hated by the Welsh and the Scots, he was much loved within England and, according to William Dawson, 'joined freely in the national sports and pastimes and kept the Christmas festival with great splendour'. He sought to emphasise his 'Englishness' through the creation of links with the legendary King Arthur; for example, he held a great Christmas feast with a 'round table' at Kenilworth at which 'a hundred lords and ladies all clad in silk renewed the faded glories of Arthur's court, and kept Christmas with great magnificence'.

Records of Edward III's Christmas celebrations in 1348, held at Guildford, are fascinating in that they suggest the reintroduction, if indeed it had ever fallen out of favour, of the Saturnalian custom of dressing up in fancy costumes. According to Louise Creighton in her *Life of Edward the Black Prince* (the Black Prince was Edward III's son), published in 1870:

> Orders were given to manufacture for the Christmas sports eighty tunics of buckram of different colours, and a large number of mask – some with faces of women, some with beards, some like angel heads of silver. There were to be mantles embroidered with heads of dragons, tunics wrought with heads and wings of peacocks,

and embroidered in many other fantastic ways. The celebration of
Christmas lasted from All Hallow's Eve, the 31st of October, till the
day after the Purification, the 3rd of February … during the period
… there was nothing but a succession of masques, disguisings, and
dances of all kinds.

Amidst all this talk of extravagant royal Christmases, we must not lose
sight of the fact that the vast majority of citizens never experienced
such grandeur, and that their seasonal celebrations were on an
altogether different scale. Dawson provides a description of what
he terms 'cottage Christmas-keeping' in the form of a quotation
from the Revd W.A.C. Chevalier's *Story of the Boyhood of William
of Wykeham*. William of Wykeham, born to a humble family in
Wickham (Hampshire) in 1320, rose to a position of great power,
becoming both Bishop of Winchester and Chancellor of England.
When he died he was one of the wealthiest men in England, but his
humble childhood is reflected in the Revd Chevalier's account of his
childhood family Christmas:

> There were great preparations in the cottage for spending Christmas
> worthily, for if there was one thing more than another that John
> Longe [William's father] believed in, it was the proper keeping of
> Christmas. It was a part of the worthy yeoman's faith. He was a
> humble and thorough believer in all the tenets of Christianity, he
> worshipped the Saviour and adored His Nativity, but his faith was
> a cheerful one, and he thought he best honoured his Master by
> enjoying the good gifts which He sent. Hence it was a part of his
> creed to be jovial at Christmas-tide. And so Dame Alice had been
> busy all that day, and a part of the day before, making Christmas
> pies, dressing Christmas meats, and otherwise making ready for
> the great festival. John Longe, too, had not been idle. He and his
> men had been working hard all day getting in huge Yule-logs for
> the great kitchen fire, whilst William and little Agnes had been
> employed in decorating the kitchen with evergreens and mistletoe,
> displaying in great profusion the red berries of the holly bushes.
> Everything was decked with evergreens, from the cups and platters
> on the shelves to the hams and bacon hanging from the ceiling …
> Christmas Day passed at the little homestead with all the social and
> religious honours that the honest yeoman could think of. The little
> household attended the service of Mass in the morning, and then,
> with clear consciences and simple hearts, spent the rest of the day
> in domestic and convivial enjoyment.

There are no authentic historical records dealing with the Longe family's Christmas, but the above account may not be a wildly inaccurate estimate of the manner in which millions of ordinary families celebrated Christmas in medieval times.

The life of the medieval peasant was not, however, all sweetness and light, especially when the 'Black Death' struck in the mid fourteenth century. Richard II was confronted with an angry mob some 10,000-strong during the so-called Peasants' Revolt of 1381, but courageously diffused the situation in person, interpreting his success as evidence of his sanction to rule as God's chosen representative on earth. His belief in his own divine right to rule is said to have been fuelled by the presence at his birth, on the Feast of Epiphany (6 January) 1367, of three kings! Richard continued the tradition of extravagant royal Christmases, spending a fortune every year on seasonal entertainment and festive fare. At Christmas 1386, he entertained the King of Armenia at Eltham, and a few years later celebrated the completion of his magnificent new roof over Westminster Hall by hosting a splendid Christmas feast there during which 'twenty-eight oxen and three hundred sheep and game and fowls without number' were consumed by thousands of guests. Richard also hosted prestigious Christmas tournaments, attracting the best jousters from all over Europe. The week-long London tournament of Christmas 1389, which saw a golden crown awarded to the best foreigner and a girdle adorned with gold and precious stones to the best Englishman, is particularly celebrated. This was followed by several further days of feasting at Windsor during which the king showered gifts upon his guests.

At Christmas 1418, during the siege of Rouen, Henry V is alleged to have called a day-long ceasefire and allowed food into the city so that the starving inhabitants might keep the feast of Christmas. The royal festive season under the troubled reign of Henry VI (who bizarrely became king at the age of eight months in 1422 and reigned until 1461, and then again, briefly, from 1470-71) does not seem to have been quite so grand as under some of the earlier kings. The reasons for this may lie partly in the Henry's pious nature, but must also reflect the perilous financial state of the royal coffers throughout much of his reign; things were so bad in 1451 that Henry apparently had to borrow his Christmas expenses! The Christmas of 1428 is worthy of particular note; during the siege of Orleans, a hugely significant event in the Hundred Years' War between England and France, hostilities are said to have been temporarily halted and Christmas celebrated with music and jousting between men of both sides, some of whom even exchanged festive gifts.

We should note at this point that our earliest known reference to a personification of Christmas dates from the mid fifteenth century. 'Sir Christmas' features within a Carol attributed to Richard Smart, rector of Plymtree, Devon, from 1435-77:

Nowell, nowell, nowell, nowell,
Who ys ther that syngith so nowell, nowell, nowell?

I am here, syre Crystesmass
Wellcome, my lord syre Christemasse
Wellcome to us all both more and lasse...

Once established, this character, also known as Captain Christmas and good old Father Christmas, would play a major role in the development of seasonal celebrations; we will meet him again in the next chapter. Similar characters evolved in other European countries and (as we will see in Chapter 6) these eventually merged with St Nicholas to produce our modern Santa Claus.

Edward IV, who became king in 1461, apparently had an inclination towards splendid and costly things and, according to an entry in the *Croyland Chronicles* (an important and generally reliable source for fifteenth-century English history, compiled at Croyland Abbey, Lincolnshire) 'at the Christmas festivities he appeared in a variety of most costly dresses, or a form never seen before, which he thought displayed his person to considerable advantage.' There are many accounts detailing the grandeur of Edward's court and the splendid hospitality offered to a range of foreign dignitaries and other visitors, and his Christmases must have been amongst the grandest of all the medieval kings.

As part of his desire for more effective law and order, Edward's first parliament, at Westminster in 1461, passed a statute prohibiting all nobles from receiving or maintaining plunderers, robbers, malefactors, or unlawful hunters, and from allowing dice and cards in their houses beyond the twelve days of Christmas. Gambling with dice and cards was extremely popular in fifteenth-century England and clearly in Edward's view had to be controlled. Any such ban must, however, have been all but impossible to enforce, and the fact that no attempt was made to ban dice and cards during the

Christmas period probably reflects Edward's acceptance that to try and do so would have been futile, rather than any desire on his part to promote their use as festive entertainment. The ineffectiveness of Edward's attempt to ban cards is reflected in the fact that Henry VIII found it necessary to pass a similar law, again restricting their use to Christmas, half a century or so later.

The marriage of Henry VII and Margaret of York took place at Westminster on 18 January 1486 and was apparently regarded as an extension of the Christmas season; the people are said to have celebrated the occasion with great joy. Subsequent Christmases were also celebrated with great extravagance by Henry and Margaret; the 'Kyng's boke of peymentis' contains many entries relating to the payment of Lords of Misrule and a variety of entertainers over several Christmases. John Leland, the famous sixteenth-century antiquary, records that at Christmas 1489 'there was an Abbot of Misrule, that made much sport and did right well in his office.' This character was paid 10 marks by the king for his services over the Christmas holidays. The duty of the Lord of Misrule, whose origin may lie in the Feast of Fools discussed in the previous section, was to oversee entertainment, including the inversion of aspects of everyday life in an amusing manner, throughout the Twelve Days of Christmas. Lords of Misrule were appointed to manage festivities within the royal court, in the houses of nobles, in the law schools of the Inns of Court, and in many Oxford and Cambridge colleges, and seem in many cases to have had real power to command anyone to do anything during their brief period in control.

While Lords of Misrule were appointed within the royal court and other institutions to ensure that festive entertainment was well planned, entertainment elsewhere was less organised and must have relied upon a large degree of spontaneity. One tradition we should note here is 'mumming', often regarded as an ancient practice with origins in pre-Christian fertility ritual. The term 'mumming' seems to have evolved from the Germanic 'Mummer', meaning 'disguised person', reflecting the fact that the mummers always performed in disguise. Mummers are known to have performed for Edward III at Christmastime, but sadly we have very little evidence relating to nature of such performances. Medieval mummers probably cavorted about in the street wearing masks and animal costumes, perhaps travelling from house to house like carol singers rather than performing set plays like those of later times.

On Christmas Day 1492, far away from British shores, Columbus reached Cuba, christening the bay where he landed 'Navidad' ('Christmas' in Spanish). Back in Britain, Henry VII held a great banquet in Westminster Hall, attended by 120 knights and squires, at which much lavish entertainment was provided. Such feasts served a political purpose as well as being great fun for participants. They helped reinforce loyalty to King and country, and, of course, while knights were feasting in the presence of the King they could not be away plotting against him as many had done over previous Christmas seasons. Dawson provides much detail of Henry VII's Christmas feasts, including the recipe for roast peacock, a feature of the royal Christmas menu:

> … the most famous dish was the peacock enkakyll, which is foremost in the procession to the king's table. Here is the recipe for this royal dish: Take and flay off the skin with the feathers, tail, and the neck and head thereon; then take the skin, and all the feathers, and lay it on the table abroad, and strew thereon ground cinnamon; then take the peacock and roast him, and baste him with raw yolks of eggs; and when he is roasted, take him off, and let him cool awhile, and take him and sew him in his skin, and gild his comb, and so serve him with the last course.

Henry VII was succeeded by his second son, Henry VIII, whose conflict with the Catholic Church would eventually have serious repercussions for the celebration of Christmas, but whose personal love of the season would ensure that royal festive celebrations reached new heights of extravagance.

5

From Reformation to Restoration and Beyond

This chapter begins with the reign of Henry VIII, during which the Reformation saw the influence of the Catholic Church much diminished throughout Britain. However, the festival of Christmas continued to thrive. After considering Christmas under Elizabeth I and James I, when festivities were perhaps celebrated with greater enthusiasm and extravagance than at any other time, we will arrive at the doomed reign of Charles I. At the start of his reign, Charles enjoyed traditionally exuberant Christmases, but the Civil War and the creation of the Commonwealth soon brought both monarchy and Christmas to an abrupt, if temporary, end. After the Restoration, Christmas bounced back, but celebrations seem never to have reached such great heights as they had under Elizabeth and James. (This chapter includes examples from many sources, but the volumes by Sandys and Dawson (cited previously), along with J.A.R Pimlott's *The Englishman's Christmas: A Social History*, have been of particular value).

Henry VIII and the Reformation

Henry VIII, at the time a dashing young man bearing no comparison to the bloated wreck he would become in later life, was crowned in the summer of 1509. Christmas at his court would reach new levels of decadence, and many records of his festive feasts survive, demonstrating the costs of such seasonal extravagance. Henry's first Christmas as king was spent with his first queen, Catherine of Aragon, at Richmond, where the entertainment included a grand jousting tournament on the green in front of the palace; such tournaments would become regular features of the royal Christmas, attracting competitors from far and wide. There was no great pageant or masque in 1509, as there would be in subsequent years, but a Lord of Misrule was appointed, at a cost of £8 6s 8d, to oversee festivities (the cost of Henry's Lord of Misrule would later rise to more than £15, reflecting the continuing importance of the role). The royal household accounts show increasing levels of expenditure on Christmas banquets and 'diversions' which render the costs of the Lord of Misrule almost negligible. For example, in 1509 a payment in excess of £450 was made to 'Willm. Buttry upon his bill for certen sylks bought by him for the disguisings', and in 1514 a sum of £247 was made 'to Leonard Friscobald for diverse velvets, and other sylks, for the disguising' and £137 was paid 'to Richard Gybson for certain apparel, & c., for the disguising at the fest of Christmes'. Elaborate costumes were clearly essential to the Christmas 'disguisings', in which the king himself sometimes played a role in the early years of his reign.

Sandys recounts that during Henry's second Christmas as king, a pageant (a portable stage, often build on a cart, which might take the form of a castle, garden or mountain) was introduced into the great hall at Richmond on Twelfth Night. This was in the form of a hill decorated with gold and precious stones, surmounted by a golden tree, itself decorated with roses and pomegranates. This

> was brought towards the king, when out came a lady, dressed in cloth of gold, and the henchmen, or children of honour, who were dressed in some disguise, and they danced a morris before the king; after which they re-entered the mountain, which was drawn back, and then the wassail or banquet was brought in, and so ended the Christmas.

The following year, at Greenwich, the pageant was in the form of a grand castle from which half a dozen fair ladies dressed in satin and gold emerged to dance with six lords, after which the castle 'disappeared' and the royal banquet commenced. A few days later, 'on the day of the Epiphanie, at night, the king with eleven others, was disguised after the manner of Italie, called a maske, a thing not seen afore in England; thei were appareled in garments long and brode, wrought all with gold, with visers and cappes of gold'.

Similar grand performances were enacted in front of the king in subsequent years, and many of the nobility put on their own Christmas shows in imitation of the court, also appointing Lords of Misrule to organise and oversee the festivities. Sandys observes that:

> The Earl of Northumberland … used to give, when he was at home, to those of his chapel, if they played the play of the Nativity

on Christmas Day, 20s.; and to his master of the revels, 20s ... to
the abbot of Misrule, 20s…Different presents also to various sets of
players; also 20s each to the barne-bishops (boy-bishops) of Beverley
and York, showing that the custom still existed.

At Christmas, the working classes were allowed privileges denied
them throughout the rest of the year. The act of Henry VII's reign
preventing people from participating in 'unlawful games' other than
at Christmas was reinforced under Henry VIII when it was decreed:

> That no manner of Artificer or Craftsman of any handicraft
> or occupation, Husbandman, Apprentice, Labourer, Servant
> at husbandry, Journeyman, or Servant of Artificer, Mariners,
> Fishermen, Watermen, or any Serving-man, shall from the said
> feast of the Nativity of St. John Baptist, play at the Tables, Tennis,
> Dice, Cards, Bowls, Clash, Coyting, Logating, or any other unlawful
> Game, out of Christmas, under the pain of xxs. to be forfeit for
> every time; and in Christmas to play at any of the said Games in
> their Masters' houses, or in their Masters' presence.

Although people were expected to enjoy Christmas, there was some
concern over illegal activities being undertaken by those disguised
ostensibly for festive fun. Sandys records that to counteract this an
act was passed to restrict the activities of mummers:

> It was, therefore, found necessary by an Act passed in the 3rd year
> of Henry VIII to order that no person should appear abroad like
> mummers, covering their faces with vizors, and in disguised apparel,
> under pain of three months' imprisonment; and a penalty of 20s. was
> declared against such as kept vizors in their house for the purpose
> of mumming. It was not intended, however, to debar people from
> proper recreations during this season…

We must now consider the Reformation and its effect on the festive
season. The Reformation was the major force for religious change
that witnessed the rise of Protestantism throughout much of Europe,
arising largely as a protest against corruption in the Catholic Church.
It effectively began in Germany in 1517 with Martin Luther who,
despite his opposition to the Catholic Church, was actually very fond
of Christmas. In England, the break with Catholicism came in 1534
with the Act of Supremacy. This followed the Pope's refusal to grant
Henry VIII a divorce from Catherine of Aragon, and saw the King

installed as head of the newly created Church of England, enabling him to proceed with the Dissolution of the Monasteries. It might reasonably be expected that this break with Catholic tradition would have a detrimental effect on the institution of Christmas, but Henry, given his fondness for the festive season, ensured that Christmas was retained as one of the new Church's three major annual festivals (along with Easter and Whitsontide). However, north of the border, Protestantism took a very different route, having a catastrophic effect on the Scottish celebration of Christmas, which in turn would have serious repercussions in England a century or so later.

In early sixteenth-century Scotland, the Catholic Church controlled more than half the nation's wealth but was exceedingly corrupt. A spontaneous popular movement of dissent, with John Knox as its main protagonist, led to the rise of Scottish Protestantism. Knox had spent several years in Geneva where he had been greatly influenced by John Calvin. Calvin developed an austere form of Protestantism that became known as Calvinism; its two main characteristics were its stress on the individual's direct relationship with God, with no need for intervention by popes or priests, and the absolute primacy of the Bible as the basis for all preaching and teaching. Calvin believed that Church and State should work hand-in-hand to create a 'godly society' within which all aspects of life were shaped by religious belief and strictly enforced codes of conduct.

In August 1560, the Scottish Parliament abolished all authority of the Pope in Scotland, and all celebration of the Latin Mass was banned. Knox and five colleagues were charged with formulating the creed and constitution of a new Scottish Church based on radical Calvinist principles. The details of this austere new Church cannot concern us here, except to say that there was no place within it for 'popish nonsense' such as Christmas. In a tradition that extends to this day, Scottish midwinter celebrations became focussed on New Year (Hogmanay) rather than Christmas, and were very much of a secular rather than Christian nature; Christmas would not be officially recognised as a holiday in Scotland until 1958.

After our brief sojourn north of the border, we must now return to the England of Henry VIII. As he grew older, his health declined and his marital problems continued, Henry's Christmas celebrations became increasingly muted. Dawson notes that 'his Christmases grew gradually duller, until he did little more than sit out a play or two, and gambol with his courtiers, his Christmas play-money requiring a special draught upon the Treasury, usually for a hundred pounds.'

While Henry's final few Christmases may have been relatively dull, they were certainly not without incident; at Christmas 1543, he entertained 21 Scottish prisoners at Greenwich before releasing them without ransom, a gesture of festive goodwill if ever there was one.

We may note in passing what must rank as one of the most fascinating Christmas gifts (or, to be exact, New Year gifts) of all time. Henry VIII appointed John Leland as Royal Antiquary, instructing him to travel the nation recording antiquities and study the nation's libraries to compile the first ever dossier on England's heritage. Leland completed his task in 1546, presenting the results to his king under the title of a 'New Year's Gift', in which he states:

> I have so traviled yn your dominions booth by the se costes and the midle partes, sparing nother labor nor costes, by the space of these vi. yeres paste, that there is almoste nother cape, nor bay, haven, creke or peers, river or confluence of rivers, breches, watchies, lakes, meres, fenny waters, montagnes, valleis, mores, hethes, forestes, chases, wooddes, cities, burges, castelles, principale manor placis, monasteries, and colleges, but I have seene them; and notid yn so doing a hole worlde of thinges very memorable.

What a gift this must have been! Sadly, Henry was deprived of the opportunity to study it, as he died in January 1547.

As Henry's desire for seasonal extravagance began to wane towards the end of his life, various institutions continued to hold exuberant Christmas festivals. Particularly worthy of note in this respect are the Inns of Court and the colleges of Oxford and Cambridge, which continued to appoint their own Lord of Misrule (sometimes referred to as the 'Master of Merry Disports') and to enjoy lavish stage performances and great banquets. Students at Queen's College, Oxford, still enjoy a festive tradition claimed to date back to the time of Henry VIII – the singing of the 'Boar's Head Carol' as the boar's head is carried into the hall at the Christmas feast. Several ancient carols reflect the importance of the boar's head at the Christmas table, and that sung at Queen's College can be traced back to 1521, when it was published as 'a carol bringing in the bores heed'. It begins:

> The boar's head in hand bring I,
> With garlands gay and rosemary;
> I pray you all sing merrily…

Henry VIII's household accounts record two separate occasions at Christmas 1529 on which a sum of 40 shillings was paid 'in rewarde for bringing a wylde bore unto the King'. The tradition extended into the reigns of Henry's successors, as recorded by the seventeenth-century antiquarian John Aubrey, who wrote in 1678 that 'before the last civil wars, in gentlemen's houses at Christmas, the first diet that was brought to the table was a boar's head with a lemon in his mouth.' The origins of the tradition are lost in time, but we know that the boar's head featured at important feasts, at various times of year, from the twelfth century onwards, and it may well have appeared at midwinter in much earlier times. Aubrey's reference to the lemon is not without significance; the boar's head was (and still is) usually served with an apple, orange or lemon placed in its open mouth as an almost subconscious symbolic representation of ancient sun-worship.

After the Reformation

Henry VIII was succeeded by his son, Edward VI, who became king at nine years of age and was effectively a puppet for his uncle and regent, the Earl of Hertford. Edward was a devout Protestant, referring at the age of 10 to the Pope as 'the true son of the Devil, an anti-Christ and an abominable tyrant'. The Archbishop of Canterbury, Thomas Cranmer, oversaw reforms that saw the banning of traditional forms of Catholic worship, but these reforms were cut short when Edward died aged just 14 in 1553 and was replaced on the throne by his Catholic sister, Mary. During her half-dozen years on the throne, 'Bloody Mary' reversed many Protestant reforms, saw nearly 300 Protestants burned at the stake and restored papal supremacy. The complexities behind this crazy swing from Catholic to Protestant and back cannot concern us here, but it is relevant to our story that throughout all this chaos both Edward and Mary continued to celebrate the Christmas season with great fervour.

Sandys records that the 1551/52 festive season at Greenwich saw 'one of the most magnificent revellings on record'. George Ferrers, a distinguished lawyer, poet and historian, was paid £100 to act as Lord of Misrule. Adopting the motto *semper ferians* ('always keeping holiday'), he provided sumptuous entertainment for the court including clowns, jugglers and dancers, appearing himself throughout the season in a series of outrageously expensive outfits of silk, fur, gold and silver. The court fool, John Smyth, played a leading role in the festivities and was supplied with a new outfit, costing in excess of £26, including a coat of yellow and gold fringed with white, red and green velvet. King Edward, appropriately attired in his own specially produced and costly garments, took part in some Christmas masques, and clearly enjoyed the festivities at each of the six Christmas seasons during which he occupied the throne.

Court festivities were curtailed somewhat under Mary's turbulent reign, although the Christmas masque was not abandoned. In 1554, there was a grand masque featuring six Venuses and six Cupids along with many other characters in fantastic costumes representing lions, goddesses, huntresses and others. On Christmas Eve, 1557, the great hall at Hampden Court Palace was lit with a thousand lamps, and the following days saw grand masques and banquets, along with a great jousting tournament. Mary was accustomed to receiving numerous valuable gifts each Christmas, including clothing, paintings and food, and her fondness for the season extended to the reintroduction of boy bishops. However, after a brief resurgence, the boy bishop expired for good along with the Queen in 1558.

Towards the end of Mary's reign, Christmas for most people can perhaps be described as a time for general merrymaking with something of a religious gloss (ancient pagan customs that did not conflict directly with Christian doctrine were not generally opposed), and with an important emphasis on charity, with landowners expected to provide a degree of festive hospitality for their tenants. The situation is neatly summed in a verse penned in 1557 by Thomas Tusser:

> Provide us good cheer, for thou knowest the old guise,
> Old customs that good be, let no man despise.
> At Christmas be merry and thank God of all,
> And feast thy poor neighbours, the great and the small.

Mary was succeeded by her half-sister, Elizabeth I, whose 45 years on the throne saw England established as a powerful, Protestant nation. The Elizabethan Christmas was an extravaganza that compared favourably with the greatest festive celebrations of earlier monarchs. Christmas 1558 was spent in preparation for the new Queen's coronation, in Westminster Abbey on 17 January 1559, and was celebrated with costly plays and pageants. Unlike her father, Henry VIII, and others of her predecessors, Elizabeth seems initially to have had some concerns over the level of expenditure on Christmas festivities, and requested a report detailing the costs involved. Subsequent events would suggest, however, that any cutbacks were of no more than temporary consequence. Dawson observes that:

> In this reign a more decorous and even refined style of entertainment had usurped the place of the boisterous feastings of former times, but there was no diminution in that ancient spirit of hospitality, the exercise of which had become a part of the national faith.

This is evident from the poems of Thomas Tusser (1515-1580) and other writers, who show that the English noblemen and yeomen of the time made hospitality a prominent feature of the Christmas season. In his *Christmas Husbandry Fare,* Tusser says:

> Good husband and housewife, now chiefly be glad
> Things handsome to have, as they ought to be had,
> They both do provide against Christmas do come,
> To welcome their neighbour, good cheer to have some;
> Good bread and good drink, a good fire in the hall,
> Brawn pudding and souse, and good mustard withal.
>
> Beef, mutton, and pork, shred pies of the best,
> Pig, veal, goose, and capon, and turkey well dressed;
> Cheese, apples, and nuts, jolly carols to hear,
> As then in the country is counted good cheer.

The traditional grand Christmas celebrations at the Inns of Court and the Universities had fallen into decline by the later sixteenth century, but there were occasional years in which a special effort was made with spectacular results. For example, the revellings of 1561 at the Inner Temple, overseen by no less than three Masters of the Revels, consisted of much feasting, music, dancing and general merrymaking that continued unabated from Christmas Eve until Twelfth Night. Dawson quotes at great length from Nichols' *Progresses of Queen Elizabeth* with regard to the plans for this Christmas at the Inner Temple, noting the following with specific regard to Christmas Day itself that after church there was planned a full breakfast and an opulent dinner:

> At the first course is served in a fair and large bore's-head, upon a silver platter, with minstralsye. Two Gentlemen in gowns are to attend at supper, and to bear two fair torches of wax, next before

the Musicians and Trumpetters, and to stand above the fire with the musick till the first course be served in through the Hall. Which performed, they, with the musick, are to return into the buttery. The like course is to be observed in all things, during the time of Christmas. The like at supper.

On the following day, St Stephen's Day, when all were seated ready for dinner, there occurred an incident which Sandys sarcastically describes as 'a pleasant Christmas amusement'. Dawson provides the following description:

> The Master of the Game entered in green velvet, and the Ranger of the Forest in green satin; these also went three times about the fire, blowing their hunting-horns. When they also had been ceremoniously seated, there entered a huntsman with a fox and a cat bound at the end of a staff. He was followed by nine or ten couple of hounds, who hunted the fox and the cat to the blowing horns, and killed them beneath the fire.

Whatever one's attitude to fox hunting, it has to be admitted that in the traditional Boxing Day hunts of more recent times the poor fox was at least given slightly more of a chance than this unfortunate beast. As for the cat, perhaps the least said the better.

On 27 December there was a grand Christmas parade through the streets of London. What the ordinary man in the street must have made of the wealth and privilege on display is not recorded, but the sight must have been impressive as there came 'Riding through the London a lord of misrule, in clear complete harness gilt, with a hundred great horse and gentlemen riding gorgeously with chains of gold'.

A few days later, Twelfth Night saw the first performance of *Gorboduc* (later published as 'Ferrex and Porrex'), a play written by two young members of the Inner Temple, Thomas Norton and Thomas Sackville, that has been described as the first English tragedy. This performance was so good that Elizabeth commanded a repeat performance a few days later at her court at Whitehall. The theme of the play was a call for unity amongst Englishmen after the strife of previous decades. It is not difficult to see why this theme would have appealed to Elizabeth, as there was still much friction between different religious groups within her kingdom. There was, for example, still much resentment amongst Puritan sympathisers over the retention of Christmas in its traditional form. During the later sixteenth century, several writers complained of the excesses of Christmas celebrations. In his *Anatomie of Abuses* (1583), an attack on the excesses of the theatre and other aspects of society, Philip Stubbes observes that 'more mischief is committed [at Christmas] than in all the year besides.' Elsewhere in the same work he provides us with a fascinating overview of contemporary Christmas celebrations, along with the reasoning behind his objections to them:

> But especially in Christmas time there is nothing else used but cards, dice, tables, masking, mumming, bowling, and such like fooleries. And the reason is, for they think they have a commission and prerogative [at] that time, to do what they list, and to follow what vanity they will. But (alas) do they think that they are privileged at that time to do evil? … But what will they say? Is it not Christmas? Must we not be merry? … But the true celebration of the feast of Christmas is to meditate … upon the incarnation and birth of Jesus Christ, God and man.

Amidst all the records of festive merrymaking, it is easy to forget that there was still a strong religious dimension to Christmas for most people, and that church services throughout the festive season were still well attended. An account survives of Elizabeth, along with members of her court, attending the chapel of Whitehall, Westminster, on Christmas Eve and Christmas Day 1565, and she probably did likewise every Christmas. However, she also sought festive fulfilment on less sacred ground; in addition to her love of theatre she was very fond of banqueting, dancing and, in particular, dicing, at which she invariably won due, allegedly, to her use of loaded dice. She also gained pleasure from the huge array of valuable presents she received from the great and the good each festive season; in 1660 she was given what were apparently the first pair of silk stockings ever worn in England, while over the years she also received many fabulous dresses, exquisite jewellery, exotic 'pets', fine foodstuffs and countless other wonderful things. The queen is said to have shown much generosity in return, showering festive gifts upon her favourites.

In addition to personal presents from friends and courtiers, Elizabeth received many 'official' gifts. Pimlott notes that:

> As far as gift giving to the Sovereign was concerned, a more or less regular tariff seems to have developed for the chief officers of state

and the lords spiritual and temporal. Under Elizabeth and her two successors the rate for an Archbishop was £40 and for other peers £20.

A fascinating glimpse into Elizabeth's attitude towards religion may be gleaned from her disapproval of a New Year gift in 1561. The festively named Dean Nowell of St Paul's presented her with a lavishly bound prayer book with images of saints and martyrs, but the Queen found these contrary to the ban on 'popish' religious images and made it clear that no such gifts should be given in future.

Evidence for festive gift-giving amongst those lower down the social hierarchy at this time is sparse, although we may assume that any gifts exchanged by the unprivileged would have been in the form of home-grown produce or home-made goods. It was customary for tenants in rural areas to present their landowners with at least a capon. Wealthy landowners could accumulate vast quantities of seasonal produce in the form of gifts from tenants and neighbouring farms. Pimlott notes that in 1636 Lord Justice Bramston recorded receipt of the following Christmas gifts at his Essex mansion: 32 turkeys, 54 capons, 3 bullocks, many other birds, a hogshead of claret (from the town of Chelmsford), puddings, oysters, a basket of apples, two doves and a silver dish. However, such gift-giving seems to have been more prevalent in some areas than in others. Sir John Oglander from the Isle of Wight received 23 New Year gifts while visiting Sussex in 1622, noting that 'Sussex is the freest place in England for the giving of New Year's gifts, and the Isle of Wight the basest.' Even allowing for the fact that gift-giving was less prevalent in some areas than in others, the festive season certainly provided a seasonal boost for many traders, notably those in exotic imported foodstuffs such as oranges, figs and various spices, as well as wine merchants.

The Elizabethan court was fortunate in being able to stage Shakespearean plays, several of which were performed at different Christmas seasons. One of Shakespeare's most studied and best loved plays, *Twelfth Night or What You Will*, while not actually about the festive season, was written to be performed as Twelfth Night entertainment. While in some ways a complex play, its themes of cross-dressing and mistaken identity provide humour accessible to all, and are clearly rooted in ancient Saturnalian tradition. Its first ever performance may have been before the court at Whitehall on Twelfth Night 1601, but the records are unclear; the earliest performance known for certain was at Middle Temple Hall on

Candlemas night (2 February) 1602. According to the English drama critic, Max Beerbohm, Shakespeare despised the festive season. In his parody, *A Christmas Garland* (1912), Beerbohm writes that Shakespeare only refers to Christmas 'now and again, but in grudging fashion, without one spark of illumination', and concludes that 'If there is one thing lucid-obvious in the Plays and Sonnets, it is Shakespeare's unconquerable loathing of Christmas …'. Whether or not Shakespeare truly despised Christmas remains unproven, but it is indeed strange that he chooses to feature it so rarely in his work.

Towards the end of Elizabeth's reign there was much concern that rural communities were being ignored by landowners who had previously provided Christmas hospitality in the country but now chose to spend their festive season in London. The problem is expressed in a late sixteenth-century song published under the rather lengthy title 'Christmas's lamentation for the losse of his acquaintance; showing how he is forst to leave the country and come to London'. The song bemoans the loss of traditional seasonal charity throughout the English countryside:

> Christmas is my name, far have I gone,
> Have I gone, have I gone, have I gone, without regard,
> Whereas great men by flocks there be flown,
> There be flown, there be flown, there be flown, to London-ward;
> Where they in pomp and pleasure do waste
> That which Christmas was wonted to feast, Welladay!
> Houses where music was wont for to ring
> Nothing but bats and owlets do sing.
> Welladay! Welladay! Welladay! Where should I stay?

In response to this problem, Elizabeth ordered the gentlemen of Norfolk and Suffolk to leave London prior to Christmas 1589 'to repair to their counties, and there to keep hospitality amongst their neighbours'. The issue was not simply one of charity, as Sandys notes that the presence of landowners in the country would:

> Not only enable them to increase the real enjoyment of their dependents, but would serve to control any tendency to riot or debauch at the country alehouses, at this time the resort of many idle strollers, under the guise of minstrels, jugglers, revellers, &c., and would, if right-minded themselves, give a proper direction to the festivities.

Several Elizabethan landowners did return to their country seats at Christmas, providing traditional hospitality for rural communities. Lord Berkeley, for example, provided great Christmas banquets for the local community around his mansion at Caludon, near Coventry. According to an account written by Sir William Dugdale:

> Such was the humanity of this Lord, that in tymes of Christmas and other festyvalls, when his neighbor townships were invited and feasted in his Hall, he would, in the midst of their dynner, ryse from his owne, & goynge to each of their tables in his Hall, cheerfully bid them welcome. And his further order was, having guests of Honour or remarkable ranke that filled his owne table, to seate himselfe at the lower end; and when such guests filled but half his bord, & a meaner degree the rest of his table, then to seate himselfe the last of the first ranke, & the first of the later, which was about the midst of his large tables, neare the salt.

Another good example is provided by the Sidney family of Penshurst in Kent, where it is recorded that all who enjoyed their hospitality were treated equally and enjoyed the same feast. The playwright Ben Jonson penned the following lines about festivities at Penshurst:

> Whose liberal board doth flow
> With all that hospitality doth know!
> Where comes no guest but is allow'd to eat,
> Without his fear, and of thy Lord's own meat
> Where the same beer and bread, and self-same wine,
> That is His Lordship's, shall be also mine.

After Elizabeth's death in 1603, the Crowns of England and Scotland were united; James Stewart, crowned James VI of Scotland in 1567 at just one year of age, also became James I of England and Ireland. He was very keen on cementing the union, introducing the Union Jack as a symbol of the new relationship between the two ancient foes ('Jack' comes from 'Jacques', the French version of his name). In 1617, the King travelled back to his native Scotland with the aim of establishing the Church of England as the state church north of the border, stating that 'the festivals of Christmas, Good Friday, Easter, Ascension Day and Whit Sunday should be observed in Scotland as in England'. The Scots, however, defied their King and flatly refused to adopt these

'Popish' and 'pagan' feasts. An act of Parliament was passed three years later to enforce the adoption within Scotland of the Church of England – this too was ignored.

It is fascinating to see how differing attitudes towards Christmas within the newly 'united kingdom' were mirrored within colonies across the Atlantic, where individual settlements tended to be dominated by one or other religious group. In 1607 at Jamestown, Virginia, Christmas was celebrated by Captain John Smith 'among the savages … with plenty of good oysters, fish, flesh, wilde fowl and good bread'. As the colony grew, its people celebrated the Twelve Days of Christmas each year with extravagant banquets and lavish entertainment according to English tradition. Contemporary accounts record yule logs, carol singing, evergreen decorations, fox-hunting, card-playing, dancing and sumptuous Christmas dinners. In complete contrast, just 500 miles up the coast, the 'Pilgrims' of the Puritan colony of New Plymouth spent their first Christmas Day, in 1620, hard at work on the construction of buildings. In subsequent years they shunned all aspects of the festival, opening their shops, going to work, and eating only ordinary meals. A few years later, the Puritan-dominated General Court of Massachusetts passed a law to punish anyone caught celebrating Christmas:

> … anybody who is found observing, by abstinence from labor, feasting, or any other way, any such days as Christmas day, shall pay for every such offence five shillings.

This law was eventually repealed in 1681, but the people of New England generally continued to ignore Christmas until the late nineteenth century. Elsewhere in America, attitudes towards Christmas varied in accordance with the distribution of different religious groups; areas dominated by Anglicans and Roman Catholics celebrated the season in traditional style, while Puritan, Baptist, Presbyterian and Quaker communities tended to ignore it.

Back at James' court in early seventeenth-century England, the magnificent Christmas masques surpassed anything that had been seen before. Some 30 plays and masques were performed at court during James' first Christmas on the throne and such theatrical extravagance was continued in subsequent years. By tradition, there was not usually a performance on Christmas Day itself, but in 1608 James wished to reverse this tradition. On being told that this was not the fashion his response left no doubt who was in ultimate control of Christmas: 'What do you tell me of the fashion? I will make it a fashion!'

It was not unusual for thousands of pounds to be spent on a single production, with mechanised stages and scenery designed by Inigo Jones, architect to the court, and poetry and music provided by the greatest talents in the land. The King, Queen, and Princes Henry and Charles all appeared on stage in court masques, as on occasion did foreign ambassadors and other dignitaries. Some of the most popular plays were written by Ben Johnson, including the famous *Christmas, His Masque*, first performed at court at Christmas 1616. This is fascinating in its use of early seventeenth-century Christmas iconography; it seeks, in its own words, to present 'A right Christmas, as of old it was.'

The opening scene sees the entrance of a personified Christmas, who then introduces himself:

> Enter Christmas, with two or three of the Guard. He is attir'd in round Hose, long Stockings, a close Doublet, a high crownd Hat with a Broach, a long thin beard, a Truncheon, little Ruffes, white Shoes, his Scarffes, and Garters tyed crosse, and his Drum beaten before him.
>
> 'Why Gentlemen, doe you know what you doe? ha! would you ha'kept me out? Christmas, old Christmas? Christmas of London, and Captaine Christmas?'

This character is then followed onto the stage by his ten sons and daughters, all splendidly attired in costumes relating to their festive names: Misrule, Caroll, Minc'd-Pie, Gamboll, Post and Paire, New-Yeares-Gift, Mumming, Wassall, Offering, and Babie-Cocke. ('Post and Paire' was a card game, popular at Christmas. 'Wassal' represents traditional wassailing, or drinking of health. Pimlott suggests that 'Offering' may refer to church offertories, as collections were normally taken on Christmas Day. For 'Babie-Cocke' read 'Baby Cake' – another term for Twelfth cake, described by Pimlott as 'the centrepiece of Twelfth Night revelry'.)

Some critics dismiss *Christmas, His Masque* as a piece of seasonal nonsense, linking it with mumming of no theatrical worth. However, close analysis suggests that it contains much satire aimed in the direction at those within Jacobean society who opposed the traditional Christmas. It must certainly have met with the approval of King James, who was very fond indeed of his Christmas.

In addition to attending, and sometimes performing in, the Christmas masques, James enjoyed gambling during the festive season, often for very high stakes. A letter dated 8 January 1608 records that on the preceding Twelfth Night 'there was great golden play at court. No gamester was admitted that brought not £300 at least.' The King went home £750 better off, while the queen lost £400 and assorted others lost similar amounts. James was also keen on hunting, often leaving London for a few days over the festive season for this purpose. There was also a revival of the traditional Christmas tournament, in which Prince Henry, heir to the throne, was a keen competitor. After Henry's untimely death in 1612, however, the tournament fell out of fashion and would not in future be a major element of the royal Christmas.

As well as having much fun at Christmas, James seems to have had great respect for the religious aspects of the festival. Sandys notes that he introduced a penalty of £10 for anyone 'making use, in plays, shows, or pageants, jestingly or profanely, of the Holy Name of God, or of our Saviour, or of the Holy Ghost, or of the Trinity.' A remarkable survival from the period is the series of 'Seventeen Sermons on the Nativity, preached before King James I at Whitehall, by the Right Honourable and Reverend Father in God, Lancelot Andrewes, sometime Lord Bishop of Winchester'. These Christmas Day sermons, ranging in date from 1605 to 1624, give a fascinating insight into the relationship between monarch and Church; they were collated and published after the deaths of both King James and Bishop Andrewes by order of Charles I.

Away from the court, seasonal banquets and entertainment continued to be arranged at the colleges and the Inns of Court. As under Elizabeth, there were some years in which a special effort was made. At the Christmas 1607 celebrations at St John's College, Oxford, a 'Christmas Prince' (Thomas Tucker, later to be Canon of Bristol) was appointed for the first time in 30 years to organise and oversee a great season of revelry including several plays, dancing, feasting and a great New Year's Day parade of the Prince and his entourage that commenced with a volley of 60 guns. Another famous incident involving the firing of guns occurred on Twelfth Day 1623, as the gentlemen of Gray's Inn brought their festive season to a dramatic end by borrowing four cartloads of 'chambers' (small signal cannons) from the Tower of London and firing them off all at once. King James was awoken by the noise and jumped out of his bed crying 'Treason! Treason!' The city was in a state of confusion and the court took up arms, the Earl of Arundel dashing with sword drawn into the king's bedchamber to rescue his king. The king's reaction on discovering the true course of the uproar is not recorded.

James followed Elizabeth in instructing the landed gentry to return to their estates at Christmas, believing it better for social stability throughout the kingdom that Christmas celebrations were held throughout the land rather than concentrated in London as they had been in earlier times. James ordered that '… as every fish lives in his own place, some in the fresh, some in the salt, some in the mud, so let every one live in his own place – some at Court, some in the city, some in the country; specially at festival times, as Christmas, and Easter, and the rest.' An ordinance enacted three days before Christmas 1622, a year which had seen a bad harvest leading to some rural disorder, stated that '… by this way of reviving the laudable and ancient housekeeping of this realme the poor and such as are most pinched in times of scarcity and want will be much relieved and comforted.' This tendency towards charity at Christmas is further illustrated by an order from the government to the Bishop of London to arrange collections in December 1627 for French Protestants seeking refuge in London, the collection being specifically arranged to take advantage of 'this festival time of Christmas when commonly men are disposed to show themselves more bountiful and hospitable towards the poor than at other times'.

An indication of the festive entertainment enjoyed by ordinary folk at this time is given by Robert Burton in his *Anatomy of Melancholy*, published in 1621:

> The ordinary recreations which we have in winter, and in most solitary times busie our minds with, are cardes, tables, and dice, shovelboard, chesse-play, the philosopher's game, small trunkes, shuttle-cocke, billiards, musicke, masks, singing, dancing, ulegames, frolicks, jests, riddles, catches, purposes, questions and commands, merry tales of errant knights, queenes, lovers, lords, ladies, giants, dwarfes, theeves, cheaters, witches, fayries, goblins, friers, &c.

Such activities, coupled with a trip to church, a splendid Christmas dinner, and perhaps a spot of mumming, would have been enjoyed by the majority of people on Christmas Day in early to mid seventeenth-century England.

James died in March 1625 and was succeeded by his second son, Charles I. As we have already noted, Charles had taken an active role in Christmas festivities at his father's court, and he inherited his father's love of the festive season. Grand masques by Jonson and others were presented during the first years of his reign, and numerous contemporary verses and other records testify to the general popularity of Christmas throughout the land. For example, Nicholas Breton, writing in 1626, says:

> It is now Christmas, and not a cup of drink must pass without a carol; the beasts, fowl, and fish come to a general execution, and the corn is ground to dust for the bakehouse and the pastry: cards and dice purge many a purse, and the youth show their agility in shoeing of the wild mare: now, good cheer, and welcome, and God be with you, and I thank you …
>
> … In sum it is a holy time, a duty in Christians for the remembrance of Christ and custom among friends for the maintenance of good fellowship.

George Wither's *A Christmas Carol*, from about the same time, begins with the verse:

> So, now is come our joyful'st feast;
> Let every man be jolly;
> Each room with ivy leaves is drest,
> And every post with holly.
> Though some churls at our mirth repine,
> Round your foreheads garlands twine;
> Drown sorrow in a cup of wine,
> And let us all be merry.

Feasting was still very much at the centre of festive celebrations, as demonstrated by this description of a 1630s domestic Christmas from the pages of the journal *Archaeologia*:

> Richard Evelyn, Esq., High Sheriff of Surrey and Sussex in 1634, held a splendid Christmas at his mansion at Wotton, having a regular Lord of Misrule for the occasion; and it appears it was then the custom for the neighbours to send presents of eatables to provide for the great consumption consequent upon such entertainments. The following is a list of those sent on this occasion: two sides of venison, two half brawns, three pigs, ninety capons, five geese, six turkeys, four rabbits, eight partridges, two pullets, five sugar loaves, half a pound of nutmeg, one basket of apples, two baskets of pears.

Robert Herrick wrote several poems about life in the Devon village of Dean Prior, where he was vicar from 1630 until 1647. Some of these refer to Christmas and demonstrate that the people treated the Twelve Days as a holiday and a time for general merrymaking. In 'A New Year's Gift', he discusses all manner of festive pastimes before closing with the lines:

> … And to the bagpipe all address
> Till sleep takes place of weariness.
> And this, throughout, with Christmas plays,
> Frolic the full twelve holy-days.

As a final example, further illustrating the importance of festive food during the Twelve Days, Breton notes that 'Capons and Hennes, besides Turkies, Geese, and Duckes, besides Beefe and Mutton, must all die for the great feast, for in twelve dayes a multitude of people will not bee fed with a little.'

For most people, the Twelve Days were the main annual holiday, but there had to be some exceptions. The Navy, for example, had to ensure that its men did not all disappear on holiday for the festive season; at Christmas 1627 the loss of two warships to the Dutch was blamed on certain officers and men having gone ashore for their Christmas holidays instead of completing their scheduled patrols.

Although most contemporary references to Christmas from this period deal with profane rather than sacred aspects of the season, many people still attended church services to celebrate the Nativity on Christmas Day, and a carol dated 1632 entitled 'Sun of Righteousness' takes us back to our observations regarding early Christian sun symbolism at the start of Chapter 5:

> Hail, O Sun, O blessed Light,
> Sent into the world by night,
> Let thy rays and heavenly powers
> Shine in this dark soul of ours;
> For most duly
> Thou art truly
> God and man we do confess.
> Hail, O Sun of Righteousness!

Many in the Church considered some Christmas traditions somewhat inappropriate, but few saw these as reason to oppose the season in its entirety. In a seventeenth-century reworking of Gregory the Great's advice to his missionaries a millennium earlier, George Herbert wrote in 1632 that:

> The country parson is a lover of old customs, if they be good and harmless; and the rather because country people are much addicted to them, so that to favour them therein is to win their hearts, and to oppose them therein is to deject them.

While many traditions could be described as 'good and harmless', there were occasions when the mark was clearly overstepped. In a Lincolnshire village in 1637, for example, serious disciplinary action had to be taken after the official marriage service was used for the mock-wedding of a Lord of Misrule and a Christmas lady! Despite such problems, the tendency within the Church of England was to adopt a generally tolerant approach. There was, however, a growing tide of extreme opposition to Christmas amongst Puritans. Writing in the early 1630s and echoing to an extent the views of Stubbes quoted earlier, William Prynne describes people at Christmas as 'engaged in amorous, mixed, voluptuous, unchristian, that I say not, pagan dancing'. He suggests that outsiders observing the usual Christmas celebrations would naturally assume the Saviour to be 'a glutton, an epicure, a wine-bibber, a devil, a friend of publicans and sinners', and expresses the view that Christmas as observed at the time would be more appropriately labelled Devil's mass or Saturn's mass!

Looking back from the comfort of the present day, this Puritan ranting may appear amusing, but the short-term consequences of such extremism were anything but. Calamity was about to befall King, country and Christmas.

Crisis for King, Country and Christmas. The banning of Christmas under the Commonwealth

In 1637 there were riots in Scotland following Charles I's imposition of what were seen as 'popish' reforms, most notably the forced introduction into the Scottish Kirk of the Book of Common Prayer. Opposition north of the border hardened and massive public protest led to the petition known as the Great Covenant. Charles recalled Parliament to raise the funds necessary to send an army north of the border, but instead of granting him the required cash Parliament countered with a series of demands that led to the dismantling of the principle of absolute royal power, including the removal of the King's right to dissolve Parliament. Relations between king and Parliament continued to deteriorate, leading in 1642 to the outbreak of the Civil War that would see the capture and execution of the king. Oliver Cromwell's Puritan-inspired parliament declared the 'Commonwealth and Free State of England', within which there would be no place for the monarchy, the House of Lords, the Church of England, or Christmas.

Puritan opposition to Christmas was two-pronged: on the one hand it was part of a part of a wider campaign that sought to rid the country of popish festivals, on the other it sought to end the excessive and immoral seasonal celebrations that were considered pagan. In other words, it was justified as an attack on both Rome and Satan. In contrast, Royalist supporters saw Christmas as an important and traditional symbol of the very English identity that their enemies were seeking to destroy. In spite of the wider political agenda, which most would agree concerned matters rather more critical to the national interest than the future of Christmas, an extraordinary amount of propaganda was circulated in support of, or opposition to, the festive season. In retrospect, this can be seen as clear evidence of the importance of Christmas in contemporary society.

There was a wide range of opinion about Christmas amongst Puritans. Some opposed it vehemently while others simply turned a blind eye; a few may even have continued to celebrate it behind closed doors. Amongst the hard-liners, the very word 'Christmas' was to be avoided due to its incorporation of the Popish term 'mass'; if it had to labelled at all then 'Christ-tide' was considered a more appropriate and acceptable term.

In Scotland, the Presbyterians had succeeded in banning Christmas back in 1583, and although this ban had been overturned by order of King James in 1618, this order had been set aside in 1638, so that Christmas was once again officially prohibited. Scottish Presbyterians demanded that Parliament should also ban Christmas in England, and although their demands were not initially heeded, they stubbornly refused to give up the cause. It was traditional for the final Wednesday in each month to be a day of fast, and in 1644 December 25 fell on a Wednesday; Parliament thus decreed that Christmas Day that year should also be a day of fast and penance. However, the law seems to have been widely flouted, and those who wished to celebrate Christmas apparently did so pretty much as normal. In the following year, 1645, the Book of Common Prayer was replaced with the Presbyterian Directory of Public Prayer, and the religious celebration of Christmas was banned. One contemporary observer recorded what must have been a popular attitude amongst less religious members of society: 'Oh blessed Reformation! The church doors all shut, and the tavern doors all open!'

Whatever one might think of its attitude towards Christmas, the Cromwellian Parliament did at least lead by example. *The Kingdome's Weekly Messenger*, a government newspaper, recorded in 1645 that on 'Thursday, Decemb. 25, vulgarly known by the name of Christmas Day, both Houses sate'. Indeed, parliament sat every Christmas Day from 1644 through to 1656.

This was a time when developments in printing technology encouraged the production and wide distribution of numerous pamphlets espousing all manner of causes; many were published in support of Christmas, while others opposed it. It was also a time when newspapers became popular. The City of London newspaper, *Mercurius Civicus*, urged its readers to disregard the nonsense of Christmas-keeping, observing in passing that Jesus was probably born in September rather than December, and quoting the opinion of an unnamed late minister that 'God did conceal the time when Christ was borne, upon the same reason that He tooke away the body of Moses, that they might not put an holinesse upon that day'. The paper went on to suggest that if people wanted a holiday, 'let them keep the fifth of November'!

In contrast, the rank absurdity of the attempt to ban Christmas is splendidly illustrated by *The Complaint of Christmas*, written in 1646 by John Taylor:

All the liberty and harmless sports, the merry gambols, dances and friscols, with which the toiling ploughman and labourer once a year were wont to be recreated, and their spirits and hopes revived for a whole twelvemonth, are now extinct and put out of use, in such a fashion as if they never had been. Thus are the merry lords of bad rule at Westminster; nay, more, their madness hath extended itself to the very vegetables; senseless trees, herbs, and weeds, are in a profane estimation amongst them - holly, ivy, mistletoe, rosemary, bays, are accounted ungodly branches of superstition for your entertainment. And to roast a sirloin of beef, to touch a collar of brawn, to take a pie, to put a plum in the pottage pot, to burn a great candle, or to lay one block the more in the fire for your sake, Master Christmas, is enough to make a man to be suspected and taken for a Christian, for which he shall be apprehended for committing high Parliament Treason ...

Parliament seems only to have been spurred on by all such argument in support of Christmas, passing in June 1647 'An Ordinance for Abolishing of Festivals':

> Forasmuch as the Feasts of the Nativity of Christ, Easter, and Whitsuntide, and other Festivals commonly called Holy-Days, have been heretofore superstitiously used and observed. Be it Ordained, by the Lords and Commons in Parliament assembled, that the said Feast of the Nativity of Christ, Easter and Whitsuntide, and all the other Festival days, commonly called Holy-Days, be no longer observed as Festivals or Holy-Days within this Kingdom of England Dominion of Wales.

The free time previously enjoyed by certain employees on these days was now to be enjoyed on the second Tuesday in the month, and was on no account to be associated with any religious festival. Christmas was now illegal, both as a religious festival and as a secular holiday, and town criers were sent out in December to warn citizens that it was not to be celebrated. Puritan politicians were very much aware of the widespread popularity of Christmas at the time, but were convinced that it must be done away with on moral grounds. Richard Kentish, a member of parliament, observed at the time that 'The people of England do hate to be reformed ... these poor simple people are mad after superstitious festivals, after unholy holidays'.

Unholy or otherwise, the people were understandably fond of their holidays, and there was considerable opposition from both the Church and the general public to the banning of Christmas. Some churches attempted to hold services, justifying their position to the authorities by stating that it was better for people to spend time in church than in the taverns! Several London churches put up seasonal evergreen decorations in time-honoured fashion, only to have them forcibly removed; in 1647, the parish officers of St Margaret's, Westminster, were arrested and fined for allowing Christmas Day services and for decorating the church with rosemary and bays. There were many public protests in London and elsewhere, most notably in Canterbury, where several days of mass rioting included the 'rescuing' of some protesters from gaol. According to a contemporary account, the Canterbury town crier proclaimed on Wednesday 22 December

Aerial view of Stonehenge, looking from the direction of the midwinter sunset over the stones and along the Avenue towards the position of the midsummer rising sun (© Skyscan Balloon Photography. Source: English Heritage Photo Library)

Winter solstice sunset at Stonehenge, 1975
(© Keith Cooper: www.northlight-images.co.uk)

Long Meg with some of her 'Daughters'

Right: Mysterious
carvings on Long Meg

Below: Winter solstice
sunset at Long Meg,
2006

Above: Aerial view of Newgrange

Below: The beautifully decorated 'entrance stone' at Newgrange, behind which is the entrance to the passage and, above this, the 'roofbox'

(Images reproduced by courtesy of the Department of the Environment, Heritage and Local Government, Dublin)

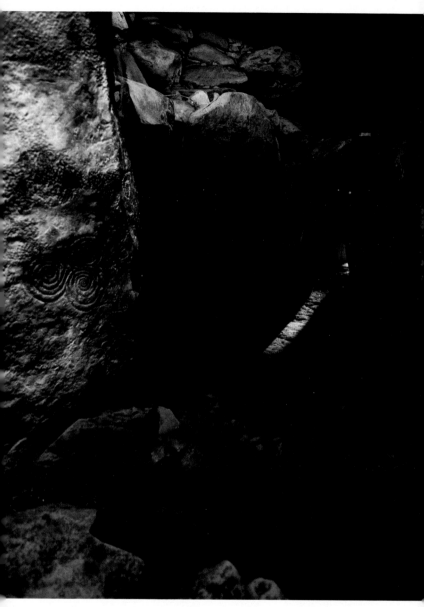

A shaft of light from the rising sun reaches the central chamber of
Newgrange at the winter solstice (Image reproduced by courtesy of
the Department of the Environment, Heritage and Local Government,
Dublin)

Above: General view of Maes Howe

Left: Looking along the entrance passage from within the chamber of Maes Howe towards the position of the setting sun at the winter solstice

Balnuaran of Clava north-east passage grave
Above: The setting sun at the winter solstice, 1998, seen from within the chamber (© Tim Phillips)
Below: A shaft of sunlight from the setting sun dramatically illuminates the chamber at the winter solstice, 1999 (© Ronnie Scott)

The Nativity has inspired many great works of art over the centuries

Above: *Adoration of the Shepherds* (detail) by Hugo van der Goes, 1430

Opposite, above: *The Adoration of the Magi* by Fra Filippo Lippi and Fra Angelico, *c.*1450
Opposite, below: *The Flight into Egypt* by Vittore Carpaccio, *c.*1515

A second- or third-century AD marble relief from Rome showing Mithras performing the tauroctony, now in the Louvre

The third-century Mithraeum at Brocolitia on Hadrian's Wall, where services celebrating the birth of Mithras were presumably held on 25 December each year

Above: Illustration
from *The Vindication of
Christmas*, a pamphlet
published in 1653. The
central figure is Old
Father Christmas

Right: *The Feast of St
Nicholas* by Jan Steen,
c.1665

Thomas Nast's illustration of Santa Claus, complete with sleigh and reindeer, entertaining Union troops during the American Civil War. From *Harper's Weekly*, 3 January 1863

Merry Old Santa Claus by Thomas Nast. From *Harper's Weekly*, 1 January 1881

Scrooge and the Ghost of Christmas Present. Illustration by John Leech for Charles Dickens' *A Christmas Carol* (1843)

The world's first Christmas card, published in 1843. This copy is signed by Henry Cole, the man who commissioned it

A flowery Christmas card from the 1890s and one from *c.*1908 featuring Santa Claus
(All three cards reproduced by courtesy of Vivian Krug of Emotions Greeting Cards: www.EmotionsCards.com)

Queen Victoria and family around the royal Christmas tree at
Windsor Castle, 1848

British and German troops fraternise in no-man's land during the 1914 Christmas truce (Photograph by Harold Robson. Reproduced by courtesy of the Imperial War Museum, London. Negative No. Q50719)

This cartoon appeared anonymously on the internet in 2006 and was widely used for electronic Christmas cards in 2007. Usually referred to as *The Chavtivity*, it has also appeared under the titles *A Glasgow Nativity Scene* and *Nativity in Crawley*

The front cover of *Private Eye*, Christmas 2006 (Reproduced by kind permission of *PRIVATE EYE*/Robert Thompson)

1647 that 'Christmas Day and all other superstitious festivals should be put downe, and that a Market should be kept upon Christmas day', whereupon the people rose in revolt and 'continued in arms till Tuesday morning: There are none as yet dead, but diverse dangerously hurt ... Master Sheriffe ... striving to keep the Peace, was knockt down, and his head fearfully broke'. Following this, 10,000 men from Kent passed a resolution that 'if they could not have their Christmas Day, they would have the King back on his throne'.

The debate was maintained within pamphlets and newspapers published by both sides. Royalist writers tended to exaggerate the decline in Christmas as representative of the generally declining situation since the loss of the king. *Mercurius Democritus* noted in 1652 that 'Old Christmas now is come to town, though few do him regard'. There must still, however, have been much support for Christmas, as that same year Parliament again considered it necessary to debate 'AntiChrist's-masse, and those Masse-mongers and Papists who observe it'. On Christmas Eve that year, it was decreed that December 25 would from now on be treated as a normal day, with no celebration to be held either in church or elsewhere. All shops and markets were to trade as normal, with the offer of protection from possible protesters. Not surprisingly, this new law met with immediate opposition, increasingly supported by a symbolic 'Old Father Christmas' who became something of spokesman for the Royalist cause, appearing in numerous propaganda pamphlets, contrasting the austere and miserable piety of the Puritans with the fun-filled Christmases of 'the good old days'. One such pamphlet, entitled *The Vindication of Christmas*, features a cartoon of Old Father Christmas announcing 'Sir, I bring good cheer', to which a Puritan replies 'Keep out, you come not here', while a supporter says 'Old Christmas welcome; do not fear.' Within the pamphlet, Old Father Christmas states 'But welcome, or not welcome, I am come' and gives an account of a fine Christmas he had just enjoyed with some Devon farmers:

> After dinner we arose from the boord, and sate by the fire, where the harth was imbrodered all over with roasted apples, piping hot, expecting a bole of ale for a cooler, which immediately was transformed into warm lambwool. After which we discoursed merily, without either prophaness or obscenity; some went to cards: others sang carols and pleasant songs (suitable to the times); then the poor labouring hinds, and maidservants, with the plow-boys, went nimbly to dancing; the poor toyling wretches being glad of

my company, because they had little or no sport at all till I came amongst them; and therefore they skipped and leaped for joy, singing a carol … early in the morning, I took my leave of them, promising they should have my presence again the next 25th December, 1653.

In practice, there seems to have been a large degree of tolerance on the part of the authorities, but this varied from place to place. Away from London, there are records of Christmas celebrations including carol singing, dancing and feasting, and even in London it proved difficult for the authorities to force shops to open. In a parliamentary debate on Christmas Day, 1656, one contributor observed that he had not slept the previous night on account of 'the preparation of this foolish day's solemnity', while another noted that it was possible to walk from the Tower of London to Westminster without a single shop being open and with hardly a soul to be seen on the streets. Interestingly, it was noted during this debate that there were many absentees from the House; surely members of parliament could not be at home celebrating Christmas? The evidence sometimes appears contradictory, but in practice, although the bans on church services and public entertainment were sometimes enforced by the authorities, most people in London and throughout the country seem to have had the option of celebrating Christmas peacefully in private.

Most Puritan leaders had more pressing issues to address than the fate of Christmas, and many were not particularly concerned about it. However, the hardliners continued to call for a total ban. One such fanatic, Hezekiah Woodward, published a pamphlet in 1656 with the rather long-winded but unequivocal title of:

> Christ-Mas Day, The old Heathens feasting Day, in honour to Saturn their Idol-God, The Papists Massing Day, The Prophane man's Ranting Day, The Superstitious man's Idol Day. The Multitudes Idle Day, Satans, That Adversarys Working-Day, The True Christian Mans Feasting Day. Taking to Heart, the Heathenish Customes, Popish Superstitions, Ranting Fashions, Fearful Provocations, Horrible Abominations, committed against the Lord, and His Christ, on that Day, and days following.

Despite such extremist views, it is clear that some people continued to ignore the law and attend Christmas Day services. It is not known how widespread such services were, but the diarist, John Evelyn, provides a dramatic account of one on Christmas Day 1657, which was raided by troops:

> I went with my wife, etc. to London to celebrate Christmas Day. Mr Gunning preaching in Exeter Chapel … as he was giving us the Holy Sacrament, the chapel was surrounded with soldiers: all the communicants and assembly surprised and kept prisoners by them, some in the house, others carried away … These wretched miscreants held their muskets against us as we came up to receive the Sacred Elements, as if they would have shot us at the altar, but yet suffering us to finish the office of communion, as perhaps not in their instructions.

After a lengthy period of interrogation Evelyn records that the soldiers found no basis on which to detain him and 'dismissed me with much pity of my ignorance'.

While it was possible to prevent people from attending church, it was much more difficult for the authorities to deprive the people of their Christmas dinner. In a pamphlet published in 1652, a leading anti-Christmas campaigner was accused of preaching against the concept of Christmas Day before returning home to his dinner of two traditionally festive mince pies! At Christmas 1655, Bishop Duppra observed that 'though the religious part of this holy time is laid aside, yet the eating part is observed by the holiest of the brethren'.

At Christmas 1657, the last of Cromwell's life, he was reputedly asked to send soldiers 'to repress some Congregations being met to observe this day, according to former solemnity'. This he initially refused to do (although he had authorised such activity many times in the past), on the basis that preventing people commemorating Christmas would be contrary to the 'Liberty of Conscience' for which he claimed great fondness – nevertheless, the soldiers were eventually sent and the congregation dispersed. Cromwell's professed vision of parliamentary liberty was not, in the end, compatible with his religious ideals, and certainly not with his views on Christmas.

Michael Harrison observes in *The Story of Christmas*, that 'Christmas, indeed has never known a bitterer enemy, since King Herod, than Oliver Cromwell; but Christmas has outlasted both.' By 1660, the Cromwellian experiment was over. The throne was again occupied by a monarch and Christmas was back. However, it seems never to have been quite the same; as we will see, Christmas after the

Restoration was in many ways a rather more subdued affair than it had been prior to the Civil War. Cromwell and his colleagues may actually have succeeded to quite a considerable extent in their desire to quash, once and for all, the extravagances of the old medieval Christmas. But Christmas, albeit perhaps slightly less gaudily clad, would soon bounce back!

The Return of Christmas. Christmas after the Restoration

Along with the return of the king came the return of Christmas. Charles II acceded to the thrones of England, Scotland and Ireland in May 1660, and people were again free to celebrate Christmas without the threat of prosecution. Charles was a great pleasure-seeker and, in stark contrast to the dour Puritans, was adamant that God would not 'damn a man for a little irregular pleasure'. Parliament reaffirmed the Supremacy of the Church of England, though the king himself supported religious freedom for all. As it happened, debate between Catholic and Protestant would have little effect on the celebration of Christmas, as both Churches continued to regard it as a key festival in the religious calendar. A popular eighteenth-century Church of England manual, written by Robert Nelson, stated that one of the ways in which people could express their gratitude for the Incarnation was through the provision of charity to those worse off than themselves. It also observed that being poor was not something to be ashamed of, 'since the blessed Jesus chose to be born in so mean and obscure a manner, and preferred it before the splendour and pomp of the rich or great.' Despite the best endeavours of the Church of England, however, church attendance at Christmas was now on the decline. There were many Dissenters within society who were influenced by Puritan ideals and refused to acknowledge Christmas, some of whom continued to campaign actively against it, denouncing everything to do with it as pagan and Popish. The Dissenters refused to accept Christmas as a holiday season and, as a matter of principle, opened their shops and businesses as usual on Christmas Day. Many others, while not so vocal in their protests, had varying degrees of sympathy for the Puritan cause and opted to celebrate Christmas quietly at home, if at all. The Methodists were notable exceptions to this general rule, with Wesley himself a supporter of Christmas. Services were held in Methodist chapels on Christmas Day throughout the eighteenth and nineteenth centuries.

Religious services after the Restoration, if rather less well attended than previously, seem to have resumed in much the same manner as before the Civil War, but the exuberance of the court festivities under Charles II and his successors would never approach that of pre-Commonwealth monarchs. Plays, masques and pageants were gradually abandoned and William Sandys observes that court festivities became reduced to 'the form of a mere state party.' However, these 'mere state parties' could still be impressive events, and within society at large, while it is fair to say that the great communal festive celebrations of earlier times were destined never to return, Christmas did just about manage to retain its status as the main annual holiday season. Whereas the Cromwellian Parliament sat on Christmas Day every year, Parliament in post-Restoration times observed the Twelve Days as a holiday, as did the universities, schools and law courts. That said, there was a general acceptance amongst writers on the subject that the festival was in decline. The reasons for this were partly religious, following the decline in influence of the Catholic Church, but also partly economic and social, as industrial development saw the gradual breakdown of the old, medieval social structure. However, we should not exaggerate this decline, as for many people, whether or not they regarded themselves as religious, Christmas remained a time for great celebration. Certainly, in the immediate aftermath of the Restoration there were many who rejoiced in their newfound freedom to enjoy Christmas, as demonstrated by verses from a ballad entitled *Merry Boys of Christmas*, written for the first festive season after Charles II's accession:

Then here's a health to Charles our King,
    throughout the world admir'd,
Let us his great applauses sing,
    that we so much desir'd,
And wisht amongst us for to reign,
    when Oliver rul'd here,
But since he's home return'd again,
    come fill some Christmas Beer.

These holidays we'l briskly drink,
    all mirth we will devise,
No Treason we will speak or think,
    then bring us brave minc'd pies
Roast Beef and brave Plum porridge,
    our Loyal hearts to chear,

Then prithee make no more ado,
  but bring us Christmas Beer.

Samuel Pepys records that Charles II visited Lincoln's Inn during
the Christmas revels of 1661, noting that these included 'according
to an old tradition, a Prince and all his nobles, and other matters
of sport and charge'. However, despite several attempts that varied
in intensity from year to year, the great Christmas festivals at the
Inns of Court were now in terminal decline and the Prince of Fools
(or Master of Revels) and the grand Christmas masque had all but
disappeared by the end of the seventeenth century.

An insight into the popularity of Christmas amongst the great
majority of the people may be gleaned from the pages of *Poor Robin's
Almanac*, published annually from 1662. Almanacs, mass-produced
using newly developed printing technology and sold for as little
as tuppence, were very popular from this time through into the
nineteenth century. They generally included astrology, including
horoscopes for the year ahead, along with all sorts of other material.
Poor Robin's Almanac (published anonymously but attributed to the
well-known author Robert Winstanley of Quendon and Saffron
Walden, and continued by others after his death) took a popular and
irreverent attitude towards astrology and proved extremely popular
from the start, its first issue selling an estimated 7000 copies. It was
always very supportive of Christmas and over the years included
many verses about the festive season which, while not necessarily
qualifying as high-quality literature, certainly do give us a flavour
of the contemporary festive season. It is tempting to give many
examples, but two must suffice. The first is from 1685:

Now thanks to God for Charles' return,
  Whose absence made old Christmas mourn,
  For then we scarcely did it know,
  Whether it Christmas were or no

To feast the poor was counted sin,
  When treason that great praise did win
  May we ne'er see the like again,
  The roguish Rump should o'er us reign.

And for the first Christmas of the eighteenth century, reference
to the Nativity is merged with the discussion of festive food and
charity:

Now that the time has come wherein
Our Saviour Christ was born,
The larder's full of beef and pork,
The granary's full of corn,
As God hath plenty to thee sent,
Take comfort of thy labours,
And let it never thee repent
To feed thy needy neighbours.

An interesting account of Christmas Day aboard an English warship, recorded by the ship's chaplain, the Revd Henry Teonge, is worthy of inclusion here as it demonstrates the exuberant nature of celebrations where one might not necessarily have expected to encounter them:

Dec 25, 1675. Crismas Day wee keepe thus: At four in the morning our trumpeters all doe flatt their trumpetts, and begin at our captain's cabin, and thence to all the officers' and gentlemen's cabins; playing a levite at each cabine door, and bidding good morrow, wishing a merry Crismas. After they goe to their station, viz. on the poope, and sound three levitts in honour of the morning. At ten we goe to prayers and sermon; text, Zacc. ix, 9. Our captaine had all his officers and gentlemen to dinner with him, where wee had excellent good fayre: a ribb of beefe, plumb-puddings, minct pyes, &c., and plenty of good wines of severall sorts; dranke healths to the king, to our wives and friends, and ended the day with much civill myrth.

It is perhaps fortunate that this particular ship was not called into action over the festive season.

Many popular ballads of the late seventeenth and early eighteenth centuries, including some penned by Poor Robin, bemoan the decline in Christmas feasting since before the Civil War, but there can be no doubt that the spirit of the Christmas feast was maintained within many private houses throughout the eighteenth century. Sir John Reresby of Thrybergh, Yorkshire, records that at Christmas 1682, between Christmas Eve and Epiphany, he provided festive fare for no less than 144 local tenants and farmers, 40 local gentlemen and traders, and half a dozen local clergymen. He notes that 'the expense of liquor, both of wine and others, was considerable, as of other provisions, and my friends appeared well satisfied'. Two years later he had even more guests, with about 80 dining with him each day and some 300 on New Year's day, when 'whole sheep were roasted and served up to feed them'. Reresby noted festive music was provided by violins, bagpipes, drums and trumpets.

A few years later, on 28 December 1712, Lord Fermanagh of Buckinghamshire wrote 'I wish you were here to see the spits and cups go round; I have already killed two oxen this week and a few sheep, and of poultry we keep no reckoning'. He had 400 guests each day over the Twelve Days, and noted that it had been a troublesome and tiresome time due in part to the vast expense and the noise of drums, trumpets, pipes and fiddles.

The hospitality of Reresby and Lord Fermanagh was a throwback to medieval times, when landowners were obliged to provide festive fare and entertainment for their tenants and others. By this time, however, such festive hospitality was becoming ever rarer as the years went by; Reresby noted that few others in Yorkshire observed the season as he did, and *Poor Robin's Almanac* for 1701 suggests that few poor people elsewhere received comparable festive hospitality from their local gentry:

> But the times are grown so bad
> Scarce one dish for the poor is had;
> Good housekeeping is laid aside,
> And all is spent to maintain pride;
> Good works are counted popish, and
> Small charity is in the land.
> A man may sooner (truth I tell ye)
> Break his own neck than fill his belly.
> Good God amend what is amiss
> And send a remedy to this,
> That Christmas day again may rise
> And we enjoy our Christmas pies.

Despite such concerns, an article in the *London Magazine* in 1754 observed that Christmas continued to be 'held sacred by eating and drinking'. A good example of a mid eighteenth-century Christmas dinner is provided in the following contribution made to *Read's Weekly Journal* of 9 January 1731 by Mr Thomas North, outlining the festive fare he enjoyed at the home of a friend in London:

> … I assure you I should have taken this dinner to have been provided for a whole parish, rather than for about a dozen gentlemen: 'Tis

impossible for me to give you half our bill of fare, so you must be content to know that we had turkies, geese, capons, puddings of a dozen sorts more than I had ever seen in my life, besides brawn, roast beef, and many things of which I know not the names, minc'd pyes in abundance, and a thing they call plumb pottage, which may be good for ought I know, though it seems to me to have fifty different tastes. Our wines were of the best, as were all the rest of our liquors; in short, the God of plenty seemed to reign here, and to make everything perfect, our company was polite and every way agreeable; nothing but mirth and loyal healths went round.

J.A.R. Pimlott notes that it was during the eighteenth century that Christmas dinner assumed its modern pattern, with mince pies, plum pudding and roast beef, turkey, goose or chicken. Cesar de Saussure in *A Foreign View of England in the Reigns of George I and George II* (1728) observes that 'everyone from the King to the artisan eats soup and Christmas pies. The soup is called Christmas-porridge, and is a dish few foreigners find to their taste.' Christmas porridge (or plum porridge) was a kind of beef broth thickened with bread and flavoured with prunes, raisins, currants, wines and spices. Staple Christmas fare during the eighteenth century, it had pretty much given way to Christmas pudding (plum pudding) by 1800. There were two kinds of pies specifically associated with Christmas. Mince pies, usually eaten at the start of the meal, were already of considerable antiquity by the eighteenth century. They were rectangular in shape and were said to represent the manger at the Nativity. Consequently, many Puritans regarded them as 'popish' and refused to eat them; the humble mince pie thus became a test of religious opinion. An early eighteenth-century recipe lists the ingredients for mince pies as 'neats' [cattle] tongues, chicken, eggs, sugar, currants, lemon and orange peel, with various spices'. As well as the mince pie, the Christmas pie was very popular, especially in northern England. Sandys describes this as 'composed of turkeys, geese, game, and various small birds, weighing sometimes half a hundred weight and upwards, and calculated to meet the attacks of a large Christmas party throughout the festival.' Pimlott notes that a Christmas pie weighing over 200lbs and containing, amongst other things, four turkeys and four geese, was consumed at a public dinner in Chester in 1811.

Dawson makes extensive reference to a little book entitled *Round about our Coal Fire, or Christmas Entertainments*, published in 1740, which gives an insight into festive celebrations during the reign of

George II. This observes that 'the manner of celebrating this great course of Holydays is vastly different now to what it was in former days', noting:

> The Geese which used to be fatted for the honest Neighbours, have been of late sent to London, and the Quills made into Pens to convey away the Landlord's Estate ... The News-Papers however inform us, that the Spirit of Hospitality has not quite forsaken us; for three or four of them tell us, that several of the Gentry are gone down to their respective Seats in the Country, in order to keep their Christmas in the Old Way, and entertain their Tenants and Trades-folks as their Ancestors used to do and I wish them a merry Christmas accordingly.

The implication that the season is in decline is again clear. However, the above account is followed by a discussion of festive entertainment, including dancing, mumming, cards and dice, storytelling, and games such as blindman's buff, forfeits and hide-and-seek. Mumming seems to have been a very popular form of entertainment throughout Britain from the early eighteenth century through into the early twentieth. Although some authorities claim that the classic mummers plays of this time have ancient pagan roots, this cannot be proved. Steve Roud, in *The English Year* (which includes much fascinating background about traditional customs and festivals) suggests that the popular nineteenth-century mummers' plays featuring characters such as Father Christmas, St George, the Turkish Knight and Dr Brown, have origins that stretch back no further than the early eighteenth century. Most villages throughout the land had their own mummers that performed at various times of the year, although Christmas performances were especially popular. These were often presented by 'Father Christmas', who introduced himself with a verse such as:

> In comes I, Old Father Christmas
> Am I welcome or am I not?
> I hope Old Father Christmas
> Will never be forgot.

Another curious custom that seems to have been in place during the eighteenth century, especially in Ireland but also in parts of England, is the Boxing Day 'wren hunt'. This involved the killing of a wren that was then carried around the village before being buried in the churchyard. As it was carried from house to house, the following verse was sung:

> The wren, the wren, the king of the birds
> St Stephen's Day was killed in the furze.
> Although he be little, his honour is great
> And so, good people, pray give us a treat.

The origins of this peculiar custom are unknown, and exactly why the wren should have been considered the king of the birds is something of a mystery; perhaps it is simply another example of 'role-reversal' at Christmas. The wren hunt seems to have died out in England by 1900, but was still practised in parts of Ireland into the twentieth century.

We will now briefly consider the nature of festive gift-giving between the Restoration and the accession of Victoria. Pimlott notes that the obligation to give presents based on official relationships all but died out during the eighteenth century. For example, at the very top of the tree, Charles II received many presents from his peers, but by the time of George III the expectation of such gifts had passed. In the seventeenth century it was the custom for judges to receive festive gifts from lawyers, but this practice was ended in the early eighteenth century as it was thought, not entirely without reason, to offer potential for indiscretion. Pimlott suggests that for most people during the eighteenth century gifts were probably in the form of produce and home-made articles. As the century progressed, however, more and more advertisements appeared featuring Christmas or New Year gifts such as jewellery and books, many of which were aimed at children as businesses sought to exploit the seasonal market. The commercialisation of Christmas, often regarded as a recent phenomenon, thus compares to most of our festive traditions in having rather ancient origins.

Back in Chapter 1 we observed that the Gregorian calendar was introduced to England in 1752; here we must note the impact this had on Christmas. The discrepancy between the old Julian calendar (within which December 25 was originally the date of the solstice) and the actual length of a year was such that the calendar found itself a full 10 days in advance of the seasons by the sixteenth century. This was solved by the introduction of the Gregorian calendar, whereby, by Papal edict, Thursday 4 October 1582 was followed immediately by Friday 15 October, and the leap year rule was tweaked so that years divisible by 100 would not now be leap years unless they were also divisible by 400 (thus the years 1600 and 2000 were leap years, while 1700, 1800 and 1900 were not). This brought the calendar back into line with the seasons, and ensured that future discrepancies between the two would be a mere 25.9 seconds each year, or one day in 2800 years. The Gregorian calendar that we take for granted today was soon adopted throughout Catholic countries, but would not be adopted by some non-Catholic nations until well into the twentieth century. In Protestant England, after two centuries of debate and confusion during which international traders and others had to maintain two calendars simultaneously and the French philosopher, Voltaire, amusingly observed that 'the English prefer their calendar to disagree with the sun than to agree with the Pope', the Gregorian calendar was finally adopted in 1752. By this time there was a need to lose 11 days, so the evening of Wednesday 2 September 1752 was followed by dawn on Thursday 14 September. This decision resulted in serious public riots as people complained about the theft of 11 days and blamed the Catholic Church, but things could have been much worse: Flanders had switched to the Gregorian calendar on 21 December 1582, meaning that the following 10 days were lost and all Belgians thus deprived of their Christmas!

The introduction of the Gregorian calendar was generally smooth, but there were some within society who refused to accept it and insisted on keeping Christmas on the 'correct' day which was now 6 January. This caused a degree of confusion, not least because, as we have seen, 6 January was already celebrated within the Church as the day of the Epiphany, and within society at large as Twelfth Day, marking the end of the festive season. In some places, services were held on 'Old Christmas Day' and people insisted on waiting until then to enjoy their Christmas dinners. Dawson gives one example, where an 'Old Christmas Day' sermon was preached for a congregation determined to celebrate the Nativity on that day; the minister, however, refused to use the official Christmas Day service and instead addressed the congregation with regard to the need for the new calendar. According to one observer, the Glastonbury Thorn, which as we have seen was thought to have grown from the staff of Joseph of Arimathea and to flower at Christmas in honour of the Lord, 'contemptuously ignored the new style and burst into blossom on 5 January, thus indicating that Old Christmas Day alone should be observed, in spite of an irreligious legislature'.

Despite such objections to the new calendar, Christmas celebrations were simply transferred to the 'new' 25 December in

1752, where they have remained, for the vast majority of people, ever since. We should note, however, that two isolated communities in the furthest reaches of the United Kingdom continue to celebrate 'Old Christmas' to this day. The *Sunday Post* on 7 January 2007 reports that communities on two of the Shetland Islands, Foula and Unst, continue to celebrate 'Auld Yule' on 6 January. All four children on Foula open their presents on this day; they are aware that people elsewhere celebrate on 25 December, but are told that Santa has to return to the North Pole to refill his sleigh before delivering their presents. A Foula resident explains that 'Auld Yule is very important to Foula's identity – it's just part of what we do here. They didn't change it in the 1700s and it won't be changed now.' People on Unst seem to have the best of both worlds, celebrating 'New Christmas' on 25 December as a family festival, followed by 'Auld Yule', a more communal affair, on 6 January.

Most people in England continued to enjoy Christmas as a holiday throughout the eighteenth century, and many continued to attend church on Christmas Day, but the sense that the festival was in decline is nevertheless clear from many late eighteenth-century sources. For example, in 1774, David Garrick introduced Old Father Christmas within his popular play *A Tale of Christmas* with the words 'Behold a personage well known to fame, once loved and honoured, Christmas is my name'. A few years later, in 1790, *The Times* reported that 'within the last half century this annual time of festivity has lost much of its original mirth and hospitality'. By the early nineteenth century, economic and social circumstances had conspired to ensure that few people still celebrated the full Twelve Days as most had done a century earlier, but Christmas Day itself was still enjoyed as a holiday by the vast majority. It was not, however, particularly newsworthy; between 1790 and the accession of Victoria in 1837, 20 Christmases received no coverage whatsoever within *The Times*, while others enjoyed no more than brief mention. The late eighteenth and early nineteenth centuries may be regarded as a quiet phase in our story of Christmas, but the season was soon to find itself rejuvenated and relaunched in spectacular fashion.

6

Santa Claus and the Invention of the 'Traditional' Christmas

Prior to the accession of Victoria in 1837, no-one in Britain had heard of Santa Claus, had sent or received a Christmas card, or had pulled a Christmas cracker; few ate Turkey for Christmas dinner, and hardly anyone outside the royal family had ever seen a Christmas tree. By the end of the Victorian era, in the early twentieth century, these were all accepted aspects of our 'traditional' Christmas, celebrated as a major festival throughout most of the western world. This chapter will explain how these developments occurred, and will consider the extent to which the Victorians actually 'invented' the traditional Christmas rather than merely repackaging and updating a number of already ancient traditions.

'Twas the night before Christmas. The saga of Santa Claus

Today, everyone knows that Santa lives in Lapland, if not actually at the North Pole. His origins, however, lie not in the Arctic, but in the Mediterranean. 'Santa Claus' is a corruption of St Nicholas, traditionally thought to have lived from AD 280-352 (although his dates are far from certain). The earliest reference we have for this character dates from the late sixth century, and refers to him only in passing as St Nicholas of Myra. Myra (known today as Demre) lies 5km inland from the Mediterranean coast of southern Turkey and in St Nicholas' time was the capital of the extensive and prosperous Roman province of Lycia, linked to the Mediterranean world through the nearby harbour of Andriake. In post-Roman times the region was hit hard by earthquakes, and the port of Andriake partly silted up through natural processes; the once grand city of Myra was largely abandoned and all but forgotten. However, a church, dating back at least as far as the early fifth century and containing the shrine of St Nicholas, survived and underwent a major restoration in the mid eleventh century. The focus for a small monastery in medieval times, this church survived, albeit in very poor condition, into the modern era. It was restored in the nineteenth century by the Russians, who had adopted St Nicholas as their patron saint. Following archaeological investigation of the church in the 1950s, Demre became widely known as the real home of Santa Claus. But what do we really know of St Nicholas, and how do we know that he is ultimately the same person as Santa? The full story has recently been presented in Jeremy Seal's excellent *Santa, a Life*, the main source for the following summary.

Other than the brief sixth-century reference mentioned above, our earliest sources relating to the life of St Nicholas date from the ninth century, half a millennium after his death. Sources such as these, written exclusively by men of the Church based in monasteries, combined oral tradition with occasional earlier (and now lost) written sources – they cannot be treated as historically reliable, but for Nicholas they are all that we have.

Tales of St Nicholas have been told and retold over the centuries and exist in many variations, although there are a number of constant elements. He was apparently born into a wealthy family in Patara (adjacent to Myra) in about 280. He demonstrated remarkable knowledge of religious matters as a young child, becoming Bishop of Myra at a very young age (thus possibly providing the inspiration for the medieval 'boy bishop' tradition). On a pilgrimage to Egypt and Palestine he worked miracles to save ships from being wrecked on both outward and return journeys, on one occasion bringing a dead sailor back to life. In the most famous of the Nicholas stories, he saved a poor man's three daughters from lives of slavery or prostitution by anonymously providing gifts of gold to be used as dowries enabling them to be married – many people cite this story (incorrectly) as the origin of gift-giving at Christmas. In another tale, Nicholas brought back to life three boys who had been murdered by an innkeeper who had hidden their bodies in a barrel. He was imprisoned during the Emperor Diocletian's persecution of Christians, but released after the accession of the Christian emperor, Constantine, returning to his duties as Bishop of Myra until his death, traditionally thought to have occurred on 6 December 352.

The major centres of the ancient Mediterranean world were linked by sea, and harbours were always busy with traders and travellers. Prior to the introduction of Christianity, sailors visiting Andriake would visit the temples of Poseidon or Artemis to pray for safe passage on the next stage of their journey. As the ancient gods were forced into retirement by Christianity, their individual remits were appropriated by saints. St Nicholas assumed responsibility for the safe passage of travellers, and his shrine at Myra became a popular attraction for those visiting Andriake. Nicholas' fame spread rapidly from Myra throughout the Mediterranean world and churches were dedicated in his honour at most ports. The stories of the three poor daughters and the three murdered boys have much to do with Nicholas' later role as patron saint of children, while the miracles at sea influenced his adoption as the patron of sailors and travellers. For various reasons, all based ultimately on rather dubious legends, Nicholas has also been adopted as the patron saint of several towns and nations as well as archers, bakers, bankers, pawnbrokers, brewers, scholars and numerous other groups. Within the Church, he is probably the most popular of all the saints, with more church and chapel dedications throughout the world than any of the Apostles: there are some 500 churches of St Nicholas in England alone.

By the early sixth century, there was a church of St Nicholas in Constantinople, a great centre of Christendom since its foundation by Constantine in 326. Constantinople occupied a key location between Asia and Europe, and from here the cult of St Nicholas spread north into Russia and west into many regions of Europe. In Russia, Nicholas became supremely important and hundreds of churches were dedicated to him, beginning in Kiev in 882. In addition to the protection of travellers, his remit expanded to include responsibility for agriculture and protection from fire. His influence in Russia was greatly diminished by the Bolshevik Revolution of the early 1920s, when thousands of churches were closed and many of their priests murdered, while back in Myra, power passed from Christians to Muslims following the creation of the Turkish nation. Nicholas, however, was far from beaten, as his influence had long since expanded into many regions of Western Europe.

In the 1070s, the Normans had captured the strategic city of Bari, in south-east Italy, from the Byzantines. Bari's patron saint was the little known Sabianus, and the Normans decreed that this important city was deserving of a more influential patron. St Nicholas' bones still lay within his shrine back in Myra, which at the time lay within a disputed area being fought over by Turks and Christians. The Normans of Bari launched a daring mission in 1087, sending, apparently with the Pope's blessing, a small force to Myra to acquire Nicholas' relics. On reaching Myra, this raiding party broke into Nicholas' shrine, guarded at the time by just four monks, then rapidly returned to Bari with the saintly bones which were soon re-housed within the crypt of a magnificent new church, the Basilica di San Nicola. The crypt was consecrated by the Pope in 1089, and Nicholas' tomb survives there to this day.

From the late eleventh century, Bari became known as the Port of St Nicholas. It functioned as the main point of departure for many crusading armies en route to the Holy Land, and no doubt all departing armies took time to pray to St Nicholas for safe passage as they prepared to set sail. As the Crusaders returned home, the cult of St Nicholas was further boosted throughout much of Western Europe.

We should note that the Venetians also claim to have recovered Nicholas' relics from Myra in the eleventh century, and that they were housed within the Church of St Nicholas in Venice. The Venetians had an established history of acquiring saintly relics from elsewhere, but their claim to possess St Nicholas seems rather less plausible than that of Bari. Nevertheless, the Venetian claim ensured that St Nicholas was unique amongst medieval saints in having three separate shrines: Bari, Venice and Myra (where the original shrine remained in operation). In addition to the three shrines, several churches across medieval Europe claimed to possess sacred relics such as teeth, fingers and various bones of Nicholas, all of which represented foci for worship and had the power to enable miracles. However, as Protestantism gained popularity in the mid sixteenth century many churches were deprived of their saintly patron. It appeared that St Nicholas was doomed, and in England his feast day (6 December) was officially banned in 1541. However, Catholicism was by no means eradicated and a number of secret churches continued to operate throughout the Netherlands, including at least one dedicated to St Nicholas in Amsterdam.

By the late sixteenth century the feast of St Nicholas had been widely celebrated throughout Europe for perhaps half a millennium, and in some places it had become the custom for parents to give presents to their children on the eve of St Nicholas' day. In an apparent throwback to the story of the Three Daughters, children were encouraged to believe that these presents were from St Nicholas himself. Nicholas was traditionally said to ride a white horse while out delivering presents to the children, and was often accompanied by a fearsome helper whose role it was to establish how well behaved individual children had been over the previous 12 months as only good children could receive presents. The feast of St Nicholas was particularly popular in Holland, as demonstrated by the well-known mid seventeenth-century paintings of Jan Steen. St Nicholas may have been shunned by the Protestant Church, but he remained very popular in the secular world.

The popularity of St Nicholas spread to the New World with Spanish, Portuguese and Dutch seafarers who named many newly discovered places, for example on Haiti and on the coast of Florida, after him. In 1624, the Dutch ship, the *Unity*, arrived at the mouth of the Hudson River. Her passengers came not to trade as others had done before them, but to settle permanently in this unexplored region of the New World. They christened their settlement New Amsterdam, though it was destined to be renamed New York by the British. New Amsterdam in the seventeenth century was in many ways a tolerant place, with many Catholics amongst its diverse population, but St Nicholas seems to have been largely forgotten. Fortunately for him, however, some Dutch families continued to celebrate the eve of his feast day every 5 December, and this was sufficient to protect his memory from total oblivion. During the later seventeenth and eighteenth centuries, Nicholas was gradually revived by the Dutch as a symbol of their identity in face of the larger British and Irish communities. This St Nicholas was, however, more of an excuse for an annual party than a sacred religious icon (a modern analogy is perhaps provided by St Patrick's Day, celebrated in exuberant style by people of Irish extraction throughout the world).

So what was it that eventually led to St Nicholas' association with Christmas and his transformation into Santa Claus? Bizarrely, a major part of the answer lies in a work of fiction that was not even intended by its author to be taken seriously. Washington Irving's *History of New York from the Beginning of the World to the End of the Dutch Dynasty*, published in 1809 under the pseudonym Dietrich Knickerbocker, was a huge success and is a key factor in the transformation of St Nicholas into Santa Claus. Irving claimed that an ancient church to St Nicholas had existed in New Amsterdam but this is fiction; the earliest settlers set up congregational halls without saintly dedications. The fact that Dietrich Knickerbocker's *History of New York* was a work of fiction did little to detract from its influence amongst local people; it provided a much needed 'historical' context for the people of New York and was widely read.

Washington Irving's St Nicholas 'would often make his appearance, in his beloved city, of a hollyday afternoon, riding jollily among the tree-tops, or over the roofs of the houses, now and then drawing forth magnificent presents from his breeches pockets, and dropping them down the chimneys of his favourites.' While many aspects of this St Nicholas are rooted in ancient tradition, the 'riding over the rooftops' is new; this ability to fly, soon to become one of Santa Claus' defining characteristics, is something to which we will return shortly. We should not forget, though, that at this point St Nicholas still had nothing whatsoever to do with Christmas; his feast day remained 6 December and his presents were delivered the previous night.

St Nicholas was in competition in early nineteenth-century New York with two other mystical midwinter gift-bringers: the German 'Christkind' celebrated on 25 December and the Italian 'Befana' traditionally associated with the Epiphany on 6 January. A further tradition, dominant within English communities, was the exchanging of gifts on New Year's Day. Somehow, although his official feast day remained 6 December, St Nicholas found himself increasingly associated with New Year in early nineteenth-century New York, but this association would be short lived.

A decade after his *History of New York*, Washington Irving published *The Sketch Book* under the pseudonym Geoffrey Crayon. This included detailed descriptions of Christmas in England and although it also included a large helping of fiction, it would prove influential in the American adoption of the 'traditional' English Christmas. However, despite his major role in the transformation of St Nicholas into Santa Claus, and his love of Christmas as demonstrated by works such as *The Sketch Book*, Irving was not responsible for the development of the now unbreakable bond between Santa and Christmas. Responsibility for this lies largely with Clement Clark Moore, a professor of Oriental and Greek literature at Columbia College (now Columbia University). Despite several other publications of considerable academic substance, Moore's main claim to fame is a poem written for his children at Christmas 1822. Actually entitled *The Visit of Saint Nicholas*, but better known by its first line, *'Twas the night before Christmas,* this exercised considerable influence over the subsequent development of Santa Claus. Whatever its literary merit, it represents an important milestone in the evolution of Christmas and is also great fun, so is included here in full:

'Twas the night before Christmas, when all through the house
Not a creature was stirring, not even a mouse;
The stockings were hung by the chimney with care,

In hopes that St. Nicholas soon would be there;
The children were nestled all snug in their beds,
While visions of sugar-plums danced in their heads;
And mamma in her 'kerchief, and I in my cap,
Had just settled our brains for a long winter's nap,
When out on the lawn there arose such a clatter,
I sprang from the bed to see what was the matter.
Away to the window I flew like a flash,
Tore open the shutters and threw up the sash.
The moon on the breast of the new-fallen snow
Gave the lustre of mid-day to objects below,
When, what to my wondering eyes should appear,
But a miniature sleigh, and eight tiny reindeer,
With a little old driver, so lively and quick,
I knew in a moment it must be St. Nick.
More rapid than eagles his coursers they came,
And he whistled, and shouted, and called them by name;
'Now, Dasher! Now, Dancer! Now, Prancer and Vixen!
On, Comet! On, Cupid! On, Donder and Blitzen!
To the top of the porch! To the top of the wall!
Now dash away! Dash away! Dash away all!'
As dry leaves that before the wild hurricane fly,
When they meet with an obstacle, mount to the sky;
So up to the house-top the coursers they flew,
With the sleigh full of Toys, and St. Nicholas too.
And then, in a twinkling, I heard on the roof
The prancing and pawing of each little hoof.
As I drew in my head, and was turning around,
Down the chimney St. Nicholas came with a bound.
He was dressed all in fur, from his head to his foot,
And his clothes were all tarnished with ashes and soot;
A bundle of Toys he had flung on his back,
And he looked like a pedler just opening his pack.
His eyes—how they twinkled! His dimples how merry!
His cheeks were like roses, his nose like a cherry!
His droll little mouth was drawn up like a bow
And the beard of his chin was as white as the snow;
The stump of a pipe he held tight in his teeth,
And the smoke it encircled his head like a wreath;
He had a broad face and a little round belly,
That shook when he laughed, like a bowlful of jelly.
He was chubby and plump, a right jolly old elf,
And I laughed when I saw him, in spite of myself;

A wink of his eye and a twist of his head,
Soon gave me to know I had nothing to dread;
He spoke not a word, but went straight to his work,
And filled all the stockings; then turned with a jerk,
And laying his finger aside of his nose,
And giving a nod, up the chimney he rose;
He sprang to his sleigh, to his team gave a whistle,
And away they all flew like the down of a thistle,
But I heard him exclaim, 'ere he drove out of sight,
'HAPPY CHRISTMAS TO ALL, AND TO ALL A GOOD
NIGHT!'

Some early versions of this poem were published with a revised opening line, *'Twas the Night before New Year*, but it was the Christmas version that caught on and from this point Santa would be forever associated with Christmas. Although many different versions of his name existed during the early nineteenth century, it would be Santa Claus (based ultimately on the Dutch, 'Sinter Klaas') that would win the day. He would ensure that the religious festival of Christmas came to incorporate the gift-giving and merrymaking of New Year in a single great centrepiece to midwinter celebrations.

Most elements of the poem are clearly rooted in earlier tradition and were not, as is sometimes thought, entirely the product of Moore's imagination. Reindeer, for example appear in an 1821 verse published in *The Children's Friend*. Moore, however, does seem to have been responsible for providing the names of the original eight reindeer, who existed quite happily for more than a century before Rudolph appeared in a booklet by Robert May, published in 1939, and went on to achieve immortality through the song *Rudolph the Red-Nosed Reindeer*, released by Gene Autry a decade later. Today, no-one questions the fact that Santa travels in a sleigh drawn by reindeer, but why reindeer? This is a fascinating question that will be considered a little later.

Moore's poem was first illustrated by T.C. Boyd, whose diminutive character, dressed in knee-breeches and a fur hat, bears little resemblance to our modern Santa. Some 40 years later, the famous cartoonist Thomas Nast was commissioned to illustrate Moore's poem for the New York-based *Harper's Weekly* magazine which had a circulation of some 200,000. Nast, a Bavarian by birth, was clearly influenced by Bavarian folk tales of Knecht Ruprecht, a version of Father Christmas's 'Dark Helper' and his original Santa has been described as 'a scary old gnome'; he certainly does not exude anything of the jollity and benevolence associated with our dear old Santa. Over subsequent years, Nast produced revised images of Santa, gradually making him less frightening and altogether more child-friendly. In 1863, during the American civil war, he illustrated Santa in stars and stripes, delivering presents to Unionist soldiers. In 1869 a compilation of his illustrations of Santa was published using new colour printing technology; whereas previous images had dressed him most often in brown, in this publication he appeared in vibrant red.

In England, the name 'Santa Claus' seems first to have been applied to a racehorse appearing on the card of a meeting at Epsom in May 1861. Gradually, over the latter decades of the century, Santa merged with Old Father Christmas, and, although English children tended to address him as Father Christmas rather than Santa, it became increasingly clear that it was the same character that visited children on either side of the Atlantic on Christmas Eve. There was no fanfare to announce Santa's arrival in Britain; he appeared gradually and nobody seemed to be aware that he had come via America. Gavin Weightman and Steve Humphries in their book, *Christmas Past*, observe that 'Santa Claus arrived silently and darkly, then emerged as a familiar figure without people having any proper understanding of his origins. It must therefore have been what he represented … that made him so popular.'

By the 1890s it was common practice for people to dress up in Santa costumes and distribute presents to children. We will consider charity at Christmas in the next section, but one example is worthy of mention here. The 'Santa Claus Christmas Distribution Fund', set up by a group of middle-class ladies in the 1890s in north London, existed to provide gifts to poor children. In 1894, this fund recorded in its journal, *The Santa Claus Gazette*, that it existed because many poor children:

> … hear a good deal about old 'Santa Claus' coming to fill the stockings on Christmas Eve and some are tempted to hang up the stockings in a prominent place, only to find that in the morning the stockings are empty and so to them, at least, the story of Santa is but a mockery.

The Santa Claus Distribution Fund appealed to the public for donations and bought real joy to thousands of poor children each year. In 1911, *The Santa Claus Gazette* records that since its foundation the fund had delivered 85,392 parcels at a value of more than £8,000.

In the 1930s, Santa was appropriated by the Coca-Cola Company in a brilliantly conceived advertising campaign that travelled the world. In contrast to Moore's elf-like character, and Nast's still rather gnome-like figure, Coca-Cola's Santa, designed by the artist Haddon Sundblom, was a rotund, jovial old man, dressed in the company's colours of bright red and white. During World War II, Coca-Cola, accompanied by Sundblom's Santa, travelled the globe along with the American military, and the Coca-Cola Company continued to use its Santa Claus advertising campaign to great effect through until the 1960s.

Sundblom's Santa, courtesy of the Coca-Cola Company, has certainly succeeded in his mission; both he and Coca-Cola are now universally recognised icons. I doubt that Santa will change much now that his image is so familiar around the globe, but his evolution, extending back through nineteenth-century America to medieval Europe and beyond, has certainly seen him go through many changes. While acknowledging that his current persona owes much to St Nicholas and Coca-Cola, we must now consider the extent to which some aspects of his character may reflect still more ancient origins.

Santa certainly seems to embody certain characteristics deemed to be of spiritual significance by human societies long before the time of St Nicholas. Let us consider first his relationship with his reindeer. The fact that he travels in a sleigh is no surprise, given that sleighs were in common use in parts of early nineteenth-century North America affected by snow each winter. These sleighs were pulled by horses, and the law in New York dictated that the horses had to wear bells to warn people of their approach; thus the association of Santa with sleigh-bells is easily explained. But why was Santa's sleigh hauled by reindeer and not by horses, or even by huskies that were used by people living further north? This is something of a mystery. Although vast herds of wild caribou, American relatives of the reindeer, were common in parts of North America in the nineteenth century, it is specifically reindeer that propel Santa. It could be that the idea of using reindeer was simply part of the desire to give Santa ancient origins, geographically and chronologically far removed from nineteenth-century America. Alternatively, perhaps someone knew something of the ancient relationship between man and reindeer in places such as Lapland and Siberia. In his book, *Reindeer People: Living with Animals and Spirits in Siberia*, Piers Vitebsky provides a detailed account of just such a relationship, in which the spiritual dimension is no less significant than the practical. The reindeer are exploited for their meat and skin, their antlers and bones are used to make a variety of tools, and they are ridden and used to haul sledges; but they also provide much of the basis for the cosmology of the people. Vitebsky observes that from 2500–3000 years ago, the Pazyryk people of north-west Mongolia erected standing stones decorated with images of flying reindeer, sometimes in association with sun symbols, and some people had similar images tattooed onto their bodies. Reindeer no longer survive in this particular region, but further north, in the Verkhoyansk Mountains of north-east Siberia, Eveny communities in historic times still performed ceremonies in which people undertook 'soul-journeys', to a mystical land of plenty near the sun, on the back of flying reindeer.

Chapter 2 discussed the role of shamans in ceremonies associated with the midwinter sun in Ancient Britain and North America; the Eveny provide another example of such shamanic activity. Within their minds, Eveny shamans could transform themselves into flying reindeer, both to survey this world to help with the planning of hunting trips, and to fly to other worlds to liaise with the spirits. The complex sacred relationship between shamans and reindeer survives to this day, and it is perfectly reasonable to assume that similar relationships existed wherever people and reindeer co-existed since the end of the Ice Age. It is also possible, of course, that the inspiration for Santa's flying reindeer came from an awareness of Native American shamanism. The caribou's significance to the subarctic tribes of North America was not dissimilar to that of the buffalo for tribes further south. The migratory habits of the caribou herds dictated the seasonal movement of the people, and caribou bones were used in shamanic rituals. Whilst it might be stretching things to claim any great relevance to the origin of Santa's reindeer, we may note in passing that reindeer are fond of mushrooms and allegedly have a particular passion for the highly hallucinogenic fly agaric (the bright red and white colours of which neatly mirror those of Santa). Jeremy Seal makes the interesting observation that Santa's choice of hauler may owe something to the possibility that 'the reindeer was not entirely indisposed to the sort of trips he had in mind'! Regardless of the reindeer's fondness for fly agaric, we know that shamans in nineteenth-century Lapland (in what were without doubt very ancient ceremonies) ingested it in order to enter trances during which they flew to other worlds to communicate with the spirits. Exactly how hallucinogenic substances like fly agaric create this illusion of flight is still something of a mystery to modern science, but to ancient shamans the experience was anything but illusory; indeed, it helped to make sense of an otherwise inexplicable world.

Another of Santa's apparently shamanic characteristics is his ability to operate outside the boundaries of conventional time. After some complicated mathematical calculations, Roger Highfield in his entertaining book *Can Reindeer Fly: the Science of Christmas*, concludes that Santa has to deliver presents down 842 million chimneys each Christmas Eve, travelling a total distance of 356 million kilometres at an average speed of 2060km per second (more than 6000 times the speed of sound, but still less than 1% of the speed of light and therefore not necessarily in conflict with Einstein's theory of relativity!). Of course, all these figures are irrelevant because Santa actually undertakes his deliveries within a shamanic timeframe, a concept entirely incompatible with the modern 'scientific' mindset.

Although its exact origins remain obscure, Santa's association with the North Pole seems also to date from the mid nineteenth century, a time when people had yet to reach this semi-mythical location. From the 1860s, a number of publications record Santa's home here, for example a poem by George P. Webster, published along with Nast's illustrations in 1869, observes that Santa lived in a 'palace of ice' near the North Pole. When the explorer Robert Peary eventually reached the North Pole in 1909 he found no sign of Santa, and Santa's traditional home was amended to 'somewhere in the Arctic'. In 1927, a claim was made on Finnish radio that Santa actually lived amongst the vast reindeer herds of Finnish Lapland. This seemed appropriate for people in America, Britain and elsewhere, and he has resided hereabouts ever since.

In recent years, Santa has received some had publicity at the hands of the Christian Church, elements of which see him as claiming some of the seasonal glory that should reside solely with Jesus. However, regardless of what the Church may think, Santa is very much here to stay. He has evolved over at least 16 centuries, possibly many more if we choose to believe that his ability to circumvent conventional time, his home near the North Pole, and his close association with flying reindeer reflect some kind of link with ancient shamanic practice.

Bah Humbug! Charles Dickens and charity at Christmas

With the possible exceptions of Jesus Christ and Santa Claus, no-one has had greater influence on the development of our 'traditional' Christmas than Charles Huffam Dickens. Born in Portsmouth on 7 February 1812, Dickens enjoyed a happy early childhood, mostly based in Chatham, Kent, showing much enthusiasm for the theatre and no little talent as an amateur performer. At the age of nine, however, his life took a serious turn for the worse as his father fell seriously into debt and moved the family to Camden Town, London. The young Dickens was not enrolled at school after the move to London, and spent much time walking the streets. Within a little over a decade he would be acknowledged as a literary genius, but there was precious little indication of his talent at this stage. Indeed, he would later remark himself that 'but for the mercy of God, I might have been … a little robber or vagabond'. He sought refuge in books, but as his father's financial plight worsened even the family library was pawned. Camden Town at the time was an overcrowded, unhealthy slum, and the contrast with the leafy streets and healthy air of Chatham, where he had been happy just months earlier, must have hit the young Dickens very hard.

At the age of 12, he was found a menial job at Warren's, a miserable shoe-blacking warehouse by the Thames. He worked a 10-hour day surrounded by uneducated, working-class colleagues. His dreams of a career on the stage seemed well and truly doomed, and things were about to get even worse. Shortly after he started work at Warren's, his father was imprisoned as a result of spiralling debts and the young Charles was sent to live in lodgings. Exactly what his father made of this dire situation is not recorded, but he managed to get out of prison after coming into an inheritance, and the story goes that while walking in Covent Garden, where Warren's had recently relocated, he caught sight of Charles working in the warehouse window. Presumably feeling a degree of shame, he removed Charles from the company and sent him to a local day school, the far from prestigious Reverend Giles' School in Chatham. Despite the apparent poor quality of this establishment, Charles enthusiastically learnt what he could and took the opportunity to participate in school plays. A couple of years later, aged 15, he left school for good, taking a job as a clerk in a lawyer's office. He went to the theatre most nights, and continued to walk the streets of London, coming into contact with underprivileged groups on a regular basis. His experience of the theatre and his hatred of poverty in society would inform much of his writing, including his work about Christmas.

Dicken's first published work about Christmas, entitled 'Christmas Festivities' was written for *Bell's Magazine* in 1835. In this he notes 'That man must be a misanthrope indeed, in whose breast something like a jovial feeling is not roused – in whose mind some pleasant associations are not awakened – by the recurrence of Christmas.' In a theme that would later be elaborated in *A Christmas Carol*, he also makes reference in this early work to the power of Christmas to encourage positive thinking, advising readers to 'Reflect upon your blessings – of which every man has many – not on your past misfortunes, of which all men have some. Fill your glass again, with a merry face and contented heart.'

By the age of 25, Dickens had achieved great fame through his first novel *The Pickwick Papers* which includes the oft-quoted passage:

> Happy, happy Christmas, that can win us back to the delusions of our childish days; that can recall to the old man the pleasures of his youth; that can transport the sailor and the traveller, thousands of miles away, back to his own fireside and his quiet home!

Dickens stresses the value of Christmas as a family occasion, bringing together family members who may rarely, if at all, see one another throughout the rest of the year. Partying, story-telling, feasting and general happiness are key elements of Christmas, which Dickens clearly regards as an altogether wonderful institution. Given his social concerns, however, he was also keen to stress the value of Christmas in terms of charity; at this time, even if at no other, the poor and disadvantaged should be well looked after.

These themes were developed in *The Pickwick Papers* and several other works, but it was in arguably his greatest masterpiece, *A Christmas Carol*, that they were most spectacularly presented. Dickens began working on the plot of *A Christmas Carol* in October 1843, shortly after a trip to America during which his campaigning against slavery caused uproar, and a tour of some northern English mines during which he was appalled by the atrocious conditions under which children were forced to work. Fuelled by indignation at such social injustices, he threw himself into the writing of *A Christmas Carol*, completing it within a mere six weeks. The book was an instant hit with the public, selling an extraordinary 6000 copies within five days of its publication on 19 December 1843. Everyone reading these words will presumably be familiar with the story of Scrooge, Bob Cratchit, Tiny Tim and the Spirits of Christmas Past, Christmas Present and Christmas Yet to Come. Its power hit a raw nerve within Victorian society; Scrooge's miraculous transformation from evil miser to generous force for good represented the changes needed in society at large if misery and poverty, especially among children, were ever to be overcome.

Dickens' fellow novelist, William Thackeray, described *A Christmas Carol* as 'a national benefit and to every man and woman who reads it a personal kindness'. Lord Jeffrey believed that Dickens had 'done more good by this little publication, fostered more kindly feelings, and prompted more positive acts of benevolence, than can be traced to all the pulpits and confessionals in Christendom'. This quasi-religious theme was echoed by Margaret Oliphant who wrote in 1871, the year after Dickens' death, that '*A Christmas Carol* moved us all those days ago as if it had been a new gospel'.

Although Dickens is generally credited with the 'creation' of the traditional Christmas, his work actually built on an already growing nostalgic desire at the time to re-engage with elements of the past. What he did, to very great effect, was to popularise, rather than invent, the idea of the 'traditional' Christmas, whilst also imbuing it with a sense of social justice. It may come as something of a surprise to some readers that Dickens can also be considered as an early expert in the art of the commercial exploitation of the festive season. Despite his genuine sense of social duty, Dickens wrote *A Christmas Carol* with personal financial reward very much in mind and over the years it earned him vast royalties. From the late 1850s until his death in 1870, his life was dominated by reading tours that gave him the pleasure of performing on stage and were also very lucrative. *A Christmas Carol* provided the most popular material for these events, and was the subject of his final public reading just six months before his death. While his public image was linked with the concept of the happy family, such as that of Bob Cratchit, he left his own wife in 1858 for an 18 year-old actress, causing a degree of moral outrage at the time. His relations with his own children became strained, and he would never again enjoy the kind of wonderful family Christmas that he describes so movingly in his work.

Dickens' work as a social campaigner should not be underestimated. We noted above that *A Christmas Carol* had a profound effect on its readers, and it had much to do with the development of charity as a key element of the Victorian Christmas. While many middle-class people were no doubt genuinely concerned for the welfare of those worse off than themselves, the growth of Christmas charity had much to do with the guilt and fear of the middle classes as the gulf between their standard of living and that of the working classes in the rapidly expanding towns and cites grew ever wider. One consequence of this situation was the decline of the 'Christmas box' – a box containing cash, and perhaps a gift, traditionally given as a form of 'Christmas bonus' to domestic and other staff on Boxing Day. This was gradually replaced by seasonal donations to various Christmas charities which ensured that some degree of festive cheer was provided for the genuinely needy. Earlier in this chapter we noted the 'Santa Claus Christmas Distribution Fund', and many similar institutions appeared during the later nineteenth century in towns and cities throughout the land, offering food and temporary shelter to the needy; there were about 1000 such charities in London alone at the end of the century. The general mood of seasonal benevolence towards the poor and the homeless is reflected in the well-known nursery rhyme:

> Christmas is coming and the goose is getting fat,
> Please put a penny in the old man's hat.

In most prisons and workhouses, inmates enjoyed a good Christmas dinner and festive entertainment was provided; indeed, inmates of such institutions generally enjoyed a far better Christmas than most working-class families 'on the outside'. In the 1860s at Hereford Prison, the Chairman of the Board of Guardians informed inmates during his Christmas address that they were 'better off than the poor people outside' – a fact reflected in their Christmas dinner of roast beef, gifts of sweets, fruit and tobacco, and entertainment including a magic lantern show and a carol concert.

During the early twentieth century, charities increasingly 'vetted' those receiving gifts and other benefits from them in an attempt to encourage church-going and temperance at the expense of anti-social behaviour and drunkenness – the 'respectable poor' should be helped to enjoy Christmas while those showing no desire to help themselves should be left to their own devices. Generally, however, it was thought that children, whatever their family background, deserved a decent Christmas. During the early twentieth century, the Salvation Army organised Christmas parties for thousands of poor children each year, recording in a report dated 1900 that:

In twenty of the slummiest districts of London nearly three thousand of the poorest children have experienced the delight of gazing upon a Christmas tree, and receiving some gifts from its toy laden branches … Poor mites! One cannot look at them, even in their merriment, without a pang of sorrow as one realises that all the glitter and brightness of this occasion is as a fleeting flash of sunlight, that relieves only for a moment the black winter of their young lives.

The desire to provide a decent Christmas for unfortunate children continued throughout the twentieth century, with orphanages, children's homes and hospitals making a special effort to provide Christmas cheer in the form of festive food, entertainment and presents. Today, the desire to help the underprivileged at Christmas acts upon the global stage, with some charities selling 'gifts' that actually consist of little more than charitable donations to communities in developing countries. The thinking behind the provision of such gifts is identical to that underlying the development of festive charity in Dickensian times; partly the genuinely altruistic desire to be kind to others at Christmas, partly the egoistic search for the 'feel good factor' generated by helping those less fortunate than ourselves.

In his discussions of Christmas, Dickens has little to say about Jesus, although he did include a conventional account of the Nativity in a *Life of Christ*, written for his children. Despite his own Christian beliefs, Dickens' Christmas has more to do with real, practical, social issues than abstract religious mythology. The second great Christmas character, Santa Claus, who, as we have seen, was coming to life in America at about the same time as Dickens was engaged in the creation of Scrooge and Bob Cratchit, likewise fails to play a key role in the Dickensian Christmas. Dickens was a keen fan of Washington Irving's *The History of New York,* so must have been aware of Santa, but presumably made a conscious decision not to present him with a starring role. Other than Jesus and Santa, however, most aspects of the 'traditional' Christmas were discussed and to a large extent influenced by Dickens, whose name will appear several more times in subsequent sections of this chapter.

Little Messenger of Friendly Thoughts. The Christmas card

Prior to the introduction of the Christmas card, it had been something of a tradition for people to exchange festive greetings by letter, and schoolchildren commonly prepared 'Christmas pieces', festively decorated printed sheets on which they wrote messages to their parents. These may have provided the initial inspiration for the development of the Christmas card. Although there are a few other contenders produced at about the same time, the first Christmas card is generally assumed to be one designed by the artist John Callcott Horsley and published by Henry Cole (the first director of the Victoria and Albert Museum) in 1843 – by coincidence the very same year that saw the publication of Dickens' *A Christmas Carol*. This depicts a family enjoying Christmas dinner, with several of the characters raising a toast towards the recipient as an absent friend. Side panels illustrate the theme of Christmas charity – to the left, a poor child is fed, while to the right another receives clothing. The combination of charity and children represents a pivotal Christmas theme which has remained influential through until the present day. To the modern eye there appears nothing untoward about this card, but, believe it or not, it was criticised by some in Victorian society for allegedly encouraging drunkenness!

Henry Cole produced a thousand of these cards to sell through a London art shop in which he had an interest, at one shilling each, which was far from cheap at the time; apparently they did not prove popular as the tradition at this time was still to exchange annual greetings at New Year rather than Christmas. However, by the 1860s printers were producing large numbers of Christmas cards with a huge variety of themes and designs. Early designs rarely depicted the Nativity, often showing scenes of no apparent relevance to Christmas; naked nymphs were strangely common. Valentine's Day was already popular and some companies produced Christmas cards simply by changing the wording on their existing Valentine cards. Towards the end of the century, now-traditional festive subjects such as holly, mistletoe, food, snowy village scenes and Father Christmas began to dominate the Christmas card market. Robins became particularly popular, their bright red breasts symbolising fire and warmth within the cold, white winter landscape. Many early cards resembled visiting cards, measuring only about 8 x 5cm, on the reverse of which personal greetings could be inscribed. As time went by the Victorians produced more and more elaborate cards, sometimes incorporating ribbon, lace, silk, scented padding or dried flowers. Many Victorian and Edwardian cards featured children, and the overwhelming impression given is of jovial, family Christmas gatherings. In 1883, an article in *The Times* observed that the introduction of the Christmas card:

has created quite a new trade, and has opened up a new field of labour for artists, lithographers, engravers, printers, ink and pasteboard makers … All the year round brains are at work devising new designs and inventing novelties. The very cheap Christmas cards come from Germany where they can be produced at a much cheaper rate, but all the more artistic and more highly finished cards are the result of English workmanship.

Soon after their introduction, Christmas cards became very popular amongst the upper classes, and after 1870, when the ½d postage rate was introduced for cards, the tradition of sending them to family and friends was soon established throughout all classes of society. During the 1880s, the cards themselves became cheaper through mass production. *The Times*, again in 1883, recorded that:

This wholesome custom has been … frequently the happy means of ending strifes, cementing broken friendships and strengthening family and neighbourhood ties in all conditions of life. In this respect the Christmas card undoubtedly fulfils a high end, for cheap postage has constituted it almost exclusively the modern method of conveying Christmas wishes, and the increasing popularity of the custom is for this reason, if no other, a matter for congratulation.

As might be expected, there were some dissenting voices; a letter to *The Times* after Christmas, 1877, complained at the 'delay of legitimate correspondence by cartloads of children's cards', and condemned the sending of Christmas cards as a social evil! This was, however, very much a minority view, and the sending of Christmas cards soon became an international phenomenon. George Budley in *The Story of the Christmas Card* observes that 'It did not take long for the Christmas card to become the acknowledged little messenger of friendly thoughts, good will and kindly greeting throughout the civilised world.' By the middle of the twentieth century (according to the *Daily Mirror* in December 1951) more than 350 million Christmas cards were sent by British people each December, a large proportion of which were sent by post using the attractive special Christmas stamps issued each year by the Royal Mail.

The Christmas card, although a relatively recent development, reflects the ancient Saturnalian custom of exchanging charms or tokens of goodwill. The card was cheap to buy and send – it was the thought behind it that was of value. Today, most friends and relatives still exchange cards, and although younger generations increasingly rely on texts and emails to send their greetings, the Christmas card will no doubt continue to evolve and to decorate our mantelpieces and window ledges for the foreseeable future.

'Oh, what a wonderful pudding!' Christmas dinner

It is no coincidence that the world's first Christmas card shows a family enjoying Christmas dinner; then, as now, this annual feast was an event to be eagerly anticipated and fondly remembered. Planning of the Victorian Christmas dinner, whether for consumption by royalty, aristocracy or working-class family, began well in advance of the big day. In early Victorian times, families in northern England tended to have roast beef while those in London and the south favoured goose. To those who could afford it, a huge variety of festive food was available from markets in the larger towns and cities. In *A Christmas Carol*, when Scrooge is visited by the Ghost of Christmas Present, Dickens uses food to help set the scene:

> Heaped up on the floor, to form a kind of throne, were turkeys, geese, game, poultry, brawn, great joints of meat, sucking-pigs, long wreaths of sausages, mince-pies, plum-puddings, barrels of oysters, red-hot chestnuts, cherry-cheeked apples, juicy oranges, luscious pears, immense twelfth-cakes, and seething bowls of punch.

Pictures of London markets published in the mid nineteenth century show huge numbers of geese, turkeys and other produce on display. Most of the turkeys and geese were reared in East Anglia. An article in the *Illustrated London News* at Christmas 1849 records that:

> Mr Valentine Fell, poulterer, of Louth, near Boston, assisted by forty-five persons, commenced his annual slaughtering of poultry for the Christmas market. No fewer than 4000 geese ... as well as 1500 ducks, turkeys and fowls, comprised the number to be slaughtered. They were all consigned to Leadenhall market, and were calculated to weigh upwards of thirty tons. Many of the geese were of remarkably large kind, and weighed from 16lb to 20lb.

Dickens, in *A Christmas Carol*, describes the preparation and consumption of the Cratchit Christmas dinner in great detail, starting with the cooking of the goose. Working-class families like the Cratchits obtained their geese through participation in a goose club, to which a few pennies were paid each week in the months leading up to Christmas. The goose clubs were often organised in pubs and were very popular, sometimes providing members with a bottle of spirits in addition to their seasonal bird. Many bakeries, closed for the day, made their ovens available for local families to cook their geese; this was how Bob Cratchit's goose was cooked. Increasingly, though, as families became wealthier and obtained their own ovens, the Christmas dinner was cooked at home.

Turkeys, originally from Central America, were being farmed in East Anglia by the sixteenth century, but did not become widely popular until Victorian times. They were traditionally given a coating of tar on their feet, or little leather boots, before being force-marched to London for slaughter, although as the roads improved it became possible to slaughter them at the farm and transport them to London by stagecoach, a journey of two or three days. As families grew in size and the railways enabled dispersed families to come together for the festive season, the turkey, which provided meat for a dozen plates, grew in popularity. By the 1880s it had displaced beef and goose as most people's favourite Christmas dish.

The vegetables served with the Victorian Christmas dinner were quite conventional, including the infamous Brussels sprout. Quite why something so revolting should have retained its place on our Christmas plate is something of a mystery, but in Victorian times sprouts were important seasonal vegetables at midwinter. They are very nutritious and recent research suggests that they can help to prevent some forms of cancer. The tradition of cutting a cross in the base of the sprout has the practical purpose of ensuring the sprout is cooked throughout, but was also thought to keep out the devil, the sprout presumably acting as a suitable representative of the devil on account of its evil taste.

The sweet course of the Victorian Christmas dinner was invariably plum pudding. Dickens provides the following account of Mrs Cratchit's plum pudding:

> The pudding was out of the copper. A smell like a washing-day! That was the cloth! A smell like an eating-house and a pastry cook's next door to each other, with a laundress's next door to that! That was the pudding. In half a minute, Mrs Cratchit entered – flushed, but smiling proudly – with the pudding, like a speckled cannon-

ball, so hard and firm, blazing in half-a-quartern of ignited brandy, and bedight with Christmas holly stuck into the top. Oh, what a wonderful pudding. Bob Cratchit said, and calmly too, that he regarded it as the greatest success achieved by Mrs Cratchit since their marriage.

Mrs Cratchit had borne Bob six children, yet he considered her greatest achievement to have been a Christmas pudding – a very fine pudding it must have been! Today, most of us get our Christmas puddings from the supermarket and microwave them in minutes, but in Victorian times the preparation was done at home with the mixture traditionally stirred by all members of the family. Sixpences and threepenny bits were often hidden within the pudding to bring good luck to those fortunate enough to receive them within their helpings – assuming, of course, that they managed to avoid swallowing them. The tradition of setting the pudding alight recalls ancient midwinter fire worship, while the use of alcohol for this purpose reminds us that drink was no less important than food at the traditional Christmas feast! There were many different recipes, but a traditional pudding might consist of chopped beef suet, bread crumbs, flour, cornflour, raisins, almonds, currants, sultanas, apple, mixed peel, sugar, lemon juice, nutmeg, rum, brandy, ale, milk, eggs and baking powder.

Another Victorian seasonal delicacy was the mince pie. Traditional mince pies, containing a mixture of savoury and sweet ingredients, had been made for centuries, but during Victorian times they generally contained 'mincemeat' of apple, lemon, orange, suet, sugar, nutmeg, ginger, mace and a good dose of brandy. In early Victorian times, cakes were generally associated with Twelfth Night rather than Christmas or New Year; their consumption marked the close of the festive season rather than its start. Traditionally, very large twelfth cakes were displayed in confectioners' windows, and Queen Victoria had a splendid one made for the royal family each year. From the 1870s, the tradition became transferred to Christmas, and smaller 'family-size' cakes became the norm, as they still are today.

Victoria treated Christmas dinner as a family event, but the tradition of eating to excess at Christmas was still very much in force. The 1840 Christmas dinner menu at Windsor Castle included six courses: turtle soup; haddock or sole; beef or roast swan; veal, chicken, partridge or curried rabbit; pheasant or capon; mince pies and Christmas pudding. On a side table, available to those still feeling a little peckish after the set menu, were beef, mutton, turkey, pork, turkey pie (including lark and pheasant as well as turkey), partridge, brawn, sausages and the traditional boar's head. Today, few boar's heads are prepared at Christmas, but the little sausages we serve up with our turkey each year are perhaps token representations of this ancient tradition. As the number of vegetarians in society continues to grow (partly in response to the horrendous conditions under which much of our meat is produced), the humble nut-roast has almost become a 'traditional' option on the Christmas menu. For most of us, however, festive fare comes in the form of roast turkey, followed by a healthy dollop of Christmas pudding, with mince pies and Christmas cake to look forward to a little later in the day.

One of the most extraordinary Christmas dinners in human history was enjoyed by only three people: the astronauts aboard the *Apollo 8* spacecraft who, on Christmas Eve 1968, became the first men to orbit the moon. The next day they became the first to enjoy a Christmas dinner, of turkey and stuffing, in outer space. Back on earth, as we have seen, feasting has been an essential element of midwinter festivals since Roman times, and probably ever since the Stone Age. Whether eaten with our work colleagues during an extended lunch-break in the run-up to Christmas, in the school canteen on the last day of term, or with our families on Christmas Day itself, the traditional Christmas dinner remains essential to our enjoyment of the festive season.

Tom Smith – King of Crackers. The Christmas cracker

The cracker is another feature of our traditional Christmas that originates from the mid nineteenth century. Although claims have been made on behalf of others, its inventor seems to have been Tom Smith, a London-based confectioner. In the 1840s his company successfully marketed double-wrapped bon-bons with mottos (usually of a romantic nature) included between the wrappers. The novelty of these bon-bons was further enhanced through the inclusion of small trinkets along with the mottos. Exactly when Tom had the idea to develop his novelty bon-bons into crackers is not known, but during the 1850s he invented the so-called 'snap' which formed the heart of the cracker. This consisted of two tough strips of paper or card, each coated on one end with a mildly explosive chemical, 'saltpetre' (potassium nitrate), with the two pieces tied together so that the explosive ends were in contact with each other (today's crackers use the same basic design, but, being subject to modern health and safety regulations, use small quantities of silver formulate rather than potassium nitrate). When the two ends of the snap were tugged in opposite directions, friction caused a small explosion or 'crack'. It is rumoured that the inspiration for Tom's idea of the cracker was a spitting log on his fire, but, while far from unlikely, we will never know for sure whether this is true.

Whatever their ultimate inspiration, Christmas crackers were on sale to the British public from about 1860. There is little evidence for their popularity in the early years, but they featured on Christmas cards in the 1870s, suggesting they had become an established part of Christmas festivities. Despite rumours that some early crackers had a tendency to catch fire when pulled, such risks could not dim the British public's enthusiasm for them and by far the most popular manufacturer was Tom Smith. Towards the end of the nineteenth century, one newspaper article recorded that 'Tom Smith is the King of Crackers, he stands alone and needs no backers', while another review advised readers to 'Go for Tom Smith, he is the Cracker par excellence'. *The Daily Telegraph* recorded at about the same time that 'Tom Smith's Christmas Crackers … are characterised by ingenuity of invention and felicitous taste', while *The Echo* noted that 'Tom Smith has elevated the manufacture of crackers to a fine art'. In 1910, George V granted Tom Smith's the royal warrant as cracker supplier to the royal family.

As illustrated in *Tom Smith's Christmas Crackers*, a fascinating book by Peter Kimpton who worked for the company in the late twentieth century, a huge variety of crackers was produced. Tom Smith's 1891/92 catalogue includes (at a rather extravagant 24 shillings for a box of a dozen) the following options, amongst many others:

> *Ye Olden Times Crackers.* 'Containing in place of the usual love motto, an old English love verse … together with old-fashioned Head-dress'.
> *Musical Toy Crackers.* 'The greatest novelty for juniors ever produced. In the twelve crackers are found twelve different musical toys'.
> *The Enchanted Box.* 'A novel box of surprise crackers of superb and chaste design, containing startling surprises including Japanese Insects, Flexible faces, Moustaches …'

Over subsequent years an extraordinary range of themed boxes appeared, most in good taste but sadly including some very offensive examples ('Darkies Surprise' from the 1925 catalogue is almost inoffensive by comparison with several others) illustrating the latent racism of the times.

Despite competition from other British manufacturers, and several in Germany, Tom Smith's remained the premier brand. During the early twentieth century, the company produced some 13 million crackers a year, most for the British market. Production was very labour intensive, with all crackers made by hand. The workers, mostly female, were capable of making about 100 standard crackers an hour, although more time was taken over the production of the more complex examples containing more valuable novelties.

Across the Atlantic, the earliest crackers seem to have been imported from Germany during the 1880s, although factories were soon manufacturing them in New York and other locations throughout the States. However, crackers in the States (generally known as 'snappers') did not enjoy the same degree of popularity throughout the twentieth century as they did in Britain.

Although many crackers, some with very patriotic themes, were produced by Tom Smith's during World War I, production ceased during World War II. In the 1950s, Tom Smith's merged with Caley's of Norwich, another long-established cracker manufacturer. The company continued to trade as Tom Smith's, and in the 1980s was producing 50 million crackers a year, many of which were now made by machines capable of churning out up to 40 crackers a minute! In October 1963 the Norwich factory was razed to the ground by a fire fuelled by millions of crackers that created a spectacular 'firework' display. The factory was rebuilt the following year and production continued into the 1990s when, following further mergers, the factory was eventually closed. The current owners of the Tom Smith's brand name still hold the Queen's warrant for cracker production and continue to provide the royal family with crackers each Christmas. (Readers wishing to learn more about the history of the cracker are referred to *Tom Smith's Christmas Crackers*, a fascinating and well-illustrated book by Peter Kimpton who worked for the company in the late twentieth century.)

In their book, *Christmas Past*, within a chapter engagingly entitled 'Misrule and Morality', Gavin Weightman and Steve Humphries observe that:

> … the Christmas cracker was tailor-made for the Victorian family Christmas dinner – a feeble spark which perfectly suited the demure

sensibilities of the class, and mimicked the more ancient communal fire festivals which were rapidly disappearing from the scene. Once paper hats were added, it became the perfect little package of pagan ritual for the family table: fire and funny hats without the Saturnalian excesses.

Today, Christmas crackers continue, albeit subconsciously, to recall the boisterous nature of Saturnalia.

That pretty German toy. The story of the Christmas tree

An ancient legend links the origin of the Christmas tree to St Boniface, responsible for the introduction of Christianity throughout much of what is now Germany in the eighth century. Boniface became aware that a local chief was planning to sacrifice his son to the gods on Christmas Eve in the year 723. The sacrifice was due to take place beneath a great oak, sacred to the god Thor. Boniface took it upon himself to fell this oak and did so with a single strike of his axe, aided by a great gust of wind. The local people were, not surprisingly, amazed by what they saw, and happily embraced Christianity. Boniface pointed to a little fir tree growing close to the felled oak and explained that it represented Christ; the old gods, like the great oak, were now of the past, and Christianity represented the way forward. The apex of the fir tree, he observed, pointed towards heaven, while its evergreen leaves symbolised eternal life. He told the people to call this fir tree 'the tree of the Christ-child', and to set one up in their homes and decorate it with 'loving gifts and lights of kindness'. The fallen oak was used to build a church dedicated to St Peter, and the little fir was cut and set up in the chief's great hall where it became the first ever Christmas tree. These events are traditionally said to have occurred at what is now the town of Fritzlar, 160km north of Frankfurt, and Fritzlar Cathedral is said to occupy the site of the Boniface's original church, built from Thor's great oak. Much as we might like to believe it, this quaint story is unlikely to be historically authentic and we cannot really claim to have traced the origins of our Christmas tree back to the time of St Boniface.

According to Daniel J. Foley, in his book *The Christmas Tree*, the origins of our modern tree can be found in medieval Paradise Plays. These plays, which were very popular in fifteenth-century Europe, and especially so at Christmas time, presented dramatisations of miracle scenes from the Bible. They usually opened with the story of Adam and Eve, for which the main prop was a fir tree hung with apples – the immediate precursor of our Christmas tree.

The Paradise Plays were performed at various public locations, but not in church, and over time became increasingly frowned upon by the church authorities. When they eventually slipped out of fashion, the tradition of decorating trees at midwinter did not die out, but found itself transferred to the domestic sphere. To begin with, these Paradise trees (as they were still called) were set up adjacent to tiered wooden pyramids on which ornaments were displayed and candles lit; before long, the paradise trees and pyramidal stands were combined to produce the Christmas tree. By the seventeenth century it was customary in Germany to place a tree in the home and to decorate it not only with fruit but also with cookies of various shapes and sizes, and candles. The earliest record of such Christmas trees, referring to trees in Strasbourg decorated with apples, wafers, sweets and paper flowers, dates from 1605.

Although the custom was frowned upon as pagan by the religious authorities, it caught on to such an extent that by the mid eighteenth century it was thought necessary to introduce a law banning the taking of small evergreens from the forests around Salzburg. Some people overcame this ban by growing their own trees in tubs and retaining them from year to year (preceding by two and a half centuries the modern drive towards 'sustainable' or 'environmentally friendly' Christmas trees).

There are many references to Christmas trees in later eighteenth-century Germany, but how was this essentially German tradition transferred to Britain? It is recorded that German merchants in Manchester had Christmas trees in the 1830s, and there are occasional references to trees being decorated by British families around this time; well-known examples include the Dickens family prior to 1820 and Lord Ravensworth's family at Durham in 1831. However, the tree did not really catch on in Britain until the middle of the century when the catalyst for its widespread uptake throughout the land was provided by the royal family, which itself included much German blood. Trees are recorded in the courts of George III and William IV, but it was Victoria and her German husband, Prince Albert, who were largely responsible for the spread of the Christmas tree to the British living room. In probably the most famous image of a Christmas tree ever published, in the *Illustrated London News* on 23 December 1848, Victoria and Albert are pictured with their family around their Christmas tree at Windsor. Along with the picture, a detailed description of the tree is provided:

> The tree, which stands upon a table covered with white damask, is supported at the root by piles of sweets of a larger kind, and by toys and dolls of all descriptions, suited to the youthful fancy, and to the several ages of the interesting scions of Royalty for whose gratification they are displayed. The name of each recipient is affixed to the doll, bonbon, or other present intended for it, so that no differences of opinion in the choice of dainties may arise to disturb the equanimity of the illustrious juveniles. On the summit of the tree stands the small figure of an angel, with outstretched wings, holding in each hand a wreath.

From here there was no going back – the loyal British public sought to emulate their monarch and the Christmas tree was soon a regular annual fixture in humble rural cottages, urban terraces and grand country houses throughout the land. For families unable to acquire a 'proper' tree, a small holly bush might be harvested from local woodland as a suitable alternative; the principle was the same – a 'live' evergreen provided the focus for celebrations within the home (although, of course, the act of cutting the tree had the immediate effect of killing it – a conveniently overlooked contradiction!). In towns and cities, trees in a variety of sizes were available from vendors. One vendor in London's Covent Garden Market (described in the December 1895 edition of *The English Illustrated* magazine as 'the high priest of the Christmas tree trade') claimed to sell 30,000 trees each Christmas, ranging in size from 18in to 40ft and in price from 4*d* to £6.

The tree was a particular hit with children. In a letter to his father, Prince Albert noted of his own children that while 'they know not why' they 'feel a happy wonder at the German Christmas tree and its radiant candles.' Such happy wonder would be experienced by millions of British children over subsequent decades. While children may grow out of a belief in Santa Claus, it is a sad child indeed that ever outgrows a belief in the Christmas tree.

Charles Dickens, who as we have already seen did more than anyone to popularise Christmas in the nineteenth century, wrote a sentimental and nostalgic story entitled *The Christmas Tree* in 1855. This served to reinforce the tree's growing role as the centrepiece of domestic Christmas celebrations. In an oft-quoted passage, he begins:

I have been looking on, this evening, at a merry company of children assembled around that pretty German toy, a Christmas Tree. The tree was planted in the middle of a great round table, and towered high above their heads. It was brilliantly lighted by a multitude of little tapers; and everywhere sparkled and glittered with bright objects.

Trees were traditionally lit with candles, which, despite the introduction of 'non-slip' candle-holders in the 1880s, represented a serious fire risk. In some large houses a member of the domestic staff would be allocated the position of 'Christmas tree guard' – responsible for inspecting the tree regularly and removing and replacing candles as necessary. As electricity was increasingly introduced into houses from the late nineteenth century, little electric 'fairy lights' became popular additions to the Christmas tree. After World War I, these artificial lights became more readily available and in some cases were used in association with artificial trees that could be reused year after year. Some of the earliest such artificial trees were manufactured by Izal using technology developed for the manufacture of toilet brushes! In the latter half of the twentieth century, the provision of Christmas trees, lights and decorations became big business and today most families enjoy setting up a tree of some description each December, usually leaving it up until after the traditional end of seasonal festivities on Twelfth Night. Some 7 million natural trees are purchased in Britain each Christmas, in addition to all the artificial examples, now available in a range of garish colours alongside various shades of green.

Although this section is particularly concerned with the Christmas tree, we should note that the tree itself was but one example of the seasonal use of evergreen decoration within the Victorian home. In a clear throwback to ancient pagan tradition, twigs of holly, mistletoe and ivy would be arranged around the living room, and sometimes incorporated into carefully manufactured wreaths which might be hung on the front door. Mistletoe's ancient association with fertility was and still is reflected in the tradition of kissing beneath it, a tradition that owes much to very ancient customs of bawdiness at midwinter. The tradition is neatly summed up in an article published in the *Home Companion* magazine in 1913:

Kissing under the mistletoe is a very old custom, and no girl should feel indignant or hurt if one of her admirers shows a keen desire to salute her in the way that Cupid so strongly approves. Girls should remember that because a man wishes to kiss her under the mistletoe he does not necessarily mean to propose to her! Very often a man will purposely avoid kissing the girl to whom he is most attached in front of other people because he considers his love too sacred for public display.

Every year since 1947, a giant Christmas tree has been sent to Trafalgar Square in London by the people of Norway as a token of their gratitude for British support during World War II and as a symbol of continuing friendship. This tree, a Norwegian spruce about 25m in height and anything up to 50 years old, is felled amidst great ceremony in November from woods near Oslo, and carefully transported to London where it is erected and its lights switched on at a ceremony attended by many dignitaries from both countries. In addition to the Trafalgar Square tree, Newcastle receives one from Bergen, and Sunderland one from Stavanger; these trees function not only as icons of Christmas, but also as powerful statements of friendship between cities and nations.

Weightman and Humphries list three reasons why the Christmas tree caught on as an essential ingredient of the Victorian Christmas:

1. It could be displayed within the home, providing the focus for domestic celebration.
2. Presents could be hung from, or laid out beneath, the branches, thus linking the tree to the growing popularity of present giving.
3. It was particularly appealing to children, who were becoming the focus of Christmas celebrations.

All of these factors are undeniably true, but the main factor underlying the popularity of the tree was surely the (perhaps subconscious) desire to perpetuate ancient traditions associated with evergreens and fire (represented by candles or fairy lights) at midwinter. Today, the Christmas tree provides the focus for seasonal celebrations from the living room to the national stage. We will leave the final words in this section to Daniel J. Foley, who writes in the introduction to *The Christmas Tree*:

The best stories about the Christmas tree have probably never been written and may never be put on paper, for much of the feeling imbued by a glistening evergreen, at this hallowed time of year, is difficult to put into words. It is a kind of co-mingling, or blending, if you will, of sentiment, awe, and wonder. To capture, or as it were, to recapture on cold type that warmth and mirth is not easy. Nor should it be. It is something we sense from within and it belongs happily in the realm of memories – not real perhaps – an image too bright and too colourful for our everyday world, for 'it sings its own song without words in all our hearts'.

O Come all ye Faithful! The Christmas carol

Whether sung at the school Nativity play, at church on Christmas Eve, at one of the great annual televised carol services, in the street, or (perhaps rather less pleasantly, at least for the poor workers who have to listen to them day after day) piped incessantly throughout shopping centres, carols contribute much to the festive atmosphere each December. We have already seen that the carol has medieval origins; this section will focus on the re-emergence of the carol during Victorian times and its subsequent popularity, before briefly considering the impact of Christmas 'pop' songs in the twentieth century.

David Willcocks, one-time organist at King's College, Cambridge, and Director of the Royal College of Music, writes in the introduction to his book *Carols for Christmas* (1983):

> It is remarkable that carol singing, the gathering of singers around the fireside or in the streets at Christmas time, should still prosper in our own age. This innocent and delightful ritual survives in our secular society, despite the commercialisation of Christmas and the age of television and mass entertainment. It has outlasted many other customs that have disappeared in the face of modern pressures, and other rites that had a less certain hold on people's true feelings. It still symbolises to us the spirit of peace and brotherhood, the unity of the family, and the values of stable community life – ideals that transcend its Christian meaning.

The carol's ability to transcend Christianity is clearly a key element in its popularity, but should come as no surprise given that its origins are to be sought in folk rather than church music. While much classical music has been written on the theme of Christmas, very little of this is well known, and despite the introduction of recorded music and the production of many new Christmas 'pop songs' over recent decades, our dozen or so best known carols continue to play a major role on the festive stage.

Perhaps surprisingly, several sources record that carols were falling out of favour in the early 1800s, being sung less and less as the years went by. This was due in part to changes in society as people flocked to the cities, gradually losing touch with their long-established rural roots. William Sandys observed in 1852 that carols were no longer sung in church, and in 1868 William Henry Tusk noted that people spoke in the singular of '*the* Christmas carol', referring solely to *God Rest ye Merry, Gentlemen*. Although the demise of the carol may have been exaggerated by some sources, the fear that many carols were being lost was certainly very real among those concerned with the conservation of English tradition at the time.

Many projects were initiated by folklorists, clerics, musicians and others in the first half of the nineteenth century to record as many carols as possible before they were forgotten. The first systematic attempt to collect carols was instigated by Davies Gilbert, MP for Bodmin, who recorded many from the West Country, noting that they had been very popular during the late eighteenth century and had given him much pleasure during his childhood. In 1825 he asked people all over England to collect every carol they heard that Christmas and send them to him. There was a desire in some religious quarters to bring more traditional carols into Christmas celebrations, but also concern at the pagan nature of others; the author of a book of carols compiled for the Society for the Promotion of Christian Knowledge in 1839 described some carols as 'the veriest trash imaginable'. Despite such objections, several collections of carols were published between 1840 and the end of the century.

In 1869 Revd H.R. Bramley and John Stainer of Magdalen College, Oxford, published *Christmas Carols Old and New*, and a slightly later edition of this, published in 1878, included 70 carols. This book proved popular in both Anglican and non-conformist churches and the carol was reborn as part of the 'official' celebration of Christmas. In their preface to the book, Bramley and Stainer observe that:

> The Editors and their friends have used every effort to obtain traditional Carol Tunes and Words which have escaped the researches of previous collectors ... The Editors hope that this collection of Carols of various kinds may promote and elevate, amongst different classes of persons, the time-honoured and delightful custom of welcoming with strains of harmony the Birthday of the HOLY CHILD.

Richard R. Chope published *Carols for Use in Church* in 1871, within which he observed that 'It has been an arduous, prolonged and costly work to restore the use of Carols in Divine Service, and thus make into an act of worship what was well-nigh considered only as a recreation at a social gathering.' A.H. Bullen published a collection of carols as *A Christmas Garland* in 1885, stating within this that 'for some time past it has been a growing practice to sing carols in church instead of in the open air.' By the turn of the century, carols were again an integral part of Christmas, heartily sung by congregations in church and families gathered around the piano in the parlour. Carol singing also remained popular in the street, with groups of singers either travelling from door to door or performing in town centres, often collecting for church or charity rather than just for themselves. By the early 1930s, carol singing was irreversibly re-established as part of popular culture and it seems that people needed no invitation to commence with it each year; *The Times* published a letter on 16 December 1931 complaining that carol singing had been in progress for several weeks and suggesting that it should be restricted more closely to Christmas! All of today's popular carols are included within the *Oxford Book of Carols* (1928), edited by England's premier composer at the time, Ralph Vaughan Williams, along with P. Dearmer and M. Shaw. This contains a scholarly introduction covering the history of carols as well as advice on the organising of carol concerts. It has been through more than 30 editions and remains the definitive volume on the subject.

The hauntingly beautiful *Silent Night,* of which versions exist in some 130 different languages, is probably the world's favourite carol. It was written by Friar Joseph Mohr (words) and Franz Xaver Gruber (music), and first performed in their village church in Oberndorf, Austria, on Christmas Eve 1818. The origins of *Silent Night* have given rise to several legends, including one that the words and music were written in just a few minutes on Christmas Eve to provide a song that could be sung without the church organ, which had broken down as the result of some mice having chewed through its bellows! In fact, the words were penned by Fr Mohr a couple of years earlier, and the fact that the score was written for guitar rather than organ owed less to a malfunctioning organ that to Mohr's prowess as a guitarist. *Silent Night* went through several alterations over subsequent years and was being performed at major concerts by the 1930s; the first recorded performance in America took place outside Trinity Church in New York in 1939. One can only wonder as to the impact the original *Stille Nacht, Heilige Nacht* sung by the choir accompanied only by Fr Mohr's guitar, may have had on the congregation of St Nicholas' church, Oberndorf, back on Christmas Eve 1818.

Once In Royal David's City began life as a poem, published in 1848 by the prolific Irish hymn writer Cecil Francis Alexander; this was set to music a year later by the famous organist, Henry John Gauntlett. Since 1919, it has provided the opening for the world-famous Festival of Nine Lessons and Carols at King's College Chapel, Cambridge, with the first verse sung as a solo, the second by the choir, and the rest by the entire congregation. *O Come All ye Faithful* is a translation by Frederick Oakeley and William Thomas Brooke of John Francis Wade's mid eighteenth-century Latin *Adeste Fidelis*; it was first published in its present form in *Murray's Hymnal* in 1852. *Good King Wenceslas* was translated from its original German and set to a traditional English tune by J.M. Neale in 1860; it proved very popular but generated much rather snobbish controversy amongst reviewers who, while acknowledging the quality of the tune, thought the lyrics to be untraditional and, in the case of one reviewer, 'poor and commonplace to the last degree'. The Irish Poet Laureate, Nahum Tate, wrote *While Shepherds Watched* in about 1700 and for a while this was the only Christmas hymn authorised by the Anglican Church. Several versions of it evolved over the eighteenth century, with the current most popular version arranged by William Henry Monk in about 1870. *Hark! The Herald Angels Sing*, an old favourite originally written by Charles Wesley (co-founder of Methodism) in 1739, was set to music adapted from Felix Mendelssohn by W.H. Cummings (Waltham Abbey organist) in 1885.

Several of today's most popular carols have mid nineteenth-century American origins. Both *Jingle Bells* and *We Three Kings of Orient Are* were written in 1857, the former by James S. Pierpoint for a Sunday school class in Boston, originally for Thanksgiving rather than Christmas, the latter as a Christmas gift for his nephews and nieces by Dr John H. Hopkins. Having recently returned from a trip to the Holy Land, Philadelphia clergyman Phillips Brooks wrote the lyrics to *O Little Town of Bethlehem* in 1868, with the music provided by the organist Lewis H. Redner; in England the same words were set to a traditional tune adapted for the purpose by Vaughan Williams and this is the version most popularly sung today. The lyrics of *Away in a Manger* (traditionally but dubiously attributed to Martin Luther) were first published anonymously in Philadelphia in 1885; a couple of years later they were set to music provided by James Ramsey Murray.

Carol singing has flourished over the past couple of centuries, proving popular in churches of various denominations and in numerous secular contexts. Carols have been recorded by the world's most brilliant classical artists and pop singers, and are sung by millions of amateur choristers every year. They are sung with equal gusto by non-believers and by the most active churchgoers. The current repertoire of popular carols includes some with medieval origins and others from the nineteenth century when carol singing underwent a great revival.

Today, our repertoire of carols is supplemented by a number of festive 'pop' songs of twentieth-century date that now qualify in their own right as essential elements of our traditional Christmas. Probably the best loved of these is *White Christmas*, written by Irving Berlin and originally recorded by Bing Crosby in 1942 (and re-recorded in 1947 due to the original master copy being worn out through excessive use!). According to the 2008 *Guinness Book of Records*, this remains the world's best-selling single of all time. The *Sunday Express* on Christmas Eve 2006 featured a list of most played Christmas songs in Britain:

1. White Christmas (Bing Crosby, 1942/1947)
2. Merry Christmas Everybody (Slade, 1973)
3. Fairytale of New York (Pogues & Kirsty MacCall, 1987)
4. Santa Claus is Coming to Town (Bruce Springsteen, 1985)
5. Last Christmas (Wham, 1984)
6. Rudolph the Red-Nosed Reindeer (Gene Autry, 1949)
7. I Wish it Could be Christmas Every Day (Wizzard, 1973)
8. Do They Know it's Christmas (Band Aid, 1984)
9. I Believe in Father Christmas (Greg Lake, 1975)
10. Merry Christmas Everyone (Shakin' Stevens, 1988)

Everyone will have their own favourite from this list; for me it has to be *Fairytale of New York*, a timeless classic that somehow managed to be brutal, melancholy, poignant and high-spirited at one and the same time. New songs may occasionally force themselves into the 'Festive Top Ten', but the above classics, along with all our favourite carols, seem destined to provide the musical background to Christmas for the foreseeable future.

Peace and Goodwill to All Men. Christmas and War

While Christmas is amongst humankind's most beautiful creations, war is probably its most hideous. There are few concepts in life less compatible with each other than war and Christmas, yet every festive season there are conflicts in progress in which people are consciously engaged in the killing of others. An in-depth consideration of the history and philosophy of links between Christmas and war could easily fill a book of this size on its own; here we will restrict ourselves to a brief discussion of a few examples.

Although it seems to have been largely disregarded from the mid fifteenth century, there existed during medieval times an unwritten code of chivalry precluding the fighting of wars over the festive season. Sadly, no such code has been in place over recent centuries. Elsewhere in this chapter we have noted the close interaction between Britons and Americans in the development of our traditional Christmas during the nineteenth century. It is easy to forget that just a few decades earlier the two nations were at war. The American War of Independence (1775-1781) saw the Americans emerge from under British rule, but only after much bloodshed. The Battle of Trenton, fought on Boxing Day 1776, is often cited as a key event in this war. The future first president, George Washington, led his small army of just 2500 men across the freezing Delaware River on Christmas night, overpowering the Trenton garrison of some 1500 men in a surprise dawn attack. Almost perversely, in the light of later conflicts that would be fought between Britain and Germany, Trenton was actually garrisoned at this time by German mercenaries fighting for the British. It is said that these mercenaries were no match for the American troops as most of them were suffering severe hangovers as a result of their Christmas celebrations the night before! Whether or not this is true, the Battle of Trenton, although in itself of minor strategic importance, was the first American victory of the war and galvanised the patriot troops into achieving further victories, resulting ultimately in independence. It may be stretching the evidence to suggest that the most powerful nation on earth, responsible (amongst other things) for the invention of Santa Claus, owes its origin ultimately to excessive Christmas partying on the part of a few German mercenaries, but the fact remains that the Battle of Trenton is regarded as a key event in the history of the United States.

We noted earlier that one of Thomas Nast's early illustrations depicted Santa dressed in the stars and stripes handing presents to

Union troops. This is perhaps the earliest example of Santa being used for propaganda purposes, bringing a degree of goodwill to men forced to spend what should be one of the most joyful days of the year fighting, far away from home. A rather more sinister image of Santa was published in *The Graphic* magazine in December 1879. This was part of a feature about British troops on the battlefront during the Afghan wars and showed a menacing-looking Santa brandishing a rifle and trampling over snow in which the words 'peace' and 'goodwill' had been written. Santa was, of course, fighting on the side of the British.

In the run up to Christmas 1899, British forces suffered serious losses during the early stages of the second Boer War in southern Africa. Despite the fact that the war was being fought on the other side of the world, news of these losses was soon relayed back home and caused much public dismay. Queen Victoria, now aged 81, responded to the situation in a most British way: she invited the families of soldiers serving in the war to a Christmas Day tea party at Windsor Castle. She records in her diary:

> All the women and children trooped in, and after looking at the tree they all sat down to tea at two very long tables, below the tree … I was rolled up and down round the tables, after which I went away for a short while to have my own tea, returning when the tree was beginning to be stripped, handing myself many of the things to the wives and dear little children … It was a very touching sight, when one thinks of the poor husbands and fathers, who are all away, and some of whom may not return.

Whatever the horrors taking place on the other side of the world, and whether or not this tea party actually made things any better for the wives, daughters and children in the longer term, it certainly seems to have helped generate some festive cheer and serves once again to emphasise the Victorian ideal of the family Christmas.

Earlier in this chapter we discussed the key role played by Queen Victoria and Prince Albert, in the introduction of the Christmas tree to England. The English were delighted to adopt this ancient German custom, and the Anglo-German royal family gathered around the Christmas tree at Windsor Castle presented a perfect picture of domestic bliss. How things would change. Just a few decades later, two of Victoria's grandchildren, King George V of England and Kaiser Wilhelm II of Germany, found themselves the figureheads of opposing sides in the most miserable conflict the world had ever seen: the so-called 'Great' War of 1914-18.

This war, known to history as World War I, extended over four Christmases, eventually ending just six weeks short of a fifth. Some 65 million men were directly engaged in the fighting, of whom 8.5 million were killed and another 21 million seriously injured. In addition, the deaths of an estimated 6.6 million civilians are attributable directly to the war. A few months after the outbreak of hostilities, Pope Benedict XV called on both sides to arrange a temporary truce for the festive season, but this was never a realistic option for the wartime leaders. Had such a truce been arranged it would have been a marvellous thing, but what actually happened on the ground, in the absence of any direction from on high, was perhaps even more marvellous. After the major battles of the autumn and early winter, troops on both sides found themselves bogged down in more or less static positions, with further advances unlikely for some time. Along a 30-mile frontier through Belgium and northern France, opposing forces reinforced their trenches, often within easy shouting distance of each other across no-man's land. Quite apart from the risk of being shot, the conditions in the trenches were dire; the weather alternated between heavy rain, when the trenches flooded with waist-high mud, and freezing cold. These thoroughly miserable conditions provided the context for the so-called 'Christmas truce'.

The best way to tell the story of the Christmas truce is in the words of those who experienced it for themselves. (Many such first-hand accounts are provided by Stanley Weintraub in his vivid and poignant *Silent Night – The Remarkable 1914 Christmas Truce*, from which several of the following examples are taken.) We begin with a letter written to his mother, on Christmas Day 1914, by Second Lieutenant Dougan Chater of the 2nd Gordon Highlanders:

> I think I have seen one of the most extraordinary sights today that anyone has ever seen. About 10 o'clock this morning I was peeping over the parapet when I saw a German, waving his arms, and presently two of them got out of their trenches … We were just going to fire on them when we saw they had no rifles so one of our men went out to meet them and in about two minutes the ground between the two lines of trenches was swarming with men and officers of both sides, shaking hands and wishing each other a happy Christmas.

A member of the London Rifle Brigade sent a letter to *The Times* in which he records:

We had an interesting time in the trenches on Christmas Eve and Christmas Day. We were in some places less than 100 yards from the Germans and held conversations with them across. It was agreed in our part of the firing line that there would be no firing and no thought of war on Christmas Eve and Christmas Day, so they sang and played to us several of their own tunes and some of ours such as 'Home Sweet Home', 'Tipperary' etc., while we did the same for them. The regiment on our left all got out of their trenches and every time a flare went up they simply stood there, cheered, and waved their hats and not a shot was fired on them. The singing and playing continued all night, and the next day (Christmas) our fellows paid a visit to the German trenches, and they did likewise. Cigarettes, cigars, addresses etc were exchanged and every one, friend and foe, was real good pals. One of the German officers took a photo of English and German soldiers arm-in-arm with exchanged caps and helmets. On Christmas Eve the Germans burned coloured lights and candles along the top of their trenches, and on Christmas Day a football match was played between us and them in front of the trench. They even allowed us to bury all our dead lying in front, and some of them, with hats in their hands, brought in one of our dead officers from behind their trench so that we could bury him decently. They were really magnificent in the whole thing and jolly good sorts. I have now a very different opinion of the Germans. Both sides have started firing and are already enemies again. Strange it all seems, doesn't it?

Sir H. Kingsley Wood, a major at Christmas 1914 and later a cabinet minister, recorded that he and his men:

> … went over in front of the trenches, and shook hands with many of our German enemies … I came to the conclusion that I have held very firmly ever since, that if we had been left to ourselves there would never have been another shot fired. For a fortnight the truce went on.

A German schoolteacher, Kurt Zehmisch of the 134th Saxon Regiment, noted in his diary that shooting ceased on Christmas Eve and men from both sides met in no-man's land where they agreed to extend their impromptu ceasefire throughout Christmas Day. That night, he wrote:

> … we placed even more candles than before on our kilometre-long trench, as well as Christmas trees. It was the purest illumination

– the British expressed their joy through whistles and clapping. Like most people, I spent the whole night awake. It was a wonderful, if somewhat cold night.

The following day he recorded that:

… the English brought a football from their trenches, and pretty soon a lively game ensued. How marvellously wonderful, yet how strange it was … Thus Christmas, the celebration of love, managed to bring mortal enemies together as our friends for a time.

There are several other recorded references from both sides to the playing of football matches in no-man's land. Some describe the use of makeshift footballs, while others bemoan the appalling state of the pitches, frozen solid and littered with shell holes and barbed wire!

Sadly, the truce was not observed uniformly along the front. Stanley Weintraub makes reference to two cases where, despite the best intentions of the Germans, it did not:

Toward the southern anchor of the British line, Major George Darrell Jeffreys of the 2nd Grenadier Guards had endured, with his men, a violent Christmas Eve and very unfriendly fire. The next morning 'a few Germans put their heads up and shouted "Merry Xmas". Our men, after yesterday, were not feeling that way, and shot at them. They at once replied and a sniping match went on all day.' Captain Billy Congreve of the 3rd Division, to the north at Kemmel, needed no upscaled animosity to maintain his belligerence. 'We have issued strict orders to the men', he noted in his diary, 'not on any account to allow a "truce", as we have heard they will try to. The Germans did try. They came over toward us singing. So we opened rapid fire on them. Which is the only sort of truce they deserve.'

In other cases there were similar attitudes in reverse. Weintraub records one such example in which a German officer provided the following response to a British suggestion of a truce:

Gentlemen, you are not, it is true, the responsible leaders of English politics, and so you are not directly responsible for their baseness; but all the same you are Englishmen, whose annihilation we consider to be our duty. We therefore request that you take such action as will prevent your mercenaries, whom you call 'soldiers', from approaching our trenches in the future.

In some cases, men were shot while believing that a truce was in operation, sometimes deliberately and sometimes apparently by accident. In one case, a British soldier was shot while returning to his trenches after delivering gifts of cigarettes to the German lines; the bullet was duly followed by an apology – an extraordinary incident given that so many millions of others would be deliberately shot, with no expectation of apology, before the war had run its course.

An article in *The War Illustrated* noted that 'Phenomenal as it may appear that soldiers fight to the death one day and fraternise the next, it is after all only strictly in accordance with human nature.' Human nature or not, the truce would soon be over and would never be repeated. From place to place along the front, the fighting recommenced, sometimes on Boxing Day or shortly thereafter, but occasionally weeks later. In one documented case, Capt Stockwell of the 2nd Welsh Fuseliers ordered three shots fired harmlessly into the air at 8.30am on Boxing Day, then raised a sign reading 'Merry Christmas' and climbed up onto his parapet. The Germans promptly replied with a sign saying 'Thank you', and their captain likewise climbed onto his parapet. The two commanding officers then bowed, saluted and descended back into their trenches. The German officer fired two shots into the air, and the carnage recommenced.

Men were threatened with execution by their own officers if they didn't begin firing again at the 'friends' with whom they just been celebrating Christmas. The powers that be on both sides made it absolutely clear that no such unofficial truce, either at Christmas or any other time, would be permitted in future. A German order dated 29 December stated that any fraternisation with the enemy would be punishable as treason, and the British issued strict instructions in advance of Christmas 1915 that there were to be no repeats whatsoever of the previous year's events.

Stanley Weintraub observes that the Christmas truce:

> … appears in retrospect somehow unreal, incredible in its intensity and extent, seemingly impossible to have happened without consequences for the outcome of the war. Like a dream, when it was over, men wondered at it, then went on with the grim business at hand. Under the rigid discipline of wartime command authority, that business was killing.

For the next four Christmases, efforts were made to ensure that British troops had as good a time as possible to discourage any thought of fraternisation with the enemy. Wherever possible, troops were given a decent Christmas dinner, even if it had to be delayed a few days for operational reasons. The men enjoyed carol services and inter-regimental football matches, and special efforts were made to ensure Christmas deliveries of post from loved ones. In an age-old custom that has its origins back in Roman Saturnalia celebrations, when slaves were to some extent waited upon by their owners, British army officers served the men at Christmas dinner, giving rise to much festive mirth. In contrast to the events of 1914, Christmas was now used as a platform for the delivery of morale-boosting rallying calls, as illustrated by King George V's message to the troops in 1916:

> I send you, my sailors and soldiers, hearty good wishes for Christmas and the New Year. My grateful thoughts are ever with you for victories gained, for hardships endured, and for your unfailing cheeriness. Another Christmas has come around, and we are still at war, but the Empire, confident in you, remains determined to win. May God bless you and protect you. At this Christmastide the Queen and I are thinking more than ever of the sick and wounded among my sailors and soldiers. From our hearts we wish them strength to bear their sufferings, speedy restoration to health, a peaceful Christmas and many happy years to come.

World War I included four Christmases, but World War II would extend over no less than six. During this conflict Christmas was used as propaganda to justify the war and stress the need for the enemy to be defeated as soon as possible. For example, King George VI stated in his Christmas radio broadcast to the Empire in 1939 that:

> The festival which we know as Christmas is above all the festival of peace and of the home. Among all free peoples the love of peace is profound, for this alone gives security to the home. But true peace is in the hearts of men, and it is the tragedy of this time that there are powerful countries whose whole direction and policy are based on aggression and the suppression of all that we hold dear for mankind. It is this that has stirred our peoples and given them a unity unknown in any previous war. We feel in our hearts that we are fighting against wickedness, and this conviction will give us strength from day to day to persevere until victory is assured.

Christmas 1941 is worthy of special mention here in the light of two key events which took place on opposite sides of the world. The United States had entered the war following the Japanese bombing of Pearl Harbour earlier in the year, and Prime Minister Winston Churchill travelled to Washington to meet with President Roosevelt to discuss tactics; good relations between the allies would be crucial to the eventual outcome of the war. Churchill arrived in Washington on 22 December, attended the lighting of the White House Christmas Tree along with 30,000 Americans on Christmas Eve, went to church with Roosevelt on Christmas Day, and addressed both Houses of Congress on Boxing Day. During the Christmas Eve festivities, Churchill's moving address to the American people included the following:

> Let the children have their night of fun and laughter. Let the gifts of Father Christmas delight their play. Let us grown-ups share to the full in their unstinted pleasures before we turn again to the stern task and the formidable years that lie before us, resolved that, by our sacrifice and daring, these same children shall not be robbed of their inheritance or denied their right to live in a free and decent world.

While Churchill and Roosevelt were enjoying their Christmas in Washington, on the opposite side of the world in Hong Kong things were altogether less convivial. Christmas 1941 is referred to here as 'Black Christmas'. Following a ferocious invasion during which a third of the men making up the 10,000 strong British garrison were killed, the Governor had no option other than to surrender, which he duly did at 3.30pm on Christmas Day – truly a 'Black Christmas', as subsequent atrocities during the brutal Japanese occupation would result in the deaths of thousands of prisoners of war and civilians.

Much has been written on the subject of Christmas on the 'home front' during World War II. Such accounts generally stress the desire of people to have as good a time as possible in the face of a shortage of provisions and the absence of loved ones (menfolk were away on service, while many children had been evacuated from the cities). Despite the difficulties, much ingenuity was applied to ensuring that people, and especially children, had a decent Christmas; the Ministry of Food provided advice on the preparation of festive food using available ingredients, including Christmas cakes made with potato instead of fruit! A 1941 Ministry of Information film entitled *Christmas under Fire*, stated that

> The nation has made a resolve that war or no war, the children of England will not be cheated out of the one day they look forward to

all year. So, as far as possible, this will be an old-fashioned Christmas, at least for the children.

This desire to celebrate Christmas in the face of adversity was not restricted to Britain, as the festive season also continued to play an important role in Germany during the War. In *The Making of the Modern Christmas*, Golby and Purdue make the important observation that according to German propaganda the war was necessary to protect German culture from both western capitalism and Russian communism, quoting the following passage from an official German publication:

> Let us bear in mind for a moment, as we stand before our pine tree, that Bolshevism has eradicated the feast of Christmas root and branch, and that Americanism has distorted it into a racket with jazz and drinking. This makes us realise that even in wartime, we must celebrate Christmas within the family, because one of the reasons our soldiers are standing guard is to ensure that we may retain this festival and celebrate it in our own way.

It is fascinating to note that both the English and German propaganda machines were using Christmas in precisely the same way – stressing it as an essential element of their own traditional cultures that were worth fighting to protect.

Sadly, the end of the war did not bring to an end the phenomenon of conflict at Christmas, although the concept of fighting over the festive season continued to provoke feelings of unease. In December 1972, during closing stages of the Vietnam War, President Nixon ordered a huge bombing raid over North Vietnam. Whatever its supposed justification, this caused unimaginable carnage and grief to the people on the ground. The campaign became known back in America as 'the Christmas Bombings', and hardened further the considerable opposition to the war. There had already been much opposition to earlier bombing raids, and to the war in general, but the fact that this raid took place over the festive season (one senator condemned it as 'a sorry Christmas present') seems to have struck a particular chord amongst the American people, and not just those vehemently opposed to the war. Whether or not it was acceptable to bomb the enemy into defeat, it certainly was not acceptable to do so at Christmas.

In the early twenty-first century, many of our festive news bulletins and newspapers were dominated by accounts of our troops in action in Afghanistan and Iraq; articles covering troops celebrating Christmas being interspersed with horrendous stories of death and destruction. During the 2006 festive season, our television screens were dominated by the grizzly spectacle of Saddam Hussein's execution, on 30 December. A year later, on 27 December 2007, the season was interrupted by news of the assassination of Benazir Bhutto in Pakistan. These events, ghastly in their own right, were somehow given extra poignancy by the fact they occurred during the supposed 'season of goodwill'.

We will leave the final words on war at Christmas to Stanley Weintraub, who ends his *Silent Night* with the following poignant and perceptive passage:

> A celebration of the human spirit, the Christmas Truce remains a moving manifestation of the absurdities of war. A very minor Scottish poet of Great War vintage, Frederick Niven, may have got it right in his 'A Carol from Flanders', which closed
>
> > 'O ye who read this truthful rime
> > From Flanders, kneel and say:
> > God speed the time when every day
> > Shall be as Christmas Day.'

A Merry Christmas and a Rubbish New Year! Christmas and climate change

We have no way of knowing how frequently white Christmases occurred in the ancient past, although occasional references to particularly cold Christmases have found their way into the history books. Symeon of Durham writes of a year in the mid eighth century when 'deep snow hardened into ice unlike anything that had ever been known in previous ages and oppressed the land from the beginning of winter until almost the beginning of spring.' During medieval times, it was not unusual for major rivers to freeze at midwinter, and frost fairs were often held on the Thames; the last such example was in 1813-14 when the entertainment included an elephant walking across the river. Things seem very different today. An article in *The Journal* (the local daily newspaper for Newcastle upon Tyne and north-east England) on 23 December 2006 notes that average Britons see a white Christmas only eight times in their lives; the lucky residents of Aberdeen enjoy a white Christmas every

2.24 years, but snow falls on Christmas Day only once in 16.5 years for the good folk of Sunderland. Niall Edworthy in *The Curious World of Christmas* records that Christmas Day snow fell on London just 10 times during the twentieth century, and, perhaps more surprisingly, on Glasgow only 10 times since 1918. Snow's intimate association with Christmas seems unjustifiable on climatological grounds alone; indeed, it can be statistically demonstrated that Britain is as likely to experience a white Easter each year as a white Christmas. It is unlikely, though, that Easter Bunny will ever be challenged by the snowman: each is an icon of its own season, and the snowman's season is undoubtedly Christmas. (Incidentally, although we have no space to delve into it here, the snowman has a fascinating history of his own, apparently stretching back to medieval times and perhaps beyond.)

The survey in *The Journal* records that of 2000 adults interviewed, 29% claimed never to have experienced a white Christmas, yet 75% hope for snow every Christmas while 86% 'reckon a white Christmas makes the day perfect'. Presumably, some of this 86% are among those who decorate their homes, both internally and externally, with electrically powered icicles and snowflakes, along with all manner of other 'festive' illuminations. In an amusing article in *The Guardian* (11 December 2007), Jon Henley visits some of the most extravagantly decorated houses. The first, a terraced home in Coventry, is truly ghastly; a 'much abbreviated list' of things attached to the front of the house mentions:

> Three illuminated blow-up Santas climbing up a red drainpipe; two lit-up snowmen on a yellow, moving see-saw; a couple of nice bright "Santa Stop here" signs in the (red and white) windows; a pair of oversized flashing church bells (gold); a Father Christmas on a motorbike (ditto); a range of wildly refulgent pine trees (green); another few snowmen on sleighs (yellow); and heaven knows how many yards of rope and strip lights (red, blue and white, mainly) draped artistically over the roof.

Believe it or not, this exterior pales into insignificance in comparison with the interior, but we will resist the temptation to step inside. The second featured example, in Wiltshire, is possibly even worse. With apologies to the owners, who clearly see the festive decoration of their home as a labour of love (and who commendably raise substantial sums for charity each year through donations from visitors), this is possibly the most appalling example of festive light pollution I have ever seen. Highlights include:

> A giant blow-up Homer Simpson dressed up as Santa, a cello-playing snowman, a particularly fine set of glowing Victorian carol-singers, Father Christmas driving a small sports car, and a magnificent illuminated reindeer…

The lights add about an extra £500 each year to the family's electricity bill, but low-power LED features (such as two newly introduced bright blue reindeer on the shed roof) are being phased in to try and prevent the costs from spiralling out of control, and 'a big effort' is made to minimise energy consumption throughout the rest of the year. Residents in the vicinity of both these houses apparently love the annual illuminations and many have invested in smaller scale versions themselves. Sadly, such seasonal cheer appears to be in rather shorter supply amongst the residents of Sonning (Berkshire) where one man's dazzling display of 22,000 lights drew complaints and a death threat from angry neighbours. After an expensive court case and a day in jail, this unfortunate chap's festive illuminations are now limited to a paltry 300 lights.

Apparently the 'art' of illuminating our houses was imported in the 1960s from (you've guessed it) America, and judging by the number of lights sold each year it seems destined to be with us indefinitely. When asked 'why?', most people who invest so heavily in festive illuminations tend to reply 'for the kids', which I suppose is fair enough, though I suspect in most cases the kids could think of better things to spend the money on. Of course, it isn't just private houses that are illuminated at Christmas. Most towns and cities provide communal illuminations, some of which, it has to be said, can be very attractive. The more traditional examples often include snowmen, reindeer and other wintry themes, but of course they are all contributing, every moment they are lit, to global warming and the seemingly irreversible trend away from real snow at Christmas. And this is only the tip of the (rapidly melting) iceberg regarding Christmas's contribution to global warming.

These days, everyone seems to be on the move at Christmas, attempting to negotiate clogged-up motorways or suffering overcrowded trains to reach relatives or get to the airport to escape for some Christmas sunshine; all this travelling about succeeds, of course, in providing a further festive boost to the causes of climate change. *The Observer* on Christmas Eve 2006 reports that 'One of the crowning glories of the festive season – holly trees groaning with clusters of crimson berries – is being destroyed by a combined assault from car exhausts and global warming.' Sadly, even those of us who opt to spend Christmas at home are far from blameless in the pollution stakes. An article in *The Independent* on 23 December 2006, entitled 'High environmental price of a very merry Christmas', outlines some of the environmental consequences of the modern British Christmas. The Liberal green spokesman, Chris Huhne, is quoted as saying that 'Having a Merry Christmas could end in a rubbish New Year', and examples of rubbish generated at Christmas are provided: 6 million Christmas trees, enough to reach, laid end to end, from London to the North Pole and back; more than a billion Christmas cards, enough to form a continuous line reaching five times around the world; 83 square kilometres of wrapping paper, enough to wrap the island of Jersey; and 125,000 tons of plastic packaging, which according to the Liberals equates to the weight of more than a million John Prescotts. The article also estimates that more than 40% of toys given as Christmas presents will be broken within three months, most of which will find their way to the local tip.

According to *The Independent*, some 16 million turkeys and 830 million sprouts are purchased for British Christmas dinners, but some 40% of all festive food is wasted. On Christmas Eve 2005, *The Independent* published several letters from readers on festive themes. One of these, quoting data from the Soil Association, claims that the average Christmas dinner consists largely of cheap imports: 'the turkey may be from Norfolk, but your carrots are likely to have come from Morocco ... and the Brussels sprouts from the Netherlands.' Adding in wine and other vegetables, the total 'food miles' bill for the average Christmas dinner is estimated at 43,674. Another contributor sums up the environmental cost of Christmas, citing the energy used in the production of gifts that are often of poor quality and disposable, the transport of these from production sites (often in the Far East) to the shops, and the environmental damage done by intensive farming to produce our Christmas dinner. We could also mention the production and transport costs associated with our beloved Christmas lights, before we even begin to count the cost of lighting them! It is estimated that Britons generate some 3 million tons of domestic rubbish each Christmas, barely a quarter of which is recycled, the rest being incinerated or dumped, resulting in further environmental pollution. The current move towards recycling of festive rubbish is certainly encouraging, but the waste generated by our 'throw-away' society each Christmas is still outrageous and certainly does nothing for the prospects of future white Christmases.

Children in Charge! The family at Christmas

Perhaps the most surprising aspect of this chapter has been the relative lack of consideration of anything to do with the Christian Church; the celebration of Christmas seems to have developed its own momentum almost without the need to refer to Christ. Although many people still go to church at Christmas (a sizeable proportion of whom attend at no other time) Christmas in many people's minds has become more a celebration of the family than of the birth of Jesus. Indeed, the development of the family Christmas, with its focus on children, has been in many ways the dominant theme throughout this chapter.

Initially, as we have seen, it was the middle classes that adopted the new family Christmas, with working-class children dependent on charity if their Christmas day was to be in any way special. Of course, many working-class people had to be at work in order for the middle and upper classes to enjoy Christmas; some 1½ million people were employed in domestic service in the early twentieth century, and their Christmases were certainly spent hard at work, even if they did receive Christmas dinner and other seasonal bonuses.

Within the Victorian middle classes, extended family reunions became the norm at Christmas, especially as the ever improving rail network made such reunions easier. Children would return from boarding school, and adults would leave their city jobs for at least a couple of days to enjoy a festive family reunion. By the mid twentieth century, many working-class folk also enjoyed a family Christmas, although not on such a grand scale; the working-class family Christmas tended to be more about the immediate family than a gathering of far-flung relatives.

As the family Christmas became the norm, children increasingly found themselves the focus of festivities and the receiving of presents became crucial to their enjoyment of the season. In the mid nineteenth century, according to the social investigator Henry Mayhew (quoted in Weightman and Humphries) only about fourpence-halfpenny (about one pence in today's money) was spent on toys for the average child *each year*. Several types of toy were available at a cost of an old penny, but any that were given in midwinter were more likely to be given at New Year than on Christmas Day. From the middle of the century, however, as Christmas grew in popularity, present-giving found itself gradually transferred from 1 January to 25 December (this change would not occur in parts of Scotland for another century). As the years went by, the middle classes spent more and more on Christmas presents, and new types of toys, games and books were mass-produced to cash in on this market. Toy shops, and toy sections within department stores, did a roaring trade in the run up to Christmas, as they still do today. Among the working classes, demand grew for cheap toys at Christmas, a demand that was met in large part by Woolworths, which opened in 1907 offering a huge range of presents for just a few pennies each. Before World War I, most of these cheap toys were imported from Germany, but during and after the war they were increasingly manufactured at home.

By the mid twentieth century, Christmas had become the favourite time of year for most children, and the emphasis within the family Christmas was very much on the provision of presents and entertainment for them. There were some who seem to have struggled to come to terms with this, amongst the most eloquent of whom was the famous English writer, Evelyn Waugh. As a young man, his view of Christmas was less than flattering, as demonstrated an entry in his diary for 1914: 'Like birthdays, Christmas gets duller and duller. Soon it will merely be a day when the shops are inconveniently shut.' In later life, his unfestive ire seems to have become focused to a degree on his children; his diaries for Christmas Day 1945 and 1946 record:

> By keeping the children in bed for long periods we managed to have a tolerable day.

> I made a fair show of geniality throughout the day though the spectacle of a litter of shoddy toys and half-eaten sweets sickened me. Everything is so badly made nowadays that none of the children's presents seemed to work. Luncheon was cold and poorly cooked. A ghastly day.

It seems the Waugh children were lucky to get presents at all, even if they didn't work properly. Waugh was, however, very much in a minority. Most families enjoyed Christmas immensely, and throughout the latter half of the century the festival became increasingly focused upon children in the minds of parents, businessmen, entertainers and, of course, the kids themselves. Festive entertainment has certainly followed this trend, developing in line with advances in technology but increasingly focusing on children. Somehow, alongside film, television and all manner of electronic gizmos, the humble pantomime has retained its popularity. The pantomime as we know it today became popular during Victorian times, merging music hall tradition with elements of Italian *commedia dell'arte* (street theatre popular from the sixteenth to the eighteenth centuries), and incorporating the age-old Saturnalian traditions of cross-dressing and dressing up in animal costumes. The earliest pantomimes were staged as support acts to conventional plays, but proved so popular that they soon grew into full-length productions in their own right. Today, many small theatres rely on the annual pantomime season to keep them in business, while larger venues compete to attract 'star names' to play leading roles. Today's pantomimes, including classics such as Cinderella, Aladdin, Dick Whittington, Snow White, Jack and the Beanstalk, Sleeping Beauty and Peter Pan, are invariable aimed at children. Despite their plots having nothing whatsoever to do with Christmas, they seem set to remain indefinitely as a key element of our festive season.

Christmas at the movies is a huge topic which we can consider only briefly here (readers who wish to find out more should refer to Mark Connolly's fascinating *Christmas at the Movies*). Some of the earliest festive films were silent versions of *A Christmas Carol,* the earliest known of which dates from 1901, but the 'Christmas movie industry' didn't really take off until after World War II. Perhaps the greatest Christmas movie of all time, *It's a Wonderful Life* (which, according to the film critic Barry Norman, should be shown on television every year immediately following the Queen's speech) was made in 1946. Very few films feature the Nativity, but from the appearance of *Miracle on 34th Street* in 1947, Santa became increasingly popular on the big screen, reflecting society's growing obsession with consumerism. While many Christmas films were aimed at an adult audience, recent examples have tended to focus very much on children, or on families with young children, as demonstrated by the following list of the 'Top Ten' Christmas movies broadcast on ITV on Christmas Day, 2006:

1. Miracle on 34th Street (1947; remade 1994)
2. White Christmas (1954)
3. The Snowman (1982)
4. It's A Wonderful Life (1946)
5. Home Alone (1990)
6. Polar Express (2004)
7. Santa Claus the Movie (1985)
8. Elf (2003)
9. The Muppet Christmas Carol (1992)
10. The Grinch (2000)

In general terms, successful Christmas movies tend to be about children and families, and most scripts see love winning out at the end of the day. No doubt we all have our favourite Christmas movie; I think mine is probably *Love Actually* (2003), which bucks the trend somewhat in not being one for the kids. Billed as 'the ultimate romantic comedy', it exquisitely exploits the Christmas spirit to accentuate the emotional turmoil in the lives of a hotch-potch of diverse characters, expertly played by an all-star cast.

In the earlier twentieth century it was customary for people to visit the cinema on Christmas Day, but today we increasingly watch films at home on our wide-screen televisions, further adding to the domestic nature of the present-day Christmas. Television has in itself been instrumental in the development of festive entertainment; in the 1980s it was calculated that more than 70% of the population watched television on the evening of Christmas Day. While millions fewer feel the need to tune into the Queen's speech on Christmas Day than did back in the 1960s, an agenda of 'Christmas specials' and blockbuster movies, most aimed at families with young children, continues to ensure that most of us turn to our televisions for festive entertainment at some point, a habit reinforced by the fact that most sporting venues, concert halls, cinemas and shops are closed on Christmas Day. For many families today, the television also provides the platform for all manner of video games. Children (and, let's be honest, lots of adults too) often receive such games for Christmas, and spend much of the festive season engaged in winning the virtual World Cup, or saving the virtual world from hordes of invading aliens. Evelyn Waugh's attempt to have a tolerable day by keeping his children in bed would not be regarded as good practice today, but many of us are grateful for the opportunity to gain an hour or two of festive peace and quiet by sticking the kids in front of a video game!

Today's children, their demands fuelled by incessant television advertising and peer pressure, receive DVDs, video games and other presents imported at great cost from all over the world, often causing serious financial hardship for their parents. As we have seen, role reversal was an element of midwinter festivities in Roman times – today, those of us fortunate enough to have them will readily testify that it is our children who are in charge at Christmas!

7

Midwinter Mayhem!
Some thoughts on the complexity of the contemporary Christmas

One figure missing – Baby Jesus! Christmas in the modern media

Having considered the evolution of Christmas over the past 5000 years, it seems appropriate to close with a brief analysis of the contemporary festive season, if only to demonstrate how history is reflected in present-day tradition. To this end I will present some recent stories from the media, along with a few personal experiences, before considering the nature of Christmas and the extent to which modern festivities reflect ancient traditions. Over recent years, newspaper articles about the festive season have tended to focus on five interrelated themes: business, religion, conflict in the Middle East, social problems at home and the environment. The last of these was covered in some detail in the previous chapter, the others are considered here.

A tendency towards what archaeologists like to term 'conspicuous consumption' has probably been a characteristic of midwinter feasts from the earliest times, and we may recall Libanius' observation that 'he who the whole year through has taken pleasure in saving and piling up his pence, becomes suddenly extravagant' during the Kalends. The Christian story of the Nativity may be rooted in poverty, but Christmas is increasingly about big business, and commercial interests now feature prominently in modern press coverage of the festive season. *The Independent* reported on Christmas Eve 2006 that a last-minute £6 billion shopping spree had averted disaster on the high street. Elsewhere in the same paper, an article recorded the frantic activity at a Milton Keynes distribution centre for Japanese consumer goods, as giant televisions, American style fridges, state-of-the-art mobile phones, and numerous other products are despatched throughout Britain to satisfy the Christmas market. The 700 staff at the centre only get Christmas Day off over the festive season, and in January plans get underway for the following Christmas. The *Sunday*

Express Christmas Eve front page screamed '£3 million a minute shopping spree', claiming that 'Britons will throng town centres today in the biggest shopping spree in history. More than 20 million people are expected to spend £1.14 billion in six hours of frantic Sunday trading.' In addition to all this activity in the shops, the *Sunday Express* reported that more than £7 billion was spent online in the 10 weeks leading up to Christmas. It also included a feature on 'Scrooge Brown', with the then Chancellor of the Exchequer and future Prime Minister depicted as Scrooge in an article claiming that 'workers will have £80 less to spend on gifts and festive food because pay packets have failed to keep pace with soaring fuel bills and council tax hikes.'

The Guardian on 23 December reported on festive shopping at Selfridges on Oxford Street, where a team of 50 'gift gurus' was employed specifically to help shoppers navigate the store. In addition to the gurus, a team of Santas was also employed to welcome up to 1600 children a day to the store's grotto; at busy times, each child got 90 seconds with Santa. The following day, Christmas Eve, *The Observer* reported that Selfridges expected 100,000 customers that day, and had noted a 'gender switch' over the previous few days, with women shopping early and men leaving it late, though no explanation of this strange phenomenon is attempted. Christmas Eve 2006 was a Sunday, so, despite the frenzy of last-minute Christmas shoppers, Sunday trading legislation applied. This limits businesses to a maximum of six hours' trading, but in a controversial move several large stores (including Tesco, Asda and Sainsbury's) opened their doors half an hour early to enable shoppers to fill up their trolleys; campaigners against Sunday trading, including the Church of England, were not impressed. As we have seen, in Scotland Christmas was only adopted as an official holiday as late as 1958, but the Scots are clearly making up for lost time; *The Observer* article reported that Christmas 2006 was expected to be worth some £2.4 billion to traders north of the border. (Unfortunately, things were not so positive 12 months later; *The Independent* on 19 January 2008 included a range of gloomy economic forecasts under the headline 'Official: worst Christmas on the High Street for 13 years'.)

When shopping for festive food and drink, people are increasingly opting to pay extra for top quality. *The Guardian* on 11 January 2007 reported a booming trade in organic and luxury ranges at several supermarkets, while an article in *The Evening Standard* on the same day reported that sales of champagne 'shot through the roof' at Christmas. Sainsbury's reported that one of its champagnes, costing

£20.99 a bottle, had outsold tins of baked beans in the run-up to Christmas, with 2 million bottles sold in December. Many other outlets reported vast growth in Christmas champagne sales over the previous year: at Morrisons sales were up by 40%. Paying for all this quality booze and festive food, in addition to presents and other seasonal expenditure, gets many of us into financial difficulty. *The Guardian* on 23 December 2006 states:

> Christmas is a time for giving, but the pressure to impress family and friends with expensive gifts means many people will be saddled with debts until long after the decorations have gone back into the box. The average Briton spent £2,200 over the festive period last year, and 20% of people say they are often still trying to break even by the following March … One in ten are still in debt by the next Christmas.

While so many of us are struggling financially at Christmas, the festive season offers rich pickings for the criminal fraternity. As consumers have switched their attention from high street shops to websites at Christmas, so criminals have turned from traditional easy targets, such as houses heaving with newly purchased presents and homes left temporarily empty, and have begun to focus on the internet. An alarming article about online festive fraud appeared in *The Times* on Boxing Day 2007:

> While families settled down to a day of unwrapping presents and second helpings of turkey and mince pies, criminals were also indulging in another form of seasonal cheer in the most fraud-ridden Christmas Day in Britain's online history.
>
> An estimated 8,500 fraudsters went online yesterday to help themselves to electronic goods and gold-plated watches using stolen credit card details. Tracking systems for online criminal activity are now so sophisticated that fraudulent transactions can be monitored in real time and reveal in which parts of the world online bandits are based.

Online fraud increased 167% on Christmas Day compared with Christmas Eve, apparently because the fraudsters believe that many retailers' fraud detection systems are not operational on Christmas Day. Readers may be interested to learn that the top five Christmas Day hotspots for fraudsters operating within Britain were Portsmouth, Reading, Blackburn, Carlisle and Beckton, while the top five hotspots from which international fraudsters targeted British businesses were Ukraine, the Netherlands, Sweden, Switzerland and the United States. Christmas crime has become a global problem, and seems likely to grow in tandem with the increasing popularity of online trading.

While most shops are legally obliged to remain closed on Christmas Day, no such restrictions apply to the internet. The front page of *The Times* on Boxing Day 2007 reported that while 2.7 million people had attended Anglican Christmas Day services, more than 3.5 million spent part of the day shopping online, spending a total of some £53 million. Anyone reading the newspapers at Christmas with no background knowledge of the subject might be forgiven for believing that the festival is primarily about shopping rather than religion. That said, there are always several articles with a religious theme in the Christmas papers, most of which cover controversial issues such as the increasingly profane nature of Christmas cards and Nativity plays. *The Guardian's* headline on 23 December 2006 read 'Religion does more harm than good – poll'. The poll concludes that 'non-believers outnumber believers in Britain by almost two-to-one', and that more than half the people in Britain who describe themselves as 'Christian' actually claim to be 'not religious'. It seems, though, that Christians become a little more Christian at Christmas; 54% of those polled intended to attend church at least once over the festive season. Interestingly, this figure rises to 64% amongst the most well-off in society, and falls to just 43% amongst the poorest. The poverty implicit in the Nativity may have succeeded in getting medieval peasants to attend church at Christmas, but does not seem to be having the same effect in the modern world. An article in *The Independent* on Christmas Eve 2006 referred to a survey showing that 'Britons associate Christmas with kindness, not with Christ', and it certainly does appear that the Church is increasingly struggling to get its traditional message across to the majority of people. Indeed, the degree of irreverence towards Christ at Christmas would have been unthinkable in earlier times; the front cover of *Private Eye* at Christmas 2007 features a fine cartoon in which a glum Joseph, standing outside a stable, is severely informed by a police officer that 'we've had complaints about your tasteless and intrusive Christmas lights, Sir'. The offending light emanates from one particularly bright star, located directly above the stable. Such humour is, for the vast majority, completely harmless, but the same cannot be said of the thieves who stole 300 shepherds from an eighteenth-century church crib in Naples, valued at more than a million Euros. *The Independent* reported this most unfestive crime on 20 December 2006, noting that the thieves, 'showing a vestige of religious feeling, or superstitious fear' left the baby Jesus in the manger. This gesture had little impact, however, on the parish priest, who states 'there is no respect any more for the values of Christmas'. Similar views may have been reached by Christmas shoppers at Woolworths in Newcastle-upon-Tyne in 2006; in an article in the *Journal* (23 December 2006) the chairman of the Newcastle Methodists records that while Christmas shopping in the store his eyes were drawn towards the Nativity sets, where:

> Amongst them all, one particular set stood out. A neat little nativity set was packed tightly into a blue box and stuck to it, somewhat precariously, was a giant orange star upon which was printed in bold letters the words 'REDUCED – one figure missing – Baby Jesus.'

While acknowledging the humour of the story, the writer went on to observe that the baby-less Nativity set:

> spoke powerfully of our time … for too many people, Christmas is much reduced because of the failure to see or to recognise the real meaning of it – the birth of a saviour, Jesus Christ. Baby Jesus really is missing!

This article is one of several contributed to a two-page spread in which local religious leaders from various faiths offered brief thoughts on the nature of Christmas. A local rabbi explained that Jews are currently celebrating 'the festival of Chanukah, celebrating the victory of good over evil, the triumph of light over darkness', and noted that many religions celebrate a festival of light and miracles during the darkest nights of winter. A leader of the Newcastle Hindu Temple notes that the Hindu community would be joining in the festivities of Christmas, called for friendship and understanding between faiths, and wished everyone a happy Christmas and a peaceful New Year. The Anglican Bishop of Newcastle and the Catholic Bishop of Hexham and Newcastle both called for people to make time for God at Christmas, with the latter making a special plea for people to support Christmas charities.

At a time when so much conflict and misunderstanding exists between the Christian and Islamic worlds, we should recall that the Qur'an honours Jesus as one of the greatest of the prophets. Islam does not regard Jesus as divine, but the Qur'an has more to say than the Bible about the virginal conception and birth, considering it as representative of the birth of the spirit in all of us. Karen Armstrong, writing in *The Guardian* on 23 December 2006, suggests that Christmas would be a good time to reconsider the relationship between Christian and Muslim in the modern world:

> The Muslim devotion to Jesus is a remarkable example of the way in which one tradition can be enriched by another. It cannot be said that Christians returned the compliment. While the Muslims were amassing their Jesus-traditions, Christian scholars in Europe were denouncing Mohammed as a lecher and charlatan, viciously addicted to violence. But today both Muslims and Christians are guilty of this kind of bigotry and often seem eager to see only the worst in each other …
>
> … this was not always the case. In the past, before the political dislocations of modernity, Muslims were always able to engage in fruitful and stringent self-criticism. This year, on the birthday of the prophet Jesus, they might ask themselves how they can revive their long tradition of pluralism and appreciation of other religions. For their part, meditating on the affinity that Muslims once felt for their faith, Christians might look into their own past and consider what they might have done to forfeit this respect.

The Christmas press in 2006 and 2007 featured many articles covering events in the Middle East. These tended to fall into two basic categories: pieces featuring the conflict in Iraq and Afghanistan, including articles on Christmas amongst British troops on the frontline, and others covering aspects of the Arab-Israeli conflict in Palestine/Israel. On 23 December 2006, an article in *The Times* linked these two themes. Under the front page headline 'Christians suffer for Iraq, says Archbishop', the paper reports the view of Dr Rowan Williams, Archbishop of Canterbury, that Christians throughout the Middle East are being put at unprecedented risk by the British government's 'shortsighted' and 'ignorant' policy in Iraq. Writing from Bethlehem, where he was on pilgrimage along with the Archbishop of Westminster (thus at least demonstrating a degree of festive camaraderie between the Catholic Church and the Church of England), Dr Williams stated that the Israeli-built wall around Bethlehem symbolised what was 'deeply wrong in the human heart'. In an article within the paper, entitled 'Pray for the little town of Bethlehem', the Archbishop notes that Christians and Muslims have lived in harmony in many places throughout the Middle East, but this harmony is being destroyed by current western policy in the region:

The first Christian believers were Middle Easterners. It's a sobering thought that we might live to see the last native Christian believers in the region. It's not a problem we can go on ignoring if we care about the health and stability of the Middle East; we need to confront it, not by weighing in with firepower but by making real relationships with the communities there and working at trustful contacts with those Muslims who understand their own history and want to live in a lively, varied culture.

This Christmas, pray for the little town of Bethlehem, and spare a thought for those who have been put at risk by our own short-sightedness and ignorance …

On the same day, *The Independent* covered this theme in its editorial, stating that the proportion of Christians in Bethlehem's population had fallen from 85% in 1948 to the current 12%, and noting that 'In one of the unfailing ironies of the place religious believers call the Holy Land, its most famous emblem of peace – the little town of Bethlehem – is once again a symbol of its troubles.' On its front page, this edition of *The Independent* asked 'What would happen if the Virgin Mary came to Bethlehem today?' The answer is provided in the form of a chilling account of mothers being mistreated and babies dying needlessly in the West Bank. According to the United Nations, at least 37 babies have died since 2002 because their mothers were detained during labour at Israeli checkpoints. The article goes on to report that medical staff have been on strike due to a lack of funds, resulting in mothers 'giving birth in startlingly similar conditions to those suffered by Mary 2,000 years ago … with no doctors, no sterilised equipment, no back-up if there are complications.'

Few would question the Archbishop of Canterbury's right to raise concerns over such problems in the Middle East, but on Christmas Eve 2006 *The Observer* published an article under the headline 'Foreign Office rap for Archbishop'. This reported that 'A serious row between church and state broke out last night after the Foreign Office rebuked the Archbishop of Canterbury for accusing the government of putting Christians across the Middle East at risk …' The article goes on to report a special Christmas message from the Queen (who is, of course, above all such tittle-tattle between her Government and her Church) to the troops serving in Iraq and Afghanistan, praising them for their 'professionalism which is so highly regarded the world over'.

A lengthy article entitled 'Christmas on the front line' appeared in the 2006 Christmas Eve edition of *The Independent on Sunday*. This

reported that British forces celebrate Christmas as best they can, but
sometimes, for operational reasons, not on the day itself. Troops get
an extra 30 free minutes of phone calls from home, and most receive
parcels sent from home free of charge. In addition, in a tradition that
has its origins back in 1914, all 25,000 British servicemen and women
serving overseas at Christmas receive a box of 'secret goodies'. A
special effort is made to provide all troops with a traditional Christmas
dinner, and every cookhouse is provided with an artificial Christmas
tree. Some regiments maintain the ancient festive tradition of officers
and senior NCOs waiting on the men. One traditional element
of the Christmas feast is, however, missing; understandably, alcohol
is not served to troops on the front line. Where possible, festive
entertainment is laid on, including concerts, pantomimes and sports
events, and church services are held for those who want them.

Despite the potential distractions, it is pretty much business
as usual for most front-line troops on Christmas Day. All must be
constantly on their guard as danger is never far away: Christmas Day
2007 saw 34 people killed and dozens wounded in two separate
suicide attacks in towns near Baghdad. On Boxing Day 2007, *The
Times* published an article about Christmas in Baghdad, where many
churches remain closed after being bombed by Islamic extremists
and the few churches able to hold services do so under heavy police
guard on the afternoon of Christmas Eve rather than at midnight,
which is considered too dangerous. The article features a depressing
interview with a young Iraqi mother following a Christmas Eve
service. Many of her relatives have fled Iraq, and she says 'I feel
sad when I remember what Christmas used to be like … I want
my relatives to return because I hate being alone at Christmas …
without them I feel like a Christmas tree with no decorations.'

Things in Britain are nowhere near as bad as in Iraq, but there
are certainly signs of growing tension between different faiths.
In November 2007, the Institute of Public Policy Research (a
government think-tank charged amongst other things with
investigating possible ways of making Britain more multicultural)
suggested downgrading the celebration of Christmas unless equivalent
status can be applied to festivals of other religions. Apparently, some
75% of employers opted not to put up festive decorations in 2006
for fear of causing offence to non-Christians. The Institute of Public
Policy Research states in its report that 'If we are going to continue
to mark Christmas … then public organisations should mark other
major religious festivals too.' The way forward surely lies in better

mutual understanding between faiths along the lines suggested by Karen Armstrong, rather than in any unilateral attempt to downgrade Christmas which history suggests would be doomed to failure.

The Pope, according to *The Times* on Boxing Day 2006, gave his traditional Christmas Day *Urbi et Orbi* ('to the city and the world') address from a balcony in St Peter's Basilica, below which was a larger than life Nativity scene (complete with baby Jesus) and a crowd of some 40,000 people. The Pope wished everyone a happy Christmas in 63 different languages, and the address was broadcast live to 88 countries around the world. Themes covered included injustice, poverty, environmental concerns and war, and the Pope 'called upon the child Jesus to bestow upon political leaders the wisdom and courage to seek and find humane, just and lasting solutions to the troubles of the world.' One may reasonably wonder why, if Jesus has such powers, he has not exercised them long ago; he has, after all, already had more than 2000 birthdays, so it is perhaps unrealistic to expect him to do anything radically different this time around.

At Christmas 2006 a cartoon which became known as 'The Chavtivity' appeared on the internet. This was published in *The Sunday Times* on 17 December 2007, where it is described in an article by Rod Little:

> A baby Jesus in a pram is greeted by three wise chavs bearing stolen goods in a smashed-up Scottish bus shelter, waiting for the bus that will never come. Mary is a shell-suited hatchet-faced cow and sullen Joseph is replicated on the wanted poster behind him … You have your doubts, looking at the picture, that it was a virgin birth, but you're glad she's now got herself a council flat. You may be surprised to see that Joseph is there at all, rather than on the run from the CSA.

The cartoon is funny, of that there is no doubt, but like many funny things it is rooted in misfortune. The kind of social problems it represents are brought sharply into focus at Christmas, when the distinctions between the 'haves' and 'have-nots' within society become clearer than ever; Hamish McRae, in *The Independent* on 20 December 2006, writes of 'a burst of consumption that highlights the differences between us rather than bringing us together: a Christmas of greed rather than a Christmas of conviviality'. Such problems are not, of course, the *fault* of Christmas, but reflect society in general. Indeed, Christmas charities do much to help alleviate suffering amongst the poor over the festive season, continuing a tradition that, as we have seen, stretches back to medieval times.

Christmas has become a great family festival but can also play a part in family breakdown. A rather unseasonal article entitled *'Tis the season – to get divorced'* appeared in *The Observer* on Christmas Eve 2006. The article begins 'Christmas might be the season of goodwill, but for many families it can be the final straw. According to new research, more than four in five of us experiencing family problems fear that they will ruin Christmas.' Parents of broken families argue about where the children should wake up on Christmas Day, and on how much should be spent on presents. Hardly the kind of thing most us want to find ourselves reading on Christmas Eve! Such problems may well ruin Christmas for broken families, but it seems that Christmas can also be bad news for families entering the season intact. Lawyers refer to the first working Monday each year as 'D-Day' – 'Divorce Day' – as the first full working week of the year invariably sees a boom in applications for divorce. Indeed, according to a report provided by BBC News on 8 January 2007, rates of divorce proceedings in early January can be 50% higher than at other times; festive family disputes and financial problems at this expensive time of year often represent the final straw in relationships that are already under strain.

Despite such problems, it is probably fair to say that the vast majority of parents want to do their best for their children at Christmas. Given the range of presents available, this is easier said than done. The front cover of the *Times2* supplement on 20 December 2007 features the headline 'Present Imperfect. Just how rubbishy are Christmas toys?'. This relates to an article analysing a range of toys to help parents find the perfect present; it includes 'toy buying principles' provided by psychologists, and concludes that 'we've created toys that are unsocial and inflexible', and that 'often old-fashioned is best'. Regardless of what psychologists may think, most children seem to know what they want from Santa well in advance of the day, and stand to be disappointed if they don't get what they want rather than surprised and delighted if they do.

While on the subject of children, we should consider the role played by good old Father Christmas in the modern world. No longer a mysterious figure who visits unseen in the dead of night, the modern Santa is present in every shopping centre from early December, replies to letters and emails, welcomes people to his home in Lapland, and can be traced throughout Christmas Eve via an online satellite-based tracking system. Under the headline 'School says sorry for Christmas clanger', *The Times* (20 December 2006) reports that a school had to apologise after informing children aged nine and ten that Father Christmas does not exist. Irate parents berated the head teacher, who apologised unreservedly, explaining that it had all been a big mistake. Other parents seemed less concerned, one noting that Santa is very useful in that he can be blamed when children don't find exactly what they want under the tree! Despite the rigidity imposed by the national curriculum, a spokesman for the Department for Education and Skills said there was no official policy on Father Christmas and individual schools could say what they like about him. One may wonder whether such enlightened thinking will ever apply to the teaching of the Nativity.

The debate over what we should tell our kids about Santa was the subject of an article entitled 'The Santa delusion: Is it harmless fantasy or cruel deception?' in the 2007 *New Scientist* Christmas and New Year Special. Described as a 'time-honoured cultural conspiracy', the whole tradition of Santa is debated by a host of academics who offer a wide range of views on the subject. One psychologist explains 'I don't think it is lying; it's making up a very pleasant story to help children enjoy an experience.' The Nativity comes to mind once again.

'Happy' Christmas. Some personal reminiscences, the nature of God, and the pursuit of festive happiness

While the above overview of Christmas in the modern press is fascinating, it is important to stress that, for each and every one of us, our experiences and memories of Christmas are intensely personal. Think about it for a moment. I suspect you can readily recall vivid details of Christmases from periods of your life for which other memories are in increasingly short supply. Perhaps memories of favourite presents received as a young child; of being upset at the end of the Christmas season (not so much due to the return to school as to the fact that Christmas would not return for a whole year); of a first Christmas following the loss of a close relative; the first, joyous Christmas with a new partner, or following the break-up of a relationship; or (perhaps most poignantly of all) Christmases spent with young children of your own.

I remember, aged four or five, forcing myself to lie awake on Christmas Eve until Santa arrived. After an age, my father entered the room and placed a stocking of festive goodies on the end of my bed. He didn't know I was awake, and having finally solved the mystery of Santa I fell sound asleep, awaking the next morning to investigate the contents of the stocking. On accusing my father of fraud over breakfast, he instantly responded that he had heard a bang from my room and had come to investigate – finding my stocking on the floor, he had carefully replaced it on the bed. I must have been asleep when Santa came, but been woken up by the bang as the stocking hit the floor. Needless to say, I believed him; in my little mind, Santa was reborn! Rather less affectionately, I recall the seemingly endless travelling from my early childhood home in Cambridge to spend Christmas with relatives near Blackpool; despite being pumped full of travel pills, I was car-sick every time. It became something of a game each year to see how far we could get before the first uncontrollable wave of nausea hit me: half-way was a triumph. Once I nearly made it, but not quite. In general, however, my childhood memories of Christmas are of warm, family gatherings, and I was determined to ensure that my own children would enjoy similar experiences, preferably without all the travelling. The Christmas Day following the birth of my elder daughter was the first in my life that I spent in my own home. I well remember the joy of buying my first ever real Christmas tree, since when I have bought a great big one every year, becoming gradually more proficient in the art of erecting it. I love the smell as well as the sight of the tree, and my children always enjoy helping to dress it with as many chocolate baubles as possible before immediately beginning to harvest them!

Sadly, in the late 1990s, my marriage to the mother of my daughters broke down irretrievably. Anyone who has been through such an experience will know how traumatic it can be, the more so where children are involved. Fortunately, my daughters have proved remarkably resilient, prospering through having two loving parents who live their own lives in separate homes, as a direct result of which Santa comes to them twice each year: on Christmas Eve (with Mum) and New Year's Eve (with Dad). While the trauma of the breakup fades with time, one image will haunt me forever. As their mother drove away on Christmas Eve 1998, the first Christmas that we spent apart, my eldest daughter, aged nearly three at the time, turned to wave goodbye through the back window of the car, the confusion etched on her little face clearly demonstrating her sadness and bewilderment as to why daddy was not coming with them for Christmas. It is a good job she couldn't see me a few seconds later as my emotions got the better of me in rather spectacular fashion. However, the girls spent a happy Christmas at their Granny's house and all thoughts of sadness were banished just a few days later when

Dad, girls and new partner spent a fabulous New Year together. However, the memory of that little face through the car window will never leave me. Why is it ingrained so forcibly in my mind? After all, I had waved goodbye to her many times over previous months, and have done so thousands of times since. Clearly, it was something to do with what we casually describe as 'the spirit of Christmas', and it was the knowledge that my family would never again spend Christmas together as a unit that was at the heart of my distress.

Six years later, a few days before Christmas 2004, I bade a tearful farewell to a girl with whom I had fallen deeply in love shortly after the break-up of my marriage. We had spent half a dozen intensely happy Christmases together, and although the break up was unavoidable it was nevertheless excruciating. A psychologist described the whole affair as having 'the intensity of a real-life Shakespearean tragedy', which sounds jolly impressive but probably doesn't quite do it justice; apart from anything else, it is unlikely that Shakespeare, given his general avoidance of the subject, would have used Christmas as the dramatic setting for the doom-laden finale. Regardless of all that, the immediate problem was how to survive Christmas. I had not spent a Christmas without a partner for two decades. My daughters have continued the tradition of spending Christmas with their mother before joining me for a week over New Year. So I was left with the prospect of a very lonely, miserable Christmas indeed. No reason for the annual excursion to the lingerie, perfume or jewellery shops; no-one to get happily drunk with on Christmas Eve or (much worse) wake up with on Christmas morning; no-one for whom to cook Christmas dinner; no-one with whom to hold hands on long, cold Boxing Day walks. In the event, I left home on a freezing Christmas morning, driving over the Pennines through a beautiful snow-bound landscape (yes – it was a wonderful white Christmas – pity I was in no state to appreciate it!) through which the roads were just about passable, to join my mother at an aunt's house near Blackpool; the very house in which I had spent so many Christmases as a small child, but which I had not visited for three decades. It brought back vivid and generally happy memories of childhood Christmases, but neither my heart nor my mind were in festive mood this particular Christmas.

My problems, however, were of no consequence in comparison to the misery suffered by millions of people on the other side of the world. On Boxing Day, a horrendous tsunami struck southern Asia, triggered by a massive earthquake beneath the Indian Ocean. While we in Britain were enjoying our cosy Christmas holiday, perhaps as many as a quarter of a million people, spread throughout 13 different countries, lost their lives. Countless others suffered the grief of losing loved ones in circumstances of unimaginable horror. To our credit, we in the Western World, perhaps shocked even more than we might otherwise have been by the fact that the event occurred at Christmas, raised billions of pounds to help ease the suffering of communities battered by the tsunami. For millions, however, the damage was irreversible, and it does not seem unreasonable to ask why God, the birth of whose 'son' we celebrate at Christmas, should allow such abysmal suffering to occur at this or any other time. I can accept that we need to go through bad times in order to better appreciate the good things in life, and I understand the religious argument that everything we experience here on earth is merely preparation for what comes later. But I am unable to equate great suffering, whether on a personal or a global scale, with the existence of the Christian God, supposedly omnipotent, omniscient and supremely good. The great Greek philosopher, Epicurus, writing three centuries before the birth of Jesus, eloquently addresses the problem:

> Is God willing to prevent evil, but not able? Then he is not omnipotent. Is he able, but not willing? Then he is malevolent. Is he both able and willing? Then whence the evil? Is he neither able nor willing? Then why call him God?

Many theories claim to counter Epicurus and 'prove' the existence of God, generally through some kind of special pleading along the lines that God gave us free will and that evil results from our misbehaviour, sometimes at the behest of the Devil. Such arguments appear absurd in the face of the Asian tsunami and countless other natural disasters. The suffering caused over the centuries by people fighting in the name of one deity against others must also be brought into question if there truly is but one omnipotent and omniscient power. I accept that some people claim to have found contentment and happiness through their belief in God, but this does not appear to me to be a sound basis for such belief; if it is, then we might as well worship Santa Claus at Christmas time.

There is no doubt that the winter solstice was of profound ceremonial significance to the people of Stonehenge but, as we have seen, archaeological evidence suggests that they enjoyed a midwinter feast in addition to their 'religious' observance of the setting midwinter sun. Perhaps, when all is said and done, and despite the different religious trends with which it has been associated over the millennia, midwinter has always represented first and foremost a good excuse for a party. Today we readily associate the word 'joy' with Christmas, and the pursuit of happiness may always have been a major characteristic of the season. Christmas certainly brings into sharp focus two different, perhaps even opposing, approaches to the pursuit of happiness. First, we have the search for spiritual fulfilment, perhaps attainable through religious activity and an appeal to God, or, in a more down-to-earth approach, through charity to others deemed less fortunate than ourselves. Second, driven by merciless advertising campaigns in the approach to Christmas, we have the search for happiness through eating and drinking to excess and through the acquisition of more and greater material possessions. It is undeniable that children (and, let's be honest, grown-ups too) gain great pleasure from the receiving of presents from friends and loved ones at Christmas. Birthday presents and chocolates at Easter are very nice too, but there is nothing quite like the orgy of expectation and the ritual of unwrapping at Christmas. Sometimes we are disappointed with our gifts, sometimes we are delighted. Sometimes we know exactly what we are going to get, leading us to wonder as we commence with the unwrapping procedure why someone bothered with the wrapping ritual in the first place! Perhaps the wrapping of gifts for others is in itself part of the seasonal search for happiness; anthropologists would have us believe (not without good reason) that the giving of presents is ground ultimately in the generation of a personal 'feel good factor' rather than primarily in the desire to be charitable to others.

G.K. Chesterton wrote of the contradiction and 'mystical defiance' of the festive season, noting that 'Man chooses when he wishes to be most joyful the very moment when the whole material universe is most sad.' While our technological sophistication ensures that we need not suffer to the extent that our ancestors did from the mood-swings of the material universe, Christmas retains a unique power to exaggerate our own state of mind; like no other occasion, it continues to inspire the highest highs and the lowest lows. On balance, as with life in general, it may be necessary to suffer the occasional low in order to fully appreciate the highs; perhaps the ecstasy of the truly 'happy' Christmas is only accessible to those who have endured one or more thoroughly wretched festive seasons in the past. You might like to bear this in mind if you are feeling in any way unhappy this Christmas!

'A wicked, cadging, lying, filthy, blasphemous, and demoralizing subject'. Alternative angles on Christmas

The modern Christmas is a complex web of diverse but interrelated traditions, some of which can appear to contradict others. It is a Christian festival, but retains ancient pagan traditions seen by many as incompatible with Christianity. While most Christians celebrate the birth of Jesus as a time of great joy, Puritans (whose mistrust of pleasure results from the worry that people, given a little of what they enjoy, will become addicted to its pursuit) traditionally shun any form of festive fun. Despite such arguments among different Christian groups, the influence of the Church over Christmas is surprisingly minor; indeed, our modern Christmas celebrations may not have been radically different had Christ never been born, although we would of course refer to them by a different name. Christmas is often described as a great family occasion, but the festive family get-together can be the final straw for many couples who find themselves heading for the divorce courts early in the New Year. Most Britons love a white Christmas, yet the very celebration of Christmas contributes substantially to global warming each year, helping to ensure that the chances of a white Christmas become annually more remote. Crime at Christmas is a growth industry, while the commercial Christmas seems to fly in the face of traditional Christian values, especially as so many are still dependent on festive charity for seasonal goodwill. Bethlehem, the focus of the world's Christmas celebrations and supposedly a symbol of peace and goodwill, lies at the heart of a long-standing and bitter conflict that is gradually seeing it abandoned by Christians. According to the Church, the Christmas message is meant to be simple, but it seems the social complexities of our festive season could hardly be more convoluted! Perhaps this shouldn't surprise us as a range of different attitudes towards the season has probably always existed. Whereas most people enjoy it, there have always been exceptions, arguably the most eloquent and outspoken of whom was the great Irish dramatist George Bernard Shaw. In 1893, he refers to 'a ghastly general pretence of festivity', informing us that:

> Like all intelligent people, I greatly dislike Christmas ... It really is an atrocious institution this Christmas. We must be gluttonous because it is Christmas. We must be drunken because

it is Christmas. We must be insincerely generous; we must buy things that nobody wants, and give them to people we don't like; we must go to absurd entertainments that make even our little children satirical …

A few years later, in 1898, he writes:

I am sorry to have to introduce the subject of Christmas. It is an indecent subject; a cruel, gluttonous subject; a wicked, cadging, lying, filthy, blasphemous, and demoralizing subject. Christmas is forced on a reluctant and disgusted nation by shopkeepers and the press: on its own merits it would wither and shrivel in the fiery breath of universal hatred: and anyone who looked back to it would be turned into a pillar of greasy sausages.

Niall Edworthy, in *The Curious World of Christmas*, offers a perceptive analysis of Shaw's legendary loathing of the festive season, suggesting that his views were fuelled not so much by careful thought and analysis as by a number of personal circumstances which, in combination, left him little chance of ever becoming a fan of Christmas:

As a socialist, Shaw was riled by the materialism and consumerism of the holiday period and what he saw as an all-too-brief flash of middle-class charity towards the poor and less fortunate; as an atheist turned mystic, he must have been repelled by the overtly Christian dimension of the holiday; as a radical rationalist, he will no doubt have been appalled by its superstitious pagan elements and the absurdity of Father Christmas and his airborne reindeer. As a serious dramatist and man of letters, he was horrified by the immense silliness of the Christmas pantomime – and all the other quaint, unintellectual, sentimental and indulgent aspects that the season brings us by the sleigh-load. As a devout vegetarian and teetotaller, perhaps it was his physical disgust at the thought of all that roasted animal flesh and booze that excited his bile.

I can sympathise to an extent with Shaw's views, but his outright dismissal of Christmas as cruel and wicked is, I think most readers will agree, somewhat misguided. Nevertheless, there are many in the modern world who choose to adopt a similar view and that is their prerogative – the loss, however, is also theirs.

From Shamans and Stonehenge to Shopping and Santa. Some concluding thoughts on the nature of Christmas

It is now time to draw our story of Christmas to a close. We have considered a vast array of festive phenomena, and although some may have been granted undue emphasis, and others perhaps glossed over too lightly, I think we have succeeded in tracing most back to ancient roots, suggesting a remarkable degree of continuity over the centuries. The most significant theme must surely be the link between Christmas and the winter solstice; the reason we celebrate Christmas at midwinter clearly owes more to the adoration of the sun by our prehistoric ancestors than to the actual birthday of Jesus. As we have seen, the reason we celebrate Christmas a few days after midwinter, rather than on the actual day of the solstice, is simply because of the inaccuracy of the ancient Roman calendar; had Julius Caesar's calendar been more accurate then the solstice would still occur on 25 December each year as it did in Roman times. Any doubt over the link between ancient sun veneration and Christmas must surely be dispelled by the many early Christian references to Jesus as the 'Sun of Righteousness'. The Nativity has been the focus of Christian midwinter celebrations since at least as long ago as the fourth century, but the conventional story of the Nativity is at best legendary, at worst little more than a fairy story (albeit a particularly fine one). Just as our Christmas celebrations today are based on a variety of ancient themes, so the Nativity was built upon foundations provided by a wealth of already ancient legend and symbolism drawn from sources such as Old Testament prophecies and Greek mythology. Once established in Britain, the Christian Christmas found itself adopted alongside ancient pagan practice, and the balance between these two traditions provides the framework for the subsequent history of midwinter festivities. People in medieval times enjoyed the Twelve Days of Christmas and generally found no inconsistency in the merging of ancient pagan tradition with the worship of Jesus, although the Puritan movement did succeed in briefly banning Christmas in the mid seventeenth century on the basis that no justification for it exists in the Bible. After the Restoration, Christmas was reintroduced as England's main national holiday, but celebrations seem never again to have reached the levels of excess enjoyed during medieval times. It was Charles Dickens who was largely responsible for the Victorian 'relaunch' of Christmas, but, as we saw in Chapter 6, the festive traditions introduced during the nineteenth and twentieth centuries generally have very ancient origins, or were at least heavily influenced by elements of ancient seasonal celebration. Many aspects of our present-day Christmas echo those of Roman Saturnalia, while the desire for a festive midwinter feast can be traced back to the pig bones of Durrington Walls and the people of Stonehenge. Christmas has seen many changes over the centuries, but its roots will be forever planted in our prehistoric past.

By its very nature, we cannot be sure of what the future may hold. Global warming may remove all chance of England ever again enjoying a white Christmas. Christianity may continue to thrive, or may eventually fade into oblivion as other great faiths have done in the past. People may leave the earth to live on the moon, or in even more remote space stations. Some may even opt to live all or parts of their lives in virtual worlds. However, the long-term future of Christmas is, I suspect, secure. Even when we are living in outer space, many of us, by nature of our being human, will still be happy to accept any excuse for a party, and whatever the future may hold it will surely create few better such excuses than Christmas, which will continue to be celebrated in some form on 25 December (Earth time).

What exactly is it that gives Christmas its peculiar power, making it for many people a spiritually uplifting highlight of every year? The answer, we must conclude, transcends Christianity and relates to the very nature of human existence. The desire to gather around a warm fire with loved ones to reaffirm or debate ancient creation myths and celebrate the mysterious but glorious nature of life, while eating, drinking, singing and generally making merry, is a natural response of human beings to the darkest point of the year. Our present-day Christmas is the current version of a long-established tradition extending back into the mists of prehistory, to the time of shamans and Stonehenge, and, despite our current seasonal obsessions with shopping and Santa, many of the fundamental issues that concern us at midwinter are probably not greatly removed from those that exercised the minds of our prehistoric ancestors as they gathered for their solstice celebrations. Christmas remains one of humanity's greatest inventions; it will be with us till the ends of time and its celebration should be open to all, regardless of religious belief. It has the power to bring together families, local communities and nations in a spirit of cooperation and goodwill. I hope that an awareness of the material presented and discussed in this book will lead to an enhanced appreciation and love of Christmas for all who have taken the trouble to read it. Whether or not you opt to believe in the Sun of Righteousness, Santa Claus, or both, Christmas is yours to enjoy.

Have fun!

References

Thousands of books and articles about Christmas and hundreds about aspects of the winter solstice (though surprisingly few about both) have been published over the past couple of centuries. This list is restricted to publications specifically cited in this volume, together with a few others consulted by the author during his research.

Abercromby, J., 1912. *A Study of the Bronze Age Pottery of Britain and Ireland*. Oxford: Clarendon

Alexander, C., 2008. 'If the Stones could Speak. Searching for the Meaning of Stonehenge', *National Geographic* vol. 213 no. 6 (June 2008)

Armstrong, K., 2005. *A Short History of Myth*. Edinburgh: Canongate

Baker, M., 1999. *Discovering Christmas Customs and Folklore*. Princes Risborough: Shire

Beerbohm, M., 1950. *A Christmas Garland*. London: William Heinemann

Bowker, J. 2004. *The Complete Bible Handbook*. London: Dorling Kindersley

Bradley, R., 1986. *The Dorset Cursus: The Archaeology of the Enigmatic*. Salisbury: Council for British Archaeology Group 12

Bradley, R., 2000. *The Good Stones. A New Investigation of the Clava Cairns*. Edinburgh: Society of Antiquaries of Scotland

Bramley, H.R. & Stainer, J., 1871. *Christmas Carols New and Old*. London: Novello & Co

Brennan, M., 1983. *The Stars and the Stones. Ancient Art and Astronomy in Ireland*. London: Thames & Hudson

Buday, G., (undated). *The Story of the Christmas Card*. London: Odhams

Burl, A. 1976. *The Stone Circles of the British Isles*. London: Yale University Press

Burl, A., 1985. *Megalithic Brittany*. London: Thames & Hudson

Callow, S., 2003. *Dickens' Christmas*. London: Frances Lincoln

Chippindale, C., 2004. *Stonehenge Complete*. London: Thames & Hudson

Clarke, G., 1936. 'The Timber Monument at Arminghall and its Affinities', *Proceedings of the Prehistoric Society Vol. 2*, Part 1

Connolly, M., 1999. *Christmas. A Social History*. London: I B Taurus

Connolly, M. (ed.), 2000. *Christmas at the Movies*. London: I B Taurus

Cunliffe, B. & Renfrew, C., 1997. *Science and Stonehenge*. Oxford: Oxford University Press

Davidson, J.L. & Henshall, A.S., 1989. *The Chambered Cairns of Orkney*. Edinburgh: Edinburgh University Press

Dawson, W.F., 1902. *Christmas: Its Origin and Associations, Together with Its Historical Events and Festive Celebrations During Nineteen Centuries*. London: Elliot Stock

Dickens, C., 1843. *A Christmas Carol*. London: Chapman & Hall

Edworthy, N., 2007. *The Curious World of Christmas*. London: Doubleday

Ehrman, B.D., 2003. *Lost Scriptures*. Oxford: Oxford University Press

Foley, D.J., 1960. *The Christmas Tree*. Philadelphia & New York: Chilton

Golby, J.M. & Purdue, A.W., 2000. *The Making of the Modern Christmas*. Stroud: Sutton

Green, M., 1986. *The Gods of the Celts*. Godalming: Bramley

Hadingham, E., 1983. *Early Man and the Cosmos*. London: Heinemann

Harrison, M., 1951. *The Story of Christmas. Its growth and Development from the Earliest Times*. London: Odhams

Highfield, R., 2002. *Can Reindeer Fly? The Science of Christmas*. London: Phoenix

Hughes, D., 1981. *The Star of Bethlehem Mystery*. London: Corgi

Hutton, R., 1991. *The Pagan Religions of the British Isles*. Oxford: Blackwell

Jackson, S., 2005. *The Medieval Christmas*. Stroud: Sutton

Johnson, A. 2008. *Solving Stonehenge. The New Key to an Ancient Enigma*. London: Thames & Hudson

Keller, W., 1956. *The Bible as History*. London: Hodder & Staughton

Kelly, J.F., *The Origins of Christmas*. Collegeville, Minnesota: Order of St Benedict

Kimpton, P., 2004. *Tom Smith's Christmas Crackers*. Stroud: Tempus

King, C., 1999. *Christmas. Antiques, Decorations and Traditions*. Woodbridge: Antique Collectors' Club

Krupp, E.C., 1991. *Beyond the Blue Horizon. Myths & Legends of the Sun, Moon, Stars, & Planets*. Oxford: Oxford University Press

Krupp, E.C., 1997. *Skywatchers, Shamans & Kings. Astronomy and the Archaeology of Power*. New York: John Wiley

Law, S., 2003. *The Xmas Files. The Philosophy of Christmas*. London: Phoenix

Littleton, C.S. (ed.), 2002. *Mythology. The Illustrated Anthology of World Myth and Storytelling*. London: Duncan Baird

Matthews, J., 1998. *The Winter Solstice. The Sacred Traditions of Christmas.* London: Thorsons

Miles, C.A., 1912. *Christmas in Ritual and Tradition, Christian and Pagan.* London: Fisher Unwin

Miller, D. (ed.), 1993. *Unwrapping Christmas.* Oxford: Oxford University Press

Muir, F. & Muir, J., 1981. *A Treasury of Christmas.* London: Bolsover

Nettel, R., 1957. *Santa Claus.* Bedford: Gordon Fraser.

O'Kelly, M.J., 1982. *Newgrange. Archaeology, Art and Legend.* London: Thames & Hudson

Pimlott, J.A.R., 1978. *The Englishman's Christmas. A Social History.* Hassocks: Harvester

Rae, S. (ed.), 1996. *The Faber Book of Christmas.* London: Faber & Faber

Renfrew, C., 1979. *Investigations in Orkney.* London: Society of Antiquaries

Ridge, M., 2006. *Jesus, the Unauthorised Version.* London: Profile

Roud, S., 2006. *The English Year.* London: Penguin

Ruggles, C., 1999. *Astronomy in Prehistoric Britain and Ireland.* London: Yale University Press

Sandys, W., 1833. *Christmas Carols Ancient and Modern.* London: Richard Beckley

Sandys, W., 1852. *Christmas-tide, Its History, Festivities and Carols.* London: John Russell Smith

Seal, J., 2005. *Santa – a Life.* London, Picador

Siefker, P., 1997. *Santa Claus, Last of the Wild Men.* Jefferson: McFarland

Smith, G. (ed.), 1985. *The Christmas Reader. A Treasury of Christmas Prose and Verse.* Harmondsworth: Viking

Souden, D., 1997. *Stonehenge Revealed.* New York: Facts on File

Stout, G., 2002. *Newgrange and the Bend of the Boyne.* Cork: Cork University Press

Vermes, G., 2006. *The Nativity. History and Legend.* London: Penguin

Vitebsky, P., 2005. *Reindeer People. Living with Animals and Spirits in Siberia.* London: HarperCollins

Wainwright G.J. & Longworth, I.H., 1971. *Durrington Walls: Excavations 1966-1968.* London: Society of Antiquaries

Weightman, G. & Humphries, S., 1987. *Christmas Past.* London: Sidgwick & Jackson

Weintraub, S., 2001. *Silent Night. The Remarkable 1914 Christmas Truce.* London: Simon & Schuster

Wheeler, J. & Rosenthal, J., 2005. *St. Nicholas. A Closer Look at Christmas.* Nashville: Thomas Nelson

Willcocks, D., 1983. *Carols for Christmas.* London: Guild

Wilson, A.N., 1992. *Jesus.* London: Sinclair-Stevenson

Index